CLERGY
MOMS

CLERGY MOMS

A Survival Guide to Balancing Family and Congregation

ALLISON M. MOORE

SEABURY BOOKS
New York

Library of Congress Cataloging-in-Publication Data

Moore, Allison M.
    Clergy moms : a survival guide to balancing family and congregation / Allison M. Moore.
      p. cm.
    Includes bibliographical references (p.).
    ISBN 978-1-59627-080-0 (pbk.)
    1. Women clergy – Family relationships – United States. 2. Families of clergy – United States. 3. Working mothers – United States. 4. Moore, Allison M. I. Title.
    BV676.M66 2008
    253'.2082–dc22

                          2008020823

Seabury Books
445 Fifth Avenue
New York, NY 10016
www.seaburybooks.org

Seabury Books is an imprint of Church Publishing Incorporated

5 4 3 2 1

To Avery and Marin
and the people of the Church of the Good Shepherd
with love and gratitude

The interviews and stories reported and described in this book represent conversations with clergy from the Episcopal Church, the United Methodist Church, the United Church of Christ, the Evangelical Lutheran Church in America, and the Presbyterian Church USA. Except where noted, the names and some identifying details have been changed to protect clergy family privacy.

Contents

PREFACE   ix

Chapter One
THE FIRST INVITATION: RELATIONSHIP WITH GOD   3
    Multiple commitments: life-giving or crazy-making? / 3
    Clergy mothers' lives are revelatory / 5
    Saying "yes" to God / 7
    God in the world / 13
    Love is our destiny / 14

Chapter Two
COLLISIONS OF JOYS   16
    The power of race, gender, and sexual orientation / 17
    Gendered assumptions of vocation / 20
    Shift in locus of family from public to private / 24
    Shift in gendering of roles within family: male headship / 26
    Empirical challenges to devotion to work and to the family / 27
    The church as a system / 33
    Implications of the church as voluntary association / 36
    Families at work / 38
    The role of clergy in parish systems / 40
    Pressure points in church and parish / 44

Chapter Three
DIFFERENTIATING SERVICE TO GOD AND SERVICE TO THE CHURCH   49
    The tapes running in my head / 49
    Expectations in the ordination process / 50
    Expectations of women in the ordination process / 55
    Expectations of parish and church for ordained clergy / 61
    "Here is your wife, and here are your sons" / 72

Chapter Four
LIFE ON THE TIGHTROPE 74
Dating / 76
Marriage and pregnancy in the parish / 82
Pregnancy, and the conflicts and joys it raises / 82
Couples juggling work and children / 88
And what about the children? / 94
Nurturing marriage (or not) / 98
Work-home boundaries / 101
Collar stories / 102
Chronic sources of stress / 107
Self-differentiation / 110
Personal crises / 112
Midlife change for spouses out of involvement
in the parish / 113

Chapter Five
UNCHOSEN DIMENSIONS OF VOCATION 116
Corporate rather than individual understanding of
vocation and self-denial / 119
Understanding self-denial in multiple dimensions / 121
Power, self-denial, and vocation / 122
Facing human limits / 125
"Love God and neighbor" as a complement to
"deny yourself" / 127

Chapter Six
A WIDER VISION OF VOCATION 129
Why should the church care about the well-being
of clergy families? / 130
Theological and conceptual insights from
clergy mothers' lives / 131
The ethics of vocation, broadly conceived / 133
Practical steps for clergy mothers / 145
Conclusion: slouching toward vocation / 166

NOTES 169

Preface

Women gathered in the seminary library in the early eighties, compiling extensive bibliographies to answer the male professors who insisted there's nothing worth reading written about women in the Bible, or social theory, or social ethics, or anywhere else. Three women sharing "war stories" of their lives as clergy wives over the past fifty years. Six clergy women around a diner table, laughing about imagined comebacks to ridiculous questions, raging about institutional denseness, working through possible responses to the issues of small parishes, dreaming about sunny beaches with nary a church in sight. More intense one-on-one conversations at other diners or on the phone about how to take maternity leave when adoption agencies can only "guestimate" a child's arrival in months, about whether four-year-olds can or should be acolytes, about marriages in trouble, about too much stress, about aging or terminally ill parents, about partners and spouses out of work. Conversations in the church kitchen about raising children. Mothers talking over coffee about politics, schools, fatigue, fathers, and guilt, while children play.

Back to the diner again, to lament the fact that four out of six competent, experienced clergy women have come in second in search processes to less experienced, less credentialed clergy men. Back to the clergy wives, who have formed Families of Clergy United in Support, added clergy husbands, and compiled an excellent resource for clergy family members out of their frustrations and joys (but of course the day assigned for me to present this information to the Episcopal Church General Convention is also my younger daughter's birthday and the date my husband needs me to be at a dinner interview for a fellowship for him!). Back to seminaries who are beginning to look seriously at the needs of clergy family members, and who by now have mainstreamed feminist voices into many disciplines. Then off to a PTA event, and parent-teacher conferences, and the therapist, and the spiritual director, and never-ending church meetings. All set in the context of "conversations" with Scripture, liturgy, and even God on occasion about how to live faithfully and love abundantly.

These conversations have helped me become who I am, a mother and a parish priest and a practical scholar who wants to move academic ethical reflection into everyday life. Informal conversations became surveys, became interviews, became clergy family events, became research and reflection on ethical theory and sociological realities, as the stories of clergy trying to manage commitments to parenting, congregational ministry, partners, and their own well-being became ever more compelling. Jeremy Taylor, a seventeenth-century Anglican theologian and poet, used "collision of joys" to describe the meeting of newly pregnant Mary and her older "barren" cousin Elizabeth, a few months farther along in pregnancy. That is how my life feels sometimes, as if too many good things are colliding, sometimes creating a new and improved blend of family and work life and sometimes toppling a very delicately balanced house of cards.

The book is organized from the "outside in." I begin with reflection on my experience to provide a working definition of vocation. Chapter 2 explores how prevailing social, economic, and political institutions shape parish ministry, partnering, and parenting. Within the context of those institutions specific expectations of clergy and mothers have evolved, so chapter 3 identifies some of those expectations. Yet clergy and parents make their own choices based on personal psychology, experience, hopes, and fears. Chapter 4 identifies some of the personality traits that are found in many clergy and many mothers and some of the stages in clergy and parenting life. Parenting, partnering, and parish ministry all involve some degree of sacrifice, yet the notion of sacrifice has been dangerously misinterpreted in Christian tradition. Chapter 5 analyzes more and less helpful understandings of sacrifice. Chapter 6 is the most practical, offering some biblically based ethical categories to help make vocational choices, practical advice for clergy mothers, and systemic suggestions for churches and denominational leaders.

I hope these conversations will be of use to clergy who are parents, to parents who are working outside the home in other fields, to church leaders trying to support clergy and their families, to seminaries committed to the spiritual formation of the next generation of clergy, and to ethicists exploring a progressive vision of "Christian family values." I have changed names and identifying details, even when the people with whom I have spoken did not ask for anonymity. My own family members don't have the luxury of anonymity, but I have their permission and I hope their forgiveness. I am truly grateful to the people of all the parishes I have served, for their support of my family and professional life. All my conversation partners have helped "hear me into speech,"[1] and I hope I have done the same for them.

CLERGY
MOMS

Chapter One

The First Invitation: Relationship with God

Multiple commitments: life-giving or crazy-making?

I care passionately about God — God as the source of life, whose love shapes all of creation, and God as Lover/Beloved inviting me to more and more abundant life. The more of myself — presence, skills, failures, persistence — I am willing to offer, the more I grow in love. I care passionately about being a good mom, offering presence, skills, failures, commitment to keep going anyway to my children so they can become who God is inviting them to be. I care passionately about seeking health in a marriage, offering presence, skills, failures, commitment to our mutual well-being. I care passionately about being a good priest, offering presence, skills, failures, persistence to help people know God and follow God. I care passionately about making real parts of the world safer, and more just, and healthier for all people — so I work against racism and sexism and war and poverty and homophobia and violence in the home.

Those are statements made out of a prayerful place, when I have time and grace to remember what's really important. Naming the relationships and the process of attending to God in and through the relationships helps me find my center again. They are core commitments, rooted in baptism and my relationship with God. Here's another experience of those same commitments from a different place.

It's Thursday night and I'm on the phone planning the weekend with my husband, who is living in another city for a year and coming home only on weekends. I'm planning to lead a workshop Friday and Saturday (I've said "no" to most Saturday workshops because Mike is away); Saturday night we'll be home as a family (but my sermon isn't quite finished); Sunday morning I'll lead church while Mike will take teenaged Avery to a reunion with summer friends and I'll find someone for six-year-old Marin to sit with in church after Sunday School; Sunday afternoon Mike will drop off Avery and leave; both girls want to go to a band festival to see their sitter perform; and I have to get the stewardship letter out by Monday morning.

The inner tapes start playing. "If I were a good priest . . . I would have had the stewardship letter already done, and a sermon written by Thursday night, and my daughter would never miss church." "If I were a good wife . . . I'd take Mike to Starbucks for a quick cup of coffee Saturday night so we can catch up (but then I'm a bad mom because we'd leave the children alone)." "If I were a good mom . . . I wouldn't have agreed to lead the workshop (but then I'd be a bad priest)." If anyone else had said any of the above things to me about themselves, I would have immediately challenged the self-criticism, but old patterns are hard to break. My own psychology, plus a good dose of female socialization, plus some internalization of parishioners' expectations, magnify the conflicting responsibilities of my life. And "what would Jesus do?" He was either single, or the kind of man who never let anyone know he had a family, or someone with "issues" about family — not helpful!

The reality is, in Barbara Brown Zikmund's words, clergy women lead complex lives.[1] So do clergy parents with children living at home, and the spouses, partners, and children of clergy. Even mature couples of one or two clergy, who've lived with church on weekends and evenings for decades, find conflicts between home and church unsettling at times. The "work-life" blend[2] is a lively issue for all working people with family responsibilities, increasingly studied from many angles. In many ways clergy families are not unique, and their struggles can be a useful point of connection with parishioners. Yet the dimension of perceived holiness, and the especially blurry boundaries between work and family life when the family is usually expected to actively participate in the workplace and the work is about loving a parish family, sets parish clergy and clergy families apart. The gender expectations about clergy and mothers set female clergy apart from their male colleagues.

Another reality, however, beneath the complexity, is God. Faithful life is moving in and out of consciousness of our fundamental relationship with God, and trying to bring all of our life — relationships, careers, family responsibilities — into alignment with God so that we can know and share God's gift of abundant life and love. God is in the underlying commitments of committed relationships, ordination, and parenting, lifelong commitments that often include an extended period of intentional discernment. God is also in the day-to-day mess that sometimes results from multiple commitments.

I want to weave experiences of faithfulness to God and analysis of the social structures that shape commitments into one understanding of vocation. The way vocation is usually described misses many aspects of holiness that are central to faithful living. Vocation usually prioritizes prayer life or church service as holier than other aspects of life, requiring the subjugation of other commitments in God's name. It prioritizes paid work in the public sphere over family commitments. Clergy women demonstrate in their lives and choices that other paths of faithfulness are also holy. Sometimes they find these paths intuitively, sometimes they are dictated by circumstance, sometimes they are proudly claimed. They are rarely explicitly discussed. They need their day in the sun so that all people, lay and ordained, men and women, can recognize how God is present in their daily lives and how they are faithful.

Clergy mothers' lives are revelatory

This book includes stories of women and men, lay and ordained, and sometimes their children. It focuses, however, on clergy mothers in parish settings, because social expectations that mothering and parish ministry each require 100 percent attention and twenty-four hours a day/seven days a week availability illustrate by exaggeration the tensions that face most working parents. The lives of clergy mothers also reveal the sexism in church and world and the systemic difficulties of parenting, child-care, and paid work in the United States.

A clergy mother married to a clergy father lamented the fact that Holy Week fell during her child's spring vacation. Both she and her husband would need to be in their different parishes for services Wednesday through Saturday evenings and were especially busy during the week, and their regular sitter could not cover so many hours (nor could a four-year-old tolerate so much church!). She said that while she had no doubt that her husband loved her child as much as she did, she would be the one organizing all the child-care logistics. "He just doesn't get it. By the time I go through the list of what needs to be done (which I know automatically by now), he shrugs and says 'Thank you for taking care of it' or 'Gee, I hadn't thought about that.'"

In another conversation, several clergy mothers discussed the relative advantages of either trying to train their husbands to do child-care logistics or just doing the organizing themselves, because it had become second nature to them. How had it become second nature for the women and not for their husbands? Barbara Brown Zikmund et al. found that among ordained parents who had at least one child at home while they were working full-time in ministry, "clergy men are more than twice as likely as clergy women to report that it was 'relatively easy' to carry on their full-time ministry with a young child at home...three times as many clergy women as clergy men recall that it was 'very difficult.'"[3]

Clergy mothers' lives are revelatory not because they're still doing the lion's share of the housework and child-care, but because they have, by necessity, integrated responsibilities to church, family, and self into one vocation. They have experienced the problems of expecting clergy and mothers both to be available 24/7, and have refused to give up on either set of responsibilities, even as that may well have meant sacrificing some aspect of either.

From the conversations I've had, it seems that clergy women's identities as mothers are as central to their sense of self as their identities as clergy, whereas for clergy men, professional identity is more central to their sense of self than identity as a father. Men don't face the same pressures to identify as fathers, and women are often still eyed with suspicion because of social expectations, socialization, and different social and economic supports (such as higher salaries for male clergy than female clergy in equal positions, and institutional biases favoring male clergy).

Expectations of clergy and of mothers and fathers make the reality of male and female clergy lives very different. Clergy mothers challenge both the norms of male clergy and the social messages about mothers. Their stories reveal important contradictions in social and economic structures shaping life in the United States, uncover implicit assumptions about holiness and vocation, and offer new models of vocation. Clergy women have often challenged structures and expectations intuitively, following their sense of God's call and their responsibilities to family and community. Many women talked about how the ordination process made them more overtly feminist. They found themselves having to defend their sense of vocation, their choice of internships and professional positions, their commitment to the church, or their leadership style because someone thought it odd that a woman would want or be able to do what they were doing. Conversely, some women have talked about how trying to be a good enough mother and priest deepened their prayer life — sometimes intentionally and sometimes out of desperation. Clergy mothers may pray more than their male colleagues about priorities because they feel the competing pulls more keenly, as in "how much therapy will my child need to recover from her disappointment that a funeral 'trumps' my presence at her Halloween party?" because we feel guiltier, appropriately or not.

In a thoroughly unscientific survey of eight clergy, male and female, who had babies in the past few years, I found that none of the men took paternity leave, although the diocesan policy made it available to them and even though some of the men were assistants, not senior pastors. The men said that having a child made them more firm about boundaries about evening meetings, and that they found themselves more efficient at work, and that they honored their days off more faithfully. All but one of the women took at least the minimum leave, some cobbling together vacation or unpaid leave to extend the six-week minimum, to care for their new children. The one exception was a lay woman on staff of her husband's parish — the adoption agency they had been working with for over a year called to say a baby was available on December 18 in the midst of a schedule full of social events and church services. Her parents arrived the next day and stayed for a month to care for their new grandson. Her husband preached Christmas Eve about saying "yes" to God when there was "no room in the inn" and no time in the schedule for a long-expected child to arrive.

Saying "yes" to God

I begin with some theological assumptions about God heard in discussions of how to live faithfully.

"God's call"

The shape and direction of each of our lives is initiated by God. God says to Jeremiah, "Before you were born I knew you, and I appointed you." The psalmist also describes feeling known and loved, needed and desired by God from before birth.[4] Men and women describing their desire to be ordained often talk of the element of surprise and irrationality — they thought their lives were proceeding quite nicely in one direction when a number of experiences opened up an often more logistically difficult but more life-giving path. They too have the sense that God had a plan for them before they were conscious of it.

That sense of call is not restricted to ordination. I have heard lay people talk with a passion about this same sense of surprise, irrationality, and yet absolute rightness of the decisions that led them to the work they love. Stories of true love often have this same dimension, as do accounts of either deciding to try to become a parent or discovering that one was pregnant, in convenient or inconvenient times. Vocation begins with a sense of someone or something outside of oneself, yet no stranger, offering an invitation to love more. Dag Hammarskjold's famous quote describes the experience well.

> I don't know Who — or what — put the question, I don't know when it was put. I don't even remember answering. But at some moment I did answer Yes to Someone — or Something — and from that hour I was certain that existence is meaningful and that, therefore, my life, in self-surrender, had a goal.[5]

Look at some of the traditional biblical "call stories"; e.g. Noah, Abraham, Jacob, Moses, Hannah, the prophets, Mary the mother of Jesus, the disciples, Paul, and so on. Usually God or a messenger of God appears and asks someone to perform a specific task; the person offers some objection, God meets the objection, and the person assents, though often not without questions and hesitations along the way (Moses, Elijah, Jonah). Four characteristics: God asks rather than commands; the task is usually life-changing; the task is part of God's plans, needed by God to fulfill God's purposes and goals; and usually the human becomes identified by the call (Moses the leader, "the prophets," John the Baptist, Mary the mother of Jesus or the Blessed Virgin Mary, etc.). These stories have been the primary model for vocation to ordained ministry.

There's another, much more subtle kind of call story in Scripture, often found in stories of women. Leah's role as one of the matriarchs of the tribe of Israel is central, and includes all of the above characteristics. But there's no direct invitation or great fanfare recorded. God never asked Leah explicitly to overcome her jealousy of Rachel, the wife Jacob loved more, enough to help Rachel become pregnant, yet Leah interpreted events in her life as enough of a sign of God's blessing to let her help Rachel, and even raise Rachel's two sons after Rachel's death.[6] Miriam, Moses' sister, also was a powerful leader. Her conversation with God, if there was one, was also not recorded. Her sense of call seemed to have emerged from careful attending to the needs of the people in their wandering through the wilderness and her interactions with Aaron. There's no record of Mary Magdalene's being invited by God or Jesus to follow Jesus, yet she is mentioned in several accounts across different gospels as serving Jesus, sharing the news of his resurrection, and serving as "apostle to the apostles."

In these accounts, vocation seems more to be about developing qualities of love and courage in and through the struggles and joys of life than about a direct conversation with God or a particular task. Whether direct or indirect, known ahead of time or after the fact, there is a tradition in human religious experience of knowing oneself to be invited by God into particular life-changing tasks that expand awareness of God and ability to love. Often the tradition has been "gendered," so women who don't hear their stories told and who do hear either of their sin or inferiority to men or whose roles are socially prescribed are reluctant to claim that vocation publicly. More subtle examples of God's invitation to abundant life despite external circumstances may be very useful. The reality of the experiences can't be denied and can provide meaning and value for the one asked and for those in her or his community of faith. They can usefully broaden understandings of how to honor multiple commitments.

"God chooses me"

On the face of it, this claim seems either obvious or absurd. Obvious, from the way God is portrayed in Scripture as first creating humans, then loving them, teaching them, sending prophets to remind them of their responsibilities and their privilege, continually seeking them out and inviting them to love. Absurd, given the way humans disregard God and God's ways, or because the idea that the Creator of the Universe is the kind of being who even notices each individual is absurd. "Of course God wants me, I'm wonderfully made," or the more subtle assumption that God is watching and available to each of us on demand, vies with "Why would God want me?" or "Lord, I am unworthy to enter your house" or "O God, who are mortals that you are mindful of them?" in everyday life.[7] Christian faith begins with accepting the fact that we are very much wanted, loved, and known by God.

"God chooses me" includes several assumptions that are central to my notion of vocation. When I was first considering ordination, I said something to a priest about "if I choose to be ordained...." He quickly corrected me. "If you are meant to be ordained, it is because God has chosen you. And not necessarily for your virtues, but for what you can learn." Humans often connect being chosen with earning a position through grades or talent or appearance or even personal connection. Clericalism in the church elevates the vocation of ordained ministry to God choosing those who must be especially holy, or good, or worthy. The notion that God chooses each and every human being (maybe each and every part of creation) to fulfill some part of God's plan or be agents of God's love in particular ways, all of which are vital to salvation, cuts through elitism or arrogance in life-giving ways. The notion that clergy are ordained because God couldn't teach them to be faithful any other way is also appropriately humbling!

"God knows me"

Scripture is full of people called by God to do great things for God's sake who nonetheless at times turned against God, betraying God, others, and themselves. Yet I hear as a priest, and experience in my own life, the fear that God will only attend to perfect people, or will only be with us or love us when we are good. There are examples in Scripture of people killed for disobeying God, examples magnified perhaps by a history of human punishment for wrong and the voice of conscience (and/or superego) noticing the gap between what we have done and what we know we should have done. Guilt makes it hard to hear many more examples of God offering repentance, forgiveness, and another chance to choose what is right in Scripture and in life.

The more we can live into the reality of the claim that God calls each of us, as we are, the more we can let go of questions of worthiness or having to get everything together before offering ourselves to God. Thinking of vocation narrowly as a set of things to do can betray us into trying to earn acceptance, when acceptance is given. Conscious and unconscious attempts to prove my own worthiness drive me, and many clergy, and many parents, to create impossible expectations for themselves. When I can remember that God doesn't share those expectations, I can find the freedom, and also the discipline, to renounce some of them. God indeed wants us, as we are, at each and every point in our life.

"God loves me"

This simple truth can turn lives around. One male cleric talked about growing up in a Methodist church. He became increasingly fundamentalist in Christian belief as he began to suspect that he was gay. Worship and church activities reinforced the experience of God's love for him, and his faith grew and deepened around that conviction, even as he tried to ignore or suppress questions of sexuality. When he claimed his sexual orientation years later, he was clear that since God loved him for who he was, he would need to find a more inclusive church in order to be true to himself and God. His faith was strong enough to withstand and ultimately move away from damaging theology.

The internal conviction of God's love is a part of any relationship with God, but its power may be more obvious when people are more likely to be marginalized. It helps to know that God loves me and chose me to be a priest when others tell me that I've no right to be ordained because I'm female. People of color, ordained and lay, often have to rely on their internal sense of being loved by God when faced with racism in the church. For gay, lesbian, bisexual, and transgender (GLBT) people who have been the subject of controversy in mainline denominations and the wider culture, the irrefutable conviction of God's love for them, as they are, becomes a lifeline, not just an abstract belief. It enables people to acknowledge the reality of institutional prejudice and power but not be defined by it.

God chooses us, knows us, loves us. These ideas are not new or complicated. Many books about priestly vocation, and many about faithful Christian living, emphasize these theological and experiential claims. I hear less about how these convictions shape parenting, and even less about how they shape committed relationships. God loves me — and you? And you, and you? When we have to eat dinner in forty-five minutes between children's lessons and church meetings and no one is willing to even help set the table, let alone cook? God loves and knows and chooses each and every person, but God didn't design the structures within which we also live and move and have our being. Nor did any one human. Work and family structures have evolved over time in response to a host of social, economic, political forces beyond any one person's control. Yet it is in those structures, imperfect and often unjust, where we are called to remain faithful to God and to each other. Ideas of vocation have to take account of those structures, so that we can stay sane as we choose how to respond to life's joys and challenges.

"One hope"

One of the most frequent comments I hear from working mothers, clergy or not, is how torn they feel between work and home. When they're with children they remember "one more phone call" that needed to be made for work; when they're at work they want to be taking kids for a walk, or meeting their teenager after school just in case he wants to talk. The culture divides life into home and work and asks people to choose allegiance to one or the other.

God doesn't. The baptismal liturgy in the Episcopal Church's Book of Common Prayer reminds believers that what may feel like scattered and even contradictory loyalties are grounded in "one hope in God's call to us; One Lord, one Faith, one Baptism; One God."[8] Most of the clergy and clergy family members I have talked to talk about how their unions or marriages are of God, how children have been a gift of God, how work in the church and the world has been a response to God. When I need some guidance addressing the inner tapes, I try to remember that if God invited me into these relationships with spouse and children and church and wider community, then God will help me find a way to honor all of them.

This musing about vocation began with experiences of being torn by multiple commitments. It's easy to commit to one thing at a time — paths are clearer and more linear. If we remember that it took the Israelites forty years to make what could have been a thirty-day walk from the Red Sea banks to the land of Canaan, we may have some clue that God has something different in mind. Wholeness in the process is as important as the destination.

One second-career clergy woman was clear: "I am a priest and a wife and a grandmother, and those are all inseparable parts of my vocation." She and God have woven together experiences over her life into one whole. Another example: God is found in my earnest prayer on the way to the hospital that I can be fully present, listen well, pray faithfully, and get out of there in thirty minutes to go pick up kids. To systematically neglect or demean any one of these commitments for the sake of any other would deny the multifaceted people God is inviting us to become (though sometimes I fear the invitation may be to schizophrenia!). When I feel most scattered, I can return to the experience of *one* call, and look for the ways the disparate pieces fit together in a holistic response to God.

More than honoring separate commitments, God develops some other gifts in and through the intersection of these commitments. Anna, a priest with four children under the age of ten, felt that her experiences prioritizing children's needs and desires at home helps her prioritize parishioners' needs and desires at church. Parenthood helped her learn to respond proactively without reacting to parishioners' anxieties. A Lutheran pastor with two children under three years old, currently working half-time in the church's national office and part-time in a congregation, also talked about how parenting suddenly clarified priorities. She described the sleep deprivation that accompanies life with a newborn. She needed to go back to work after three months, but was still nursing on demand whenever possible until she wore herself out. Then her husband and older child got sick, and she realized that she had to take care of herself to be of use at home and in the office. "Mothering and working forces you to take enough care of yourself to be a good human in both arenas," she said. In her case, physical limits helped her set appropriate boundaries at work and routines at home. This contrasts with another kind of pastor, often male, who overfunctions at work because home obligations are either nonexistent or performed by someone else.

"One hope" also means sometimes giving up something known and satisfying for the "hope unseen" of a new way of meeting needs of home and work. Darlene was, in her words, a "suburban housewife" who went to seminary in the mid-1970s because she enjoyed theology, without planning to become ordained. She commuted to classes, unlike most of her fellow students, so that she could manage responsibilities at home. Darlene was the seventh woman ever to matriculate in her seminary with a master of divinity degree. Most of the women in her classes were more militantly feminist than she was. Darlene looked in vain for role models of suburban wife and mother and priest, and held on vigilantly to her role as "queen of the domestic sphere" at home while also embarking on this new journey. She did well, especially in clinical pastoral education (CPE), and found herself driving 130 miles each day for a year for training to be a supervisor. CPE supervisors were expected to be ordained, so she began the process in 1977, all the time wondering if she could be a "good enough" wife and mother. Eventually she found herself working full-time, found that her daughter had benefited from the day-care setting Darlene had feared initially, and found herself proud to be an effective mother and priest. Her broader vocation unfolded gradually as step by step she moved into the new hope to which God had called her.

If God is inviting us to begin a new phase of relationship with God, then we can trust that we will find grace to do faithfully what is being asked. When it feels impossible, painful, or divisive, our task is to return to the source. "God, I thought this was from you and now it feels like a dead end — what happened?" Maybe we misunderstood. Maybe there has been a change in us or in a situation and God is inviting us to a different place. Maybe sin, our own or others', has blocked God's desires and we need to move in a different direction. In any case, God's plans and desires are the foundation of our relationship and can be trusted.

The countercultural nature of relationship with God

God's call. In a culture that emphasizes individual choice and earned success, the idea that each person is chosen and invited by God into relationship before that person may even be aware of it is a countercultural but life-saving perspective. The idea that the Source of Life and Love may ask something of us contradicts cultural notions of individual self-determination, even for those of us who have experienced enough of God's love to know it for ourselves and trust its reality. The idea that the Source of Life gives abundant life to us freely, without having to earn it, is even more radical.

God in the world

"I wouldn't call myself holy. In my day I already have only an hour that's really mine, free of responsibilities to family or work or anyone else — I know I should pray but it's also the only time I can work out or write or sometimes just veg out and watch TV — and sometimes I fall asleep." This lay woman knows that time with God feeds her, and feels guilty about not devoting more time to prayer. Maybe she needs to reduce some of her responsibilities to others, but maybe she needs to accept that God knows her situation and will meet her in the midst of daily life as well as whenever she can devote her full attention to God. She, and many others, measure holiness by the amount of time devoted wholly to God in prayer, in church, or in explicitly religious activities. This measure of holiness is one of many factors that lead people to assume that ordained ministry is more holy than ministry in the world, despite a consistent thread within spiritual writings that celebrates awareness of the presence of God in all aspects of life.

Staying faithful

Holding on to awareness of a relationship with God has been a perennial human struggle, for people individually and together, in all aspects of life. Prayer gets squeezed into car rides and five minutes before or after sleep; months go by when partners only talk about logistics of work or family; relations with children or parishioners are reduced to seemingly endless demands and delays on both sides; and the church exhibits yet another particularly egregious example of racism or homophobia. All too often pressures in the culture and the church either obscure the presence of God or make life with God into one among many other activities, rather than the center or foundation of all of them.

And yet, God calls us back. I received an e-mail from a priest with a very young infant. "I love my child. He's teething, beginning to crawl, and simply adorable. It's a regular love fest," she wrote. "Neither my husband nor I do too well without sleep, however!" She went on to describe some of the exciting things she's learning about leadership in her parish. She's finding God in mothering and work, and maybe she will in marriage again, once she and her husband can sleep. Moments of being overwhelmed with love when my younger daughter still wants to hold my hand, or even when my teenager takes hours to choose the right shampoo in the grocery store, make up for the fights for the bathroom in the morning. I know the sense of "midwifing God's presence" that comes in some pastoral visits, planning parish discernment exercises, or celebrating Eucharist. A male priest can't wait to go away, with his wife and without their children, to "rekindle holy passion" in their marriage. This same priest has also spoken gratefully about the opportunity to walk with terminally ill parishioners through dying to new life.

Humans get away from God, and God calls us back. We can develop disciplines in parish life and home life that help remind us of God's presence. Psychotherapy and spiritual direction can keep clergy and parents honest about the quality of their relationships. Regular retreats and vacations restore perspective and delight in God's creation. Sometimes all of those are not enough. I expect that even in a world with reasonable work expectations; adequate salaries, housing, education and health care for all people; and work and family structures that complement and enhance each other — humans could still lose the ability to see God and need to be called back into relationship.

Therefore, we need to be very careful about the images we use to describe our commitment to living as faithfully as possible. When vocation means only or-dained ministry, and people seek to anchor their relationship with God primarily in activities that promote ordained ministry, their relationships with their families can suffer. When the vocation of parenting trumps the needs of the couple, rela-tionships with partners suffer. Vocation needs to be understood as the living out of a relationship with God in and through all the commitments into which God has invited us. That will give us the freedom to attend to whichever relationship is most out of kilter, and trust that righting one relationship will create enough space to help the others fall more neatly into their place.

Love is our destiny

Attending to the multiple dimensions of vocation is important not only because it will help us better serve the church, sustain a relationship, raise a child, or make a difference in the world. Vocation also has an intrinsic purpose of transforming believers and transforming the world so that God's desires for the world are more fully incarnated. This vocation is nurtured in the nitty-gritty details of ordinary life as much as in work explicitly labeled as holy (e.g., making pastoral calls or preaching or praying). When I really don't want to call a disgruntled parishioner or stay up to help a teenager rewrite an essay, but I do it anyway; when we take time to play joyfully with those we love; when we routinely empty the dishwasher or clean up messy dogprints — we are blessing ourselves and our world by attuning ourselves more and more fully to God's grace. Struggle, and duty, and sacrifice — all part of the language both of vocation and of love — take their rightful place in the service of love rather than as extra spiritual obligations. N. T. Wright expresses it well in an exegesis of 1 Corinthians 13, Paul's paean to love. "Love is not our duty; it is our destiny ... constantly coming to us from God's future to shape us into the people through whom God can carry out [God's] work in the world."[9] Attending faithfully to all aspects of vocation is essential for the well-being of the larger community, not only for particular individuals.

This book offers no prescriptions for a life of perfect balance between ordained ministry and parenting and committed relationships. I get tired just thinking of what I sometimes expect I should do to find God in each of these aspects of my life serially. Lisa Belkin says it well:

> Not a one of us [the readers who respond to her articles on the "collisions that happen at the intersection of life and work"] seems to be able to give 100 percent to their job and 100 percent of themselves to their family and 100 percent of themselves to taking care of themselves. . . . No one can do it, because it cannot be done.[10]

One hundred percent in at least three different dimensions cannot be done. Yet every day clergy mothers get up, attend to self, to children, to partner (when there is one), to stray e-mails and phone messages and the church's agenda, to pets and repair people and the unexpected, not necessarily in that order. We do enough, enough of the time. Sometimes we don't and the world doesn't fall apart. (Rumor has it that Jesus already saved the world, so we don't have to!) We can apologize, make amends, and try again, trusting God's forgiveness until we can forgive ourselves. Our whole life, the multiple commitments through which we live into our relationship with God, is greater than the sum of its parts. Glimpses of God in just one or two places once or twice a day, can keep us sane when we can pay attention. When we live into our God-given destiny of love, we help God transform this world into God's new creation of wholeness, justice, and peace, a bit more of God's commonwealth "on earth, as it is in heaven."

Chapter Two

Collisions of Joys

Relationships, ordination, and parenting are lived in social, political, and economic structures, many of which were not designed for the well-being of all of God's children. This chapter identifies some of the ways social institutions force commitments to church, family, and God to compete with each other, and suggests changes in church practices and social structures that could make it more possible for clergy, family members of clergy, and the church as a whole to honor God's invitations more fully.

Blair is a United Methodist clergy woman, ordained in her late twenties, with ten years of ministry experience in large and small parishes and a special-needs four-year-old. When the small urban parish she was in decided to close, she talked with her district superintendent about her need to be close to a large city, with access to special medical services for her son. The district superintendent suggested an associate position at a large urban church, which initially pleased her. An interview with the senior pastor, however, changed her mind. She described her need to work fifty hours a week, with her regular day off on Saturday, to accommodate her son's special schools and doctor's appointments, and her husband's retail work schedule. She could schedule child-care for some Saturdays, but it would have to be an exception, not the norm. The senior pastor described his needs for associate staff to be available sixty to seventy hours a week and every Saturday, and both agreed it was not a good match.

Clergy and their families make decisions about how to balance work and family life based on personality, skills and passions, internal and external expectations, and particular circumstances (proximity to extended family, or special resources or needs). Yet all of these decisions are also made within the social, economic, and religious structures of twenty-first-century United States. Barriers of race, ethnicity, gender, and sexual orientation in church and society limit some families' choices of work and honesty about family life, while privileging other families. "Full-time work" can actually mean anywhere from forty to one hundred hours a week when the employer expects employees' time, energy, and attention. Parents raising their own children or caring for their dependent family members are not compensated even when that essential work can occupy all waking hours. The school calendar, with a long summer break and afternoon dismissal, worked well for farmers' children when children were needed to bring in crops and do after-noon chores, but it hasn't changed in most of the country even though child labor laws, the nature of farming, and the proportion of farm work to other forms of employment mean most work calendars are at least nine to five, fifty weeks a year. Congregations with deficit budgets often find the clergy salary or health benefits line a tempting place to try to reduce costs (since building costs are relatively fixed and programming costs are already usually minimal). Denominational structures and the public rhetoric of Christian churches also shape clergy life, from policies about sexual orientation or denominational financial support of congregations (or vice versa), or church-state relations, or sexual misconduct and other boundary violations. All of these social structures shape choices about family and work life.

These structures are among the most pervasive, the most taken-for-granted, and the most difficult to change. They are also each the subject of volumes of research and analysis. My goal in this chapter is simply to identify some of the ways social institutions force commitments to church, family, and God to compete against each other.

The power of race, gender, and sexual orientation

In sermons preached almost fifty years ago, Martin Luther King Jr. described "the 11 o'clock hour on Sunday [as] the most segregated hour in American life."[1] While genuinely multiracial congregations have emerged in mainline denomina-tions over the past forty years, racism is still a pervasive characteristic of church life and life in the United States. The majority of the people I have interviewed are white, as are the clergy and clergy families in the Diocese of Newark, and as are clergy and clergy families in most mainline denominations. In the Episcopal Church in 2002, "only 596 (3.06 percent) of the 17,500 persons listed in *The 2001 Clerical Directory* are black. Black priests are in charge at only 2.1 percent of ECUSA's 7,347 domestic congregations."[2] A total of 46,400 communicants, or 2.5 percent, in the domestic dioceses of the Episcopal Church are African-American. In 2001, 2.5 percent of the laity are African-American, 89 percent are Caucasian, 7 percent multiracial, and 1 percent other.[3] In 2005, 19,000 clergy and professional lay leaders were serving in the Evangelical Lutheran Church of America. Of those, five hundred, or 2.6 percent, were people of color.[4] The

Presbyterian Church in the United States in 1998 included approximately 484 predominantly African-American congregations and 80,000 African-American Presbyterians.[5] All of these denominations have offices or initiatives designed to support people of color and recruit more clergy and lay leaders of color. They also have educational programs about ending racism in their denomination and their communities. However, despite significant institutional and attitudinal barriers to the full inclusion of people of color in church and society, the general public rhetoric says that all men of color (who are either straight or quiet about their sexual orientation) are welcome in all positions of leadership.

There is more debate about whether women should be ordained, and whether their primary vocation should be as caretakers of children and other dependents, in the private realm. All mainline denominations accept women's ordination in general, with resolutions opening ordination to women beginning in the late 1960s and continuing through the 1970s. In all mainline denominations there are splinter groups that challenge women's ordained leadership on the basis of Scripture, tradition, and "nature." Zikmund et al. have written the most current book about clergy women, using information they gathered in 1993–1994 from women in fourteen denominations. They found the largest *number* of ordained women in the United Methodist Church, the United Church of Christ, and the Assemblies of God. The percentages of ordained women in a particular denomination give a different picture: 30 percent of Unitarian-Universalist clergy are women, the highest percentage; followed by the United Church of Christ (25 percent), and the Christian Church (Disciples of Christ) at 18 percent. The other denominations in the sample had an average of 10 percent female clergy in 1994;[6] by 2002 this had increased to about 15 percent.[7]

The experiences of ordained women of color in predominantly white denominations differ from their white sisters because of systemic racism in the church and society. In addition, the relatively low numbers often mean isolation, tokenism as various denominational committees seek members from all ethnic groups without necessarily being able to respond proactively to their suggestions, and the need to perform perfectly in case people make a judgment about an entire ethnic group based on a single person's performance. In the Episcopal Church, "black female priests are 18.2 percent of all the black priests, yet the 24 black female priests constitute 12.8 percent of all black priests in charge of ECUSA congregations in the 100 domestic dioceses. Males are 87.2 percent of all black priests in charge."[8] The United Methodist Church has approximately 1,050 racial-ethnic clergy women in the United States among its 45,000 U.S. clergy members, which includes more than 10,000 clergy women.[9] A 2004 study found that "United Methodist clergywomen of color in the United States do not feel substantive support from the denomination, struggle with lack of opportunities for appoint-ments and visible leadership roles, and receive salaries lower than their male and female counterparts."[10] Two white clergy women married to African-American partners described their struggles working in predominantly white congregations where their children were not fully accepted — both felt racism was a compo-nent of their struggle, and both eventually chose to have their children worship elsewhere with their partner.

There is a lively rhetoric within conservative Christianity, and in the media they control, asserting that the proper role of women is in the home. Laws gov-erning marriage and divorce still often privilege men, though there are wide variations from state to state. The prevalence of rape, sexual harassment, and violence against women in the home, and relative silence about it in church cir-cles, directly endangers women's lives. Within the church women face two unique obstacles. Ordained ministry is considered a *sacred* calling, as defined by centuries of scriptural interpretation. Law and policies, liturgy and song, describe God and clergy in male language and images. Appeals to the United States' Constitution, used successfully by women seeking to enter many other male-dominated pro-fessions, are irrelevant for religious organizations that, by national and state law based on the First Amendment separation of church and state, are exempt from equal employment and affirmative action claims.[11] So counterforces to women's full inclusion are still part of the culture and exert sometimes subtle, sometimes explicit pressure on women who seek institutional or attitudinal change.

Zikmund et al. observe that "in spite of overall growth in numbers, female clergy remain a minority in almost every area of church life...numbers indi-cate that women remain significantly underpaid and underemployed relative to men. Women are more likely to serve part-time, to leave parish ministry, and to serve in specialized ministries."[12] There is some debate over whether part-time service or service in specialized ministries is due to women's choice or systemic limits on opportunities, but there is evidence that systemic limits are present and hence hinder some women's ability to serve as they would like.[13] Women still face a stained glass ceiling that blocks their movement into senior positions in churches with large attendance and large budgets.[14] Stereotypes of women and men influence daily church life in overt and subtle ways.

The public debates over whether to recognize GLBT people as full members of the body of Christ continue within most mainline denominations and in the larger culture. Most mainline denominations exclude from ordained ministry gay and lesbian people who are in committed relationships or open about their sexual orientation. The United Church of Christ General Synod accepted the ordination of "active" gay and lesbian people officially in 1980, but General Synod decisions are not binding on local congregations or associations.[15] Some dioceses, and some parishes, within the Episcopal Church accept gay and lesbian clergy in committed relationships, but controversy over what the official denominational position should be is raging. The Evangelical Lutheran Church of America, the United Methodist Church, the Presbyterian Church in the United States of America, and the American Baptist Church ordain gay and lesbian individuals as long as they remain celibate, and some lesbian and gay clergy who have been open about their same-sex commitment have been prohibited from functioning as clergy. I have not included data on clergy from the Metropolitan Community Church, a denomination founded in 1968 "with a primary, positive ministry to gays, lesbians, bisexual, and transgender persons."[16] The constant need for GLBT people to justify their existence or full humanity, or to hear their lives discussed as an object of debate, or to deny an essential part of themselves in order to be accepted, take a costly toll on their lives and on the church as a whole. Scripture and tradition are used as barriers to exclude, and the countervailing interpretations of both are often muted, especially in public discourse. The challenge to the legal and sacramental ability to marry, or have lifetime commitments affirmed, or be ordained, or secure the rights and privileges for oneself and one's family that are granted routinely to heterosexual people, shows the extent to which heterosexism is built into the fabric of church and society.

Racism, sexism, and homophobia are institutional problems that influence life in the church and the world and keep humans from knowing the fullness of God's commonwealth. The church should follow Jesus and work for a world in which all God's children are fully recognized, respected, welcomed, and granted access to resources to survive and thrive. As a Presbyterian pastor said, "I am unable to identify a model in the corporate world, in higher education, in the political arena, or elsewhere, that comes even close to the ultimate core of our faith . . . the good news of a world turned upside down by Jesus Christ."[17] Yet we live in the meantime, in structures that are less than perfect. Lives of clergy, of parents, and of clergy families take place within the struggles for full inclusion. White people, men, and heterosexual people have privileges that often are taken for granted and invisible to those who can exercise them. Yet this book can only acknowledge the power of these structures and then listen for the particular ways discrimination or privilege shape the stories included here: Other resources document the existence of institutional racism, sexism, and homophobia and identify ways to challenge them.

Gendered assumptions of vocation

There's another set of institutional structures that shapes the lives of women and men in the public and private realms. In *The Protestant Ethic and the Spirit of Capitalism,* Max Weber articulated the ways the Protestant idea of vocation as source of meaning, value, status, and livelihood in the workplace had perfectly complemented capitalism's need for motivated workers. The Protestant work ethic was the meaning system responsible for the huge increase in productivity as economic systems shifted from agricultural to an industrial base and financial industries developed.[18] His analysis, though debated and critiqued, is a foundation of social science disciplines. The literature about vocation in both religious and secular domains, from Weber on, assumes that men live out their vocation in the workplace, while women take care of the reproductive labor: care for home, husband, children, and dependent adults. Weber, writing in the early twentieth century, didn't write about reproductive labor or women's vocations at all. He didn't need to describe what church and society had conveyed for centuries, that motherhood was women's vocation.

Mary Blair-Loy is a contemporary sociologist who has considered in depth the vocation of women executives in finance, using Weber's understanding of vocation. In *Competing Devotions,* she describes two "schemas of devotion" operating in the lives of women executives considering motherhood: devotion to work and devotion to family. "Schemas of devotion promise to provide meaning to life and a secure connection to something outside of ourselves."[19] They are models conveyed consciously and unconsciously by employers, media, parents, schools, religious institutions, and other social organizations and adopted by individuals, which influence the way individuals behave. They are also built into the economic and social institutions that shape individuals' lives.

The schema of devotion to work that Blair-Loy describes is based in the sociological and economic situations of "middle class, traditionally masculine, twentieth century, urban model of an upwardly mobile managerial career."[20] As early as 1938, the U.S. Fair Labor Standards Act distinguished between hourly workers, who are eligible for overtime pay, and salaried workers who are not. Higher salaries and benefits were powerful economic incentives encouraging companies to require elite workers to work longer hours. Competition within and between companies and the use of "face time" and "billable hours" in performance reviews and compensation all contribute to a culture of long hours.[21] In time, the model of intensive commitment to work assumed independent meaning and value greater than economic considerations, both in terms of social status and self-worth. Yet Blair-Loy shows how employees, especially female employees, who challenge these expectations in order to parent as they would like are rarely able to remain in the corporate structure at any level. Evaluation, compensation, and advancement are still directly tied to the number of hours and the amount of travel expected of employees.[22] There's a social norm that people are expected to work long hours, either for professional satisfaction and advancement or for financial security, regardless of the toll that it takes on other parts of their life.

Corporate standards often generalize to clergy, who have the same educational level as many salaried professionals, and to the congregations who see the clergy they hire as professionals. Parish clergy are expected to be at least as devoted to their vocation of ministry as secular professionals are devoted to their careers. Both secular and parish careers promise meaning, value, and "a secure connection to something outside of [themselves]."[23] Both secular and clerical careers are seen by Weber as means of fulfilling divine purpose.

The differences in salary, benefits, opportunities for career advancement, and ultimate purpose between clergy and corporate managers are often forgotten in clergy job descriptions or salary and benefits packages. In the Episcopal Diocese of Newark, for example, the model clergy job description calls for fifty hours a week of work; other dioceses use a system of "units" to help clergy set limits on what can seem to be endless demands. Yet conversations with members of search committees in parishes with a high preponderance of professionals often reveal some resentment toward these limits. "Why should our rector work fewer hours [read 'be less dedicated to our parish's needs'] than we do?" When a rector, hired at the diocesan minimum salary, asked the vestry for a raise after three years of no change in salary, her warden responded that she shouldn't need one because her housing and utilities were included, making the rector's job "rather cushy." The rector was livid, for several different reasons. First, housing and utilities were part of the negotiated salary package and reflected in a lower stipend. Second, the warden's life in the corporate world meant that in addition to a better salary, she had adequate resources to do her job, while the rector struggled without a parish secretary or support to maintain an aging building, and with an annual program budget of under $5,000. Third, the rector's children often felt at a disadvantage because their family income was so much lower than the family incomes of most of their peers. Ideally, part of parish ministry should be about modeling a "more balanced life" than is possible in many professional careers. There is no financial reward for parish clergy to work so many hours that other aspects of their lives are compromised.

Blair-Loy's schema of devotion to family specifies that "it is desirable and worthwhile for women to spend most of their adult lives intentionally caring for their families."[24] It first emerged in white middle-class culture in the nineteenth century in the United States, as families attained a certain level of economic security and work moved from farms and homesteads to industries often in cities. It reemerged after World War II as a norm for all women, even as many women lived different realities. One of the major assumptions of this schema is that it "presumes a heterosexual, permanent, reciprocal marriage, in which wives are dependent on husbands for livelihood and social status, while husbands rely on wives for physical and emotional care of themselves and their children."[25] The schema completely ignores the African-American experience, where slavery could disrupt a family at any time and women were expected to do almost every kind of work in addition to raising their own children, or later when disparity in incomes due to racism meant most African-American women needed to work outside the home, and when it was often easier for women to be hired than men. It also ignores poor and working-class white women who worked long hours in factories or doing piece-work in order to support their children. The devotion-to-family model was championed by the church, civic institutions that enjoyed women's volunteer labor, and producers of consumer goods that suddenly became essential for the woman at home. Here is the schema of the "nuclear," or "traditional," family that was so celebrated in the 1950s, and that has been read back into images of United States family history for centuries.

Clergy wives were held to this traditional standard. Evelyn Kirkley wrote a master of divinity thesis reviewing the literature that defined pastors' wives roles from the 1920s through the 1980s. The expectations for clergy wives changed with the expectations of white women in the culture. She called the model for the 1950s the "home and hearth model."[26] In the 1930s and 1940s, approximately 40 percent of the bachelor's degrees granted were given to women; by 1950 only 24 percent of graduates were female.[27] More than in any other generation, being a housewife eclipsed any other opportunities for female fulfillment. Housing developments in the suburbs increased the distance, physical and emotional, between home and work for men in general. For clergy in this period, the rectory was no longer seen as an extension of the church office, but it was expected to be a home open to the needs of parishioners for entertaining and counsel.[28] Clergy wives were never to hold leadership positions in church, were to make sure their homes were clean, their husbands dressed properly, and their children well-behaved. One manual reminded wives to polish their husband's shoes.[29]

In the 1960s and 1970s, Betty Friedan's *Feminine Mystique* was published; the second wave of feminist actions began; the media, churches, and many parts of the culture reacted with horror and tried to put women "back in their place." Kirkley found that ministers' wives reacted in three ways to Friedan and her critics. Some, labeled by Kirkley as "self-fulfillers," grappled honestly with feminist issues; others reasserted the "home and hearth" model as proper role for clergy wives; and still others revived the "assistant pastor" model of the earlier generation, where husband and wife were partners, sometimes paid, sometimes not, with shared leadership in the parish.[30] Kirkley traced each group's understanding of God, of relations between men and women, and of the proper scope of responsibilities to the parish. She uncovered gendered definitions of Christian duty and vocation that still influence clergy family life today, whether families fit these molds or not. When women were ordained, devotion to work and devotion to family, both of which are holy, were suddenly embodied in one person. There were no manuals telling clergy husbands how to behave; it was expected that they would have their own careers. In general, there are many fewer manuals for male behavior in any area than there are externally imposed definitions of "women's place," because social control of women, men's subordinates, has been important for centuries.

Some clergy husbands do teach Sunday School or help maintain the property or organize church events, but there is no approbation when they don't. One male couple I interviewed fit the traditional role of clergy and clergy spouse to a tee — the spouse was independently wealthy and found great pleasure in decorating and entertaining in the church where his partner was rector. Between them they offered at least one hundred hours a week to church work, which parishioners have perceived both as a blessing and as a barrier to their own participation. Another clergy husband is an airline pilot, frequently away and uninterested in church when he's home; yet another worships with his children in the parish where his wife had worked years ago; she found a new, smaller parish as rector, but her family stayed on at the larger church because of the youth programming and music. None of the male clergy spouses felt that their parishes expected anything particular of them, but that they were welcome to do what they liked.

Shift in locus of family from public to private

The notion of a family as a unit bound together by affection, not economic or so- cial necessity, and with boundaries that provide a certain amount of privacy, has only been possible in the past few centuries.[31] For many centuries, in most if not all cultures, the household was the primary place of economic production. It was not a private realm apart from the workplace, but the place where employees, slaves, people related by blood, and outsiders doing business with the house- hold interacted. Until the eighteenth century, *familia*, in Latin, referred not to a "mother-father-child" unit as a distinct group but to a household, always headed by a man, which could include hundreds of people, including wives, children, slaves, and often livestock.[32]

During the Industrial Revolution, the first factories employed whole house- holds of people, paying wages to men, women, and children and often providing a house for them. Over time, work increasingly became an individual pursuit: Men and the poorest of women and children worked in factories, while those women who could afford to do so stayed home to educate children, sew, cook, garden, and care for the home. Women's economic contributions gradually decreased as

more and more household goods (candles, clothes, food) were produced by factories, doctors and hospitals took over care of the sick, and public schools provided
education. The concept of "breadwinner" emerged at this time, as did the short-
lived idea of a "family wage," a wage determined by the number of dependents
as well as by the type of work done, to prevent child labor and allow mothers
to care for children at home.[33] Children, and to a lesser degree women, became
economic liabilities rather than assets, and the family rather than the household
was seen as a unit of consumption rather than production.

Beginning after the Civil War and culminating in the first Gilded Age in
the United States, women's public roles became more circumscribed, and more
emphasis was placed on the creation of home as a private sanctuary and retreat
from the "nasty" world of business. The family was idealized as the source of all
virtue, and there was a general decline in participation in elections, discussions
of economic justice and social morality, and other ways to care for the common
good. When life becomes bifurcated into work and home, and participation in
the public sphere is reduced primarily to work, and participation in the private
sphere is reduced primarily to the well-being of one's nuclear family, it becomes
harder to notice, let alone tend to the structure of the social fabric sustaining
both home and work.

The distinction between the public sphere, where men lived out their economic and political responsibilities, and the private sphere, where they could
retreat from the trials of public life into relative anonymity, had hardened. In
the Victorian era in Europe and the United States, the place of morality shifted
from the Enlightenment ideal of the upright public citizen demonstrating virtue
in public actions, such as philanthropy and participation in civic associations, to
the home. Women were to teach their children moral values and altruistically
attend to the common good, while their husbands pursued economic self-interest
and status for themselves and their businesses in the work world. Women were
involved in the abolition movements, in child labor reform, in temperance movements, in hospitals, welfare, and care for dependent members of society. Women
were models of altruism, piety, and compassion, extending the caretaking work of
the home to the public realm. The economic world of men was often portrayed
as ruthless and cutthroat, and the household as a place of retreat from greed and
competition.

Ann Douglas argues that as the distinction between public and private realms
hardened, there was a parallel bifurcation of public and private morality and a
"feminization" of American culture. The process began in the United States in
the late eighteenth century with the disestablishment of religion. Clergy in established churches, who had been authoritative leaders in the political and economic
realm, now took cues about the public realm from the members on whom they

were financially dependent.[34] Douglas traces the overall trend between 1820 and 1875 of clergy in disestablished churches to mute their critique of slavery and political action in the cause of abolition. Churches who continued active political work against slavery lost constituents.[35] The authority of churches had moved from political to moral influence, from public proclamation to private persuasion, from social transformation to the changing of individual hearts and minds. The church was no longer a vital community center for worship, education, and business, but a private place for words, not deeds about moral living.[36] These words often embodied virtues of compassion, altruism, and piety attributed primarily to women. Douglas describes a similar trajectory for many women, depending on social and economic class, as they moved from economic producers to consumers.[37] So clergy men were often spending most of their time working with and preaching to groups of women. Female writers and missionary leaders and clergy men extolled the virtues of the home as a locus of morality and the private realm as the proper place for both religious leaders and women, relinquishing the role of church as prophetic public influence. It is no accident that the prominent female reformers of the nineteenth century generally distanced themselves from churches and at times critiqued them harshly.[38]

Shift in gendering of roles within family: male headship

Men were assumed to be the heads of households in ancient Near Eastern culture, Greek, and Roman societies, as evidenced in the New Testament's household codes. This assumption prevailed in medieval Europe and England, and came to the United States at the country's inception. The U.S. Census used male heads of household as an organizing principle of data collection from 1790 until 1980. Puritan men could be disciplined in church for failing to control the actions of their wives and children, and laws allowing husbands to beat their wives also were part of the United States' legal inheritance from British common law. The U.S. income tax adopted male headship at its inception in 1913.[39] An analysis of divorce decisions in states across the nation in the 1980s found that these expectations governed the division of property and awarding of custody,[40] often regardless of the actual circumstances of particular marriages.

During the Enlightenment, beginning in the eighteenth century in Europe and colonial America, mothers were given more responsibility than fathers for raising children because more men were leaving home for the workplace. The public language of rights and contracts, personal self-reliance and autonomy, and independent rational decision-making reflected economic shifts in the accumulation of capital, the flourishing of a middle class, and the need to regulate business, trade, and commerce. It was accompanied by a growing sentimentalization of women as interdependent, emotional, and relational. The family came to be understood as an escape from the ruthless and competitive public world, and as a haven for dependent women, children, and others unable to negotiate the public market.[41] Men had added both the responsibility and the privilege of breadwinning, with the increased power that it brought within the family, to the position of "head of household" even as women's moral and decision-making power within the family increased.

Women's virtue

In late eighteenth-century Anglicanism, Evangelicals linked woman's godliness to her maternal and wifely duties, as a way to make sense of increasing male participation in the public workplace. Men's duty was to provide for the family; women's duty was to care for it psychologically and emotionally. This message was incorporated into the First and Second Great Awakenings in the United States, and has become a theme of evangelical churches' family values ever since. Preachers seeking biblical texts to justify and reinforce gender differences drew on the household codes rather than the messages of equality and mutual respect also found in Scripture. Women also became responsible for the morals of the family and, by extension, for society. Women's participation in the temperance movement, the settlement house movement, and other forms of charity and social service were an extension of the domestic sphere. Women could focus on the victims of unfair economic circumstances rather than addressing their causes. The tradition of male authority in the home, coupled with increasing wage-earning power of men but not women and a change in the understanding of women's role in the home was another linchpin in the nuclear family schema described by Blair-Loy.

Empirical challenges to devotion to work and to the family

Schemas are wonderful tools of analysis, because they name the logic by which many people understand the world and make decisions. As a mother and a priest, I feel the pull to live into both schemas daily. Blair-Loy's schemas are theoretical models based on the ways professionals and mothers interpret their lives, career, and parenting aspirations. Yet schemas of interpretation sometimes do not correspond to actual empirical situations, in history or the present. Using either the model of devotion to work or family, when they used to be performed by two interdependent spouses, can make any woman feel perpetually guilty. (Male guilt is less because men are not expected to be primary caretakers, even when some of them are.) The ideal of the family has become so separated from analysis of the social and economic forces that shape it that the family is often seen as the cause rather than the victim of current pervasive social problems. The "breakdown of the traditional family" has been blamed for poverty, crime, and welfare when in fact racism, continued economic limits on women's earnings, poverty, lack of safe and affordable child-care, and wages and salaries that do not rise with increases in the cost of housing, medical care, or basic necessities are the real "family crises" in the United States today.[42] The rhetoric about gendered roles, home and family, and paid work obscures the reality of most women's lives and makes work for healthier and more just arrangements more difficult.

Not everyone lives in nuclear families

The first challenge to the schema of the nuclear family with male breadwinner and female caretaker comes historically from evidence of families who were never able to live this ideal. Poor families of any race often needed two or more full-time incomes to support their families. Until the Industrial Revolution, "families" often included servants and apprentices, and many children would leave their parents to learn a trade or earn money for the family. In the eighteenth and nineteenth centuries, when maternal mortality rates were higher, "blended families" with children of multiple mothers or fathers were more the norm than the exception in the United States. African-American family life was shaped by the reality and then the legacy of slavery. Slave marriages were not legally acknowledged in any Southern state. Owners often sold children or parents away and denied parental rights. A child born to a slave mother was a slave regardless of the status of the father.[43] Both mothers and fathers were expected to work at least full-time for their owners. Still, many slaves lived in two-parent families until the death of one spouse, and after slavery was abolished former slaves spent years reuniting families separated by white owners.[44] After the Civil War, racist hiring, firing, and salary practices meant it was never as possible for black men to earn enough money to support their families as for white men, and often black women had more opportunities to earn money as maids and in service industries than black men, so sources of family economic security were less gendered.

Economic shifts in women's wages and careers

Another challenge to schemas of devotion to work and family comes from shifts in economic opportunities. When economic work and child-care occurred in the home, women's work was central to family income. The Industrial Revolution in the United States separated economic production from family households, making it difficult for adults to combine work and child-care. Public rhetoric in media and religious institutions extolled the gendered division of labor, with men in the workplace and women at home, so that by the twentieth century, housekeeping and child-care were considered full-time occupations in the United States.[45] Yet that phenomenon was relatively short-lived. In the 1950s, many husbands could support their families on only their income, especially with help for housing and education from the GI Bill (though black soldiers were often excluded from these benefits). Succeeding generations found this more difficult. The number of two earner families rose from 39 percent to 62 percent between 1970 and 1998.[46] Approval of dual-earner marriages is as high in 2000 as approval of male-breadwinner marriage was in the 1950s.[47]

Why? By the mid-1960s, women's employment had become central to family economic advancement, replacing child labor, migration to cities, and increased investment in male training and education as sources of increased income. There was a shrinking disparity between male and female wages, so that by 2001, 30 percent of wives earned more than their husbands. The background of the twentieth-century women's movement, coupled with greater economic opportunities for women, meant that women started working for their own improvement as well as for the needs of their families. Women could make decisions to move in or out of the labor market in response to economic opportunities rather than changes in their husband's jobs and earnings.[48] "Among all mothers with children under the age of six in 2002, more than two-thirds of women with college degrees and three-fourths of women with graduate or professional degrees were in the labor force."[49]

These facts represent a challenge to the gendered division of labor, so that it is more acceptable for women and men to both devote their lives to paid work and find meaning and value in it. The greater economic, psychological, and social freedom this represents is central to women's well-being. There has not been a parallel shift in the schema of devotion to family, however. The real numbers of full-time male caretakers is still small, although social acceptance of stay-at-home fathers is rising.[50] Recently, a Nassau County, New York, district attorney prohibited women in her office from working part-time because of child-care responsibilities, perhaps a corollary example of the resistance Blair-Loy found in the financial industry to part-time work. One response to a move like that is found by the Center for WorkLifeLaw at the University of California Hastings College of Law in a study of "family responsibilities discrimination." Ninety percent of the plaintiffs are women, and a few are caring for parents or spouses instead of children. They are all claiming discrimination at work because they are giving care at home, and they are finding enough precedents in legal arguments since 1971 to carve out a niche recognized by liberal and conservative judges.[51] Women still feel more responsible for taking care of children, and studies continually show that women shoulder more of the responsibilities for taking care of home and children than men do. Garland suggests that more women might stay home longer if they had subsidized family leaves available to workers in much of Europe.[52] It would be nice if fathers also wanted and were empowered to take paid leave from work because they looked forward to caring for their children.

Reconstitution of families with "marriage/divorce revolution"

Another equally compelling challenge to the nuclear family comes from profound changes in marriage and divorce rates across all ethnic groups and economic classes. In the 1950s, 80 percent of all households were married couples. In the 2000 census, less than 51 percent of all households were married couples, and only 25 percent of families had children at home.[53] This was a fairly dramatic change after almost a century of stability, with ramifications for the church as well as society at large. Stephanie Coontz identified several factors contributing to the demise of the so-called "traditional family" and the blossoming of a host of family structures in the late twentieth century: changes in individual values, marriage laws, economic opportunities for women, and legal codes.[54]

Birth control and legal access to abortions have increased alternatives to marriage, so that more people live together without being married, or engage in sex before marriage.[55] Cohabitation rates have increased steadily over the past forty years, and many companies now extend benefits to couples, straight or gay, in domestic partnerships. Expanded reproductive options (e.g., artificial insemination and in vitro fertilization) for women, the extension of adoption rights to same-sex couples, and the legalization of same-sex marriage in Massachusetts and civil unions in several other states gives more gay and lesbian couples access to the same rights as married couples, despite the surge in marriage protection mandates in many states and the struggle for real equality of rights.[56] There is work still to be done to ensure full access to legal, social, and economic benefits, but the social norms are slowly changing.

Completing an education and finding a job have joined — if not replaced — marriage as a credential of adulthood in the culture, where until the 1950s "adulthood" implied marriage and parenting. The age of marriage is rising, more young adults are living alone (without parents or partners) than ever before, more couples are choosing not to have children, and for the first time in the 2000 U.S. Census there are more people living alone than couples with or without children.[57] There is also greater acceptance of "never-married" women having or adopting children. In 2000, one child in three was born to an unmarried woman, up from one in twenty in 1960.[58]

Garland summarizes the work of many sociologists who are no longer using a structural definition of "family" as a husband and wife living at home with children. Instead of using biological or legal connections to define family, Garland recommends a definition of families as people who fulfill certain functions of meeting needs for belonging and attachment, for mutual affection, care, and the nurturing of young, which may or may not be determined by biology or law. She argues that functional definitions of families are more consistent with Jesus' teachings about family because they focus on relationship processes such as "loving one another, being faithful to the same Lord, and adopting one another as brothers and sisters in the household of faith."[59]

The "sandwich generation"

A functional definition of family is especially helpful when analyzing the patterns of adult children caring for aging parents, a topic that came up fairly consistently in interviews and discussions with clergy mothers. A Pew Research Center study found that in 2005, 71 percent of "baby boomers," adults ages 41 to 59, have one living parent, compared to only 60 percent in 1989. Twenty-nine percent of baby boomers provide some financial support to their parent(s), while 19 percent receive some form of financial support from their parents. Fifty-six percent of boomers believe it is their responsibility to allow their elderly parent(s) to live in their children's home if their parents so desire, and 13 percent of boomers are currently caring for dependent aging parents.[60] I suspect that clergy in general and female clergy in particular may bear a disproportionate share of responsibility for care of aging parents. One clergy man said that his siblings expect him to be the primary source of advice and care for his parents, now in assisted living, because he is perceived by them to have the most flexible schedule and the most professional experience addressing the needs of elderly, ill, and dependent people.

Several clergy women felt they were assuming a larger share of responsibility because they were the daughters as well as clergy. This impression is supported by statistics from the Family Caregiver Alliance, which estimated that from 60 to 75 percent of family or informal caregivers are female, and that female caregivers spend about 50 percent more time providing care than male caregivers. The average caregiver is forty-six years old, female, married, and working outside the home.[61]

Employers in many fields are beginning to offer support to employees caring for their parents, from informational seminars to support groups on site to flexible work hours, and access to long-term care insurance coverage for employees, spouses, and dependents.[62] Most of the clergy women who were caring for elderly family felt their congregations were supportive of their needs to rearrange schedules, travel, or fulfill other responsibilities, and even to grieve the changes in parents' health and their own roles.

No parallel change in structures of parenting and child-care

The past forty years have wrought a sea change in the nature of families and of women's participation in the workplace. The women's movement changed legislation, attitudes, and entrenched practices that brought women into the workplace at wages that approach those of men for similar work. Increased economic opportunities and more liberal divorce laws and attitudes toward same-sex relationships and childbearing "outside of wedlock" changed the shape of the family. These changes revealed the extent of mothers' unpaid labor taking care of homes, children, and dependent elders by the sudden scrambling for affordable quality care for dependents young, old, and chronically ill. European countries developed state-subsidized group day-care for children two generations ahead of the United States. Perhaps the American culture of individualism blinds people to their fundamental interdependence, and a different history of human rights doesn't include access to medical care, housing, child-care and education for the United States.

Yet the question of "who's taking care of the children?" is more than a question of creating safe, nurturing, and affordable structures. Parenting provides a unique kind of joy for all who are involved in it, parents and children. For too long parenting has been unvalued because it was invisible, hidden in the private sphere. For centuries men and women were able to combine economic productivity and reproductive labor, but now the structures in which baby boomers are raising children — full-time, without engagement with other adults, in separate homes, with competition for the best test scores and highest achievements — pit parents against each other in unhealthy ways. The development of suburbs, which further separated workspace and home, exacerbates the phenomenon. School hours, child-centered community activities offered only on weekdays during usual working hours, the lack of safe, affordable child-care for all mothers, media images of caretakers and homemakers as primarily female, limited parental leave and benefit options, the paucity of research on how men are caretakers, wages for most American jobs that cannot support two adults and more than one child — all pose insuperable problems for people who want to be good employees and good parents, too.[63] When childrearing is undervalued and undersupported, its true joys can't be found.

But escape to the public realm of power through wages, status, or a chance to use education and to see measurable progress has its problems, too. In the church and the secular world, employers assume that their employee's primary loyalty, during working hours, is to the employer. Employers allot different amounts of vacation days, personal days, and sick days to employees, and some employers work with their employees to create flexible schedules, but the workplace in the

United States assumes that male and female employees leave their families and personal lives at the door when they come to work. One lay woman who directs the after-school program in the church where her husband is the rector laments the fact that while she is working hard to provide the best possible educational experiences for the children she serves, her son is being cared for by others.

The realities of jobs and marriages have changed, but the rhetoric of women's roles and the reality of child-care arrangements has not. The devotion-to-work schema now fits men and women, in the church and the secular world. There has been no parallel change in economic and social structures to enable the devotion-to-family schema to fit either men's lives or employees' lives. This is the crux of the "work-family" debate — there are hundreds of books written about the work-family balance, but until we "unbend some gendering of parenting,"[64] and restructure paid work to accommodate family needs the stress will increase, endangering women, children, and men. The lives of clergy mothers both exemplify the conflict and, with notions of the sacredness of paid work and parenting, could suggest some ways out of the conflict. The church should model different ways of honoring parenting, and actively advocate for changes in the workplace and neighborhoods to make a better balance of work and family life possible. The church has had a strong tradition of caring for poor children, organizing against child labor, of caring for the sick, widows, and orphans.

The church as a system

Changes in social and economic structures will take generations and be determined by a host of factors well outside the control of any particular individual or group. They contribute to sanity or craziness in daily life. It's important to name them to have a sense of the possibilities and limits of change in daily exercise of ministry, lay or ordained, in the home or workplace. Church leaders have more ability and responsibility to influence the actions and attitudes of people within their denominations than to rearrange the working patterns in the United States. I turn now to an analysis of the particular structures within parish ministry that influence the way ordained women and men and their families are more or less able to honor commitments to God, spouse or partner, children, and church faithfully.

Cohorts of women

Blair-Loy found in her research that there were three rather distinct cohorts of women financial executives, shaped in part by historical events in the culture. Women who completed college before 1969 came of age in an era of traditional gender-role attitudes. Women graduating between 1969 and 1973 were in college or about to enter the workforce when the resurgence of the women's movement "helped establish the enforcement of equal employment rights, fostered gender-egalitarian ideologies, and encouraged young women to enter male-dominated occupations."[65] Women finishing college between 1974 and 1980 entered the work force after many of these legal changes had been implemented, and egalitarian ideologies were more acceptable in the United States culture at large.

The same cultural changes affected women clergy, as did the implementation of legal changes in many professions (but not in the church). In many denominations throughout the eighteenth and nineteenth century, white and African-American women were missionaries, leaders, preachers, teachers, church planters, all "without benefit of ordination" but with a sense of God's call that was respected by those who heard them preach the Word. The first woman to be ordained in the United States was Antoinette Brown, who was designated pastor in 1853 in the Congregational Church in the Northeast. After a few years of service, she was forced to step down; she joined the Unitarians and was again ordained in 1863. In 1894, Julia Foote was the first woman ordained deacon in the African Methodist Episcopal Zion Church; she was ordained an elder in 1900. Mary J. Small was ordained deacon in the A.M.E. Zion Church in 1895, and elder in 1898.[66] As the suffrage movement and the first wave of activism for women's rights took place, more women were ordained.[67] By the 1960s, many mainline denominations approved women's ordination, and a handful of women responded to this change and became ordained. A study of Presbyterian women identifies the "living pioneers" as women ordained between the 1950s and 1970s, 15 percent of their sample. Thirty-eight percent of their sample were ordained in the 1980s, and almost half, 47 percent, were ordained after 1990.[68]

A second wave of women entering seminaries and then seeking ordination occurred in the 1970s. By the 1980s, between one-third and one-half of entering classes were female. Between 1973 and 1984, African-American women's enrollment in seminaries grew from 5 percent to 20 percent of total African-American enrollment.[69] Often seminary faculty were hostile, and women had to find materials and push for acceptance, but they supported each other. Many of these women were second-career women, who may not have intended to be ordained when they entered seminary. Many of them had also been involved in the women's liberation movement, and they organized students to press for more female faculty and courses dealing with feminist perspectives.[70] Parishes were even more hostile than seminaries. Charlene Kammerer, a United Methodist Church bishop in the Western North Carolina Conference, talked about the difficulties of always being the first woman. This was a central theme of her peers in *Leading Women: Stories of the First Women Bishops of the United Methodist Church*. Of the first eleven women ordained in the Episcopal Church, only three found work in parish ministry and they all faced enormous hostility at almost every turn. These "first-wave" women talked repeatedly of how it was only by the grace of God, by unshakeable conviction born of prayer, and with the support of one or two key people each, that they found themselves trail-blazing — no girl they knew as a child ever said they were going to be a pastor when they grew up.

By the 1990s, there were as many women as men in seminaries, tenured women faculty, and most seminaries had mainstreamed at least some feminist resources into required classes and offered electives focusing on feminist perspectives on religious life and scholarship. In the 1992–1993 school year, 42 percent of the students at Howard University School of Divinity and 60 percent at Harvard Divinity School were women, although at Yale Divinity School that year women made up only 30 percent of the student population.[71] A few male voices complained that "the women were getting all the cushy jobs," even when statistics showed clearly that this was not true. For many women, seminary and ordination were a second career, after years in the secular workplace full-time or part-time, and after their children were either grown or in school full-time. Many African-American women serve in denominations that do not require a master of divinity degree for ordination, so women were working secular jobs to pay the rent, pastoring churches, and attending seminary classes when they could. They too brought skills from the secular workplace to ministry. Many of these women, African-American and Anglo, were often "the first" associate or rector or senior pastor or solo pastor, but there had been enough positive response to the first wave and enough time to let the overt hostility diminish that sexism seemed to go underground. McKenzie's study of African-American women and Zikmund et al.'s or Lehman's studies are too disparate to compare the different ways sexism manifested in Anglo and African-American communities, yet it is fair to say that resistance to women's ordained leadership is still a problem in both. It seems that many of the younger women I interviewed (women in their thirties and forties, many of whom chose ordination as their first career) were more matter-of-fact about their decision to seek ordination, clearer about the home-work boundaries they needed to maintain, less aware of resistance to their gender, and often (though far from always) were in marriages where male spouses took on more home and family responsibilities.

I wish now that I had paid more attention to age or date of ordination, and that I had asked about use of inclusive language or other challenges to a patriarchal symbol system. Pamela Cooper White suggests, in ways that ring true to my experience, that clergy women who become pregnant and have children while leading parishes are more aware for themselves of feminine dimensions of God and of the conflict between their experiences of God's grace and the limits of liturgical language. Cooper White writes:

> I understood incarnation in a whole new way when I gazed at each of my infant sons....My sermons became full of womb and breast imagery, because those were the images that had meaning for me, and the ways in which God had been revealed to me....I know now how God could be both fiercely protective and exasperated with us at the same time.[72]

For Vashti McKenzie, clergy women leaders need to reclaim the historical legacy of women leaders in the church, beginning with biblical examples such as Deborah, Naomi, Miriam, the unnamed women of the gospels, Phoebe, Euodia, Syntyche and Prisca of the epistles, and moving through church history (sometimes between the lines), to help ordained women understand that "a minister who happens to be a woman is not an individual who just stumbled into leadership because no one else was available; she is part of a historical legacy."[73]

Implications of the church as voluntary association

Decreased social capital

There is another interesting dimension of the social structure of clergy careers. Blair-Loy's schemas assume a division of the world into public and private realms, work and home, career and family. The church as an institution is a workplace for clergy, but for lay people and family of clergy it is what sociologists call a voluntary association. Civic associations — religious organizations, scouting, Elks and Masons, parent-teacher organizations, recreational clubs, political parties — exist between home and work. They are voluntary activities that contribute to the common good through providing valuable services and enabling people to enjoy each other's company. Robert Putnam is a contemporary sociologist and political scientist who popularized the notion of "social capital" in *Bowling Alone*. He defines social capital as "connections among individuals — social networks and the norms of reciprocity and trustworthiness that arise from them."[74] Social capital is important because the cooperation it encourages helps citizens resolve shared problems more easily, the trustworthiness it engenders facilitates business and social transactions, and the connections it fosters help people "become more tolerant, less cynical, and more empathetic to the misfortunes of others."[75] Religious organizations have traditionally been vital places to develop social capital, and participation in religious organizations has contributed to the well-being of other social and economic institutions. When time pressures mount, and people are forced to choose between work, family, and voluntary associations, participation in voluntary associations is often the first sacrifice. Decreasing social capital diminishes both individuals and the society in which they live.

Diminished status of clergy

The role of religion in the public life is currently a subject of intense debate. Participation in religious organizations in the United States has decreased steadily over the past forty years, as has participation in many other voluntary or civic associations, from the Elks and Rotary to PTAs, political parties, and group recreational activities. Robert Putnam offers several reasons for this decline, which is felt by clergy and lay leaders alike. Pressures of time and money, especially on two-career families, reduce participation in all civic activities. Religious organizations and educational groups are less severely affected, but there is a decline nonetheless. Suburbanization, commuting, and sprawl make it more difficult for people to get together for organized activities or informal socializing. Electronic entertainment, especially televisions and computers, have privatized leisure time significantly. For Putnam, though, the most important change has been generational: Every generation since people who were adults during World War II has seen a steady decrease in the participation of the next generation.[76] This is especially true for church-going. "Over the past three to four decades Americans have become about 10 [percent] less likely to claim church membership, while our actual attendance and involvement in religious activities has fallen by roughly 25 to 30 percent."[77]

This affects congregations and clergy in several different ways. When the role of the church in society is uncertain, that uncertainty generalizes to clergy, who often perceive themselves to be irrelevant. One priest whose father was also a priest quoted his father's friends' complaints about how when they began their ministries they were consistently invited to bless public events, participate in decision-making bodies in local governments, offer opinions about and gather support for community activities. Clergy in their children's generation are much less likely to be automatically included in civic affairs. Laws now prohibit blessings at most public events, and the congregations themselves play a less significant role in community life.

Weakening of public institutions

Putnam also finds that rather than disappearing, many institutions of civic life have been "hollowed out." The external structure exists, albeit with dwindling members and support, but "decay has consumed the load-bearing beams of our civic infrastructure."[78] Fewer lay people are around to be leaders, and their time is more limited. This rings true for the many small congregations within a mile or so of each other in northern New Jersey; all had been thriving forty years ago but now are in "survival mode," competing for parishioners and denominational resources. The difference between past experience, current perception, and the reality of hours of support can demoralize clergy and lay leaders alike. It's easy for clergy and lay leaders to blame themselves (or, more dangerously, each other) for failing to rally the troops for fundraisers, or for sermons that no longer draw the crowds who used to come, or for declining membership and pledges. The potential for conflict mounts as dwindling congregations face relatively fixed costs of maintaining older buildings and even minimum clergy salaries. Financial resources diminish, too, at the parish and denominational level, often increasing competition among clergy who need to support each other in a sometimes lonely position.

This takes its toll on clergy families in terms of clergy burn-out, overfunctioning at the expense of the family, conflict often taken out on family members, and even participation in church activities. A generation ago clergy children may not have been the only children to participate in every church event; in small congregations, several clergy and their partners or spouses now find that their children are the only ones in Sunday School, or that their toddlers are the only ones running up the aisles during worship because they're the only toddlers in the congregation.

Families at work

Because of the way economic systems have structured work, parents in the corporate world (or stores or factories or classrooms or hospitals) wouldn't even think about bringing their children to work. Nannies leave their own children to go care for other people's children. Spouses or partners rarely come to work except on social occasions (although there is a history of corporate wives' contributions to their husbands' careers through home entertaining). Very few employers count the cost of the demands they make on their workers, let alone their workers' families. Employers assume that while at work employees' first allegiance is to the workplace. Why should the church be any different?

Expectation of family attendance

Unlike most other professions, there is an expectation that clergy bring their families to church, just as do the families in the congregation. Family members in both clergy and congregation who don't meet that expectation are increasingly common, but both the absence and presence of family members can become an issue in parish life. Families who don't fit the traditional mold of biological nuclear family — single mothers, divorced parents raising children alone, youngish couples without children, families with special-needs children, same-sex couples with or without children — can also become a subject of discussion or pointed nondiscussion. The schema of nuclear family life blinds many people to the existence of "differently structured" families.

Limits on family participation

Many family members of clergy worship and participate in church life, but find that there are appropriate but bothersome limits on how they can participate in leadership. Either church rules or custom often prohibit the clergy person's spouse or partner from serving as an elected lay leader, because of numerous conflicts of interest. Family members may not have a voice on some of the issues that most affect them, including salary, housing, or schedules of programs or worship, though other members of the church do. Family members of clergy often don't have a priest or counselor other than their spouse, partner, or parent to support them in crises or in their ordinary journey in faith. In an informal survey of the needs of clergy families in the Diocese of Newark, the need for both formal clergy support and informal support groups was named as the most pressing desire for family members of clergy.[79]

Moving home dynamics into church and vice versa

Recently a parish lay leader gave my family a board game called "The Nightmare before Christmas" to honor ten years of ministry with the parish. She was a "preacher's kid" and she knew how it could be: Christmas is a classic set-up for a collision of clergy and parental expectations and needs. A Jay Sidebotham cartoon illustrates the tension well — in it, the female rector asks the organist to play all five verses of a Christmas carol slowly so she can wrap some last-minute presents for her family![80] My own experience has mirrored this. One Christmas Eve day, I thought things were fairly calm. The worship was organized, Christmas shopping was done, and I even had time to wrap some presents while my husband was preparing dinner. Then a parishioner called with what felt like a serious enough issue that I agreed to meet her after dinner and before the pageant, which meant leaving home for church earlier than I expected. When I finished meeting with her, I met a crisis in the parish hall: The three kings' crowns were missing! My daughters have an extensive dress-up collection and I knew there were crowns at home, but my youngest child didn't want to share *her* crowns with the kings. My husband and daughters often resent the "drift" of home possessions to church, because sometimes they don't drift back. I was focused on church needs and impatient with old family issues, so I yelled at both husband and daughter in front of others; they yelled back; we recovered enough to say sorry, but then the show had to go on. It wasn't the best way to celebrate Christ's birth, though it helps to remember that the first Christmas couldn't have been easy for Mary and Joseph, either.

Spouses, partners, and children can offer support to clergy when in church. Someone touring with candidates for bishop in an episcopal election noticed how much family members between interviews were ready with smiles, Kleenex, water, and reassurance that helped the candidates recenter themselves. In my survey of Episcopal clergy in the Diocese of Newark, many clergy cited their spouse or partner's support for their work as one of the joys of congregational ministry. Family members can also offer less-helpful advice. Many clergy need to work out rules with their family about when constructive criticism about sermons is welcome; Sunday afternoon is often not a good time. Children see their parents giving more attention to other people's children sometimes. One man said it made him sad to see that his clergy partner was rather uncomfortable with even a kiss or squeeze of his hand when he was "on duty" in church.

The role of clergy in parish systems

Institutional power

Jackson Carroll identified four types of power working in the church. God is the ultimate source of authority, based on the church's convictions about God and God's purposes for the world in history, in Jesus, and in life.[81] There are two dimensions of authority: *representing the sacred*, when by personal attributes and/or institutional recognition people are seen as "men and women of God," and *expertise*, a body of knowledge and skills that contribute to effectiveness in ministry. There are two sources of authority: *official authority* granted by an institution and *personal authority* given by through basic integrity, charisma, character, and piety. Authority to represent the sacred is conveyed officially by the institution, through ordination or licensing, or conveyed personally, by a reputation for piety and holy life. Think of the woman in the pew who has never held a church office but who is known for her spiritual wisdom and the power of her prayer. Expertise comes through certified competence (e.g., a master of divinity degree or other recognized certification), or through demonstrated competence, when specific gifts for ministry are developed over time and through experience. Carroll shows how different denominations expect different balances of personal and official authority in their clergy in both dimensions.[82] Carroll doesn't explore what most all clergy women know: that given historical resistance to granting official authority to women, and given the gendered ways women and men have been socialized to exercise personal power, there are nearly constant challenges to women's exercise of power and authority in the church regardless of the number of degrees or years in ministry. Yet this is the context in which power and authority are exercised.

In *Leaving Church*, Barbara Brown Taylor eloquently describes the loss of institutional power she felt when she moved from rector of Grace-Calvary to an academic position at Piedmont College. Suddenly she was sitting in the pews on Sunday morning, seeing the backs of everyone's head rather than all the faces, singing hymns someone else had chosen, "watching the play" rather than starring in it.[83] When one or even a few people routinely lead those gathered for worship, pray aloud and on behalf of everyone, interpret Scripture, give instructions, consecrate bread and wine, and pronounce blessings, they come to be seen as holier than others despite all the rhetoric of "the ministry of the baptized." When the system designates one person as holy, and then expects that person to represent the institution in all places where a "holy person" is required, it distorts the basic understanding of holiness because it has equated holiness with ordination. When the clergy person was male, there was an implicit assumption that the family he headed was also holy; this is less true for female clergy who aren't typically seen as the heads of their households (even when they are). This process establishes expectations of clergy presence at events even when the clergy's real expertise and gifts may not be needed, and can draw clergy away from the family where they are also needed.

Vague job descriptions for rectors

"What do you do all day?" "Do clergy have other jobs during the week?" are questions often asked of clergy. They're also asked of "stay-at-home" moms, one indication that the work of nurturing and pastoral care is often undervalued. Jane Austen or Anthony Trollope novels portray clergy as seemingly only required to lead services (or delegate them to others to lead), attend teas, find wives, and negotiate church politics. The separation of workplace from residences mean that clergy are usually only seen by parishioners on Sundays, or evenings when the parishioners are not working, or by retired people, sick people, or people who work or are active in the place of residence. All of these feed the impression that clergy really only work on Sundays. Letters of agreement that spell out responsibilities are really helpful, but they don't always match the implicit expectations of either clergy or parishioners, such as who takes out the recycling? How many Saturday meetings are too many? How often should hospitalized people be visited, and how do clergy get notified? Contrary to popular belief, clergy don't usually receive messages in prayer about who was admitted to what hospital and when.

Some lay people who are working full-time and then volunteering at church scoff at the notion that clergy can work too hard: If lay people can put in all these hours, so can the clergy. How can work for the church be a "real job" if lay people can fulfill all the responsibilities of their secular work and still give significant amounts of their "free time"? But clergy and lay people get fed differently from participation in church activities. Lay people generally come to church to deepen their relationship with God. Clergy often need to go elsewhere (somewhere where they are not in charge) to be fed and renewed by God. Even if lay people are teaching a class or leading a program, clergy participate with one eye on how things are going or what new corner of the ceiling is peeling. Lay people use the work of the clergy to be "equipped for the work of ministry."[84] Clergy may also find that worship depends on their relationship with God, but whether they want to come or not, whether they're feeling in tune with God or distant, their job, first and foremost, is to preside over the space where worship (or program) happens.

Overdependence on clergy, especially in times of parish growth or change

Donald is the rector of an urban parish with a huge community development center, and where his wife Marlene, a professional social worker, is one of many staff people. The church had a history of decline and then, with the previous rector, experienced fairly dramatic growth and expansion of worship and social services. As often happens when a "founder" begins a new institution or a new era, the system tends to revolve around the founder. The successor is left to move the institution from one centered on personality to one that depends on new administrative structures. Yet even when rector and parish leaders know this consciously, the process of change is slow, awkward, and often full of resistance. The parish Donald inherited was big enough to function as a corporate or resource parish, but in practice it still functioned as a program or even family system highly dependent on clergy. Neither lay leaders nor staff were strong enough to share leadership, despite systematic training, which meant that Donald often worked seventy- to eighty-hour weeks. If he refused, he ran the risk of jeopardizing part of the program and — given intertwined finances — the church as a whole. His very real question to me was, "I know I'm not indispensable. No one is. But until people are willing and able to do the work, can I really risk letting a whole program close, when that may be the card in the house of cards?" Many clergy berate themselves for having terrible boundaries, or being inefficient time managers, and while sometimes that's true, sometimes there are real pressures that make "just saying no" potentially dangerous. Marlene wants to have another child, however, so her desire to change this situation is increasing rapidly.

More congregations can only afford to pay their clergy part-time. Yet there's a minimum amount of work that a clergy person needs to do to maintain even a part-time parish — it takes the same amount of time to write a sermon for twenty people as for fifty. When Janet was called to her current parish, her contract was for two-thirds time, and she needed a second part-time job (two days a week) to make ends meet. Two jobs added enormously to time constraints — easily more than fifty hours a week. The parish grew enough to pay her four-fifths time, so she could quit the second job. Sharing finances with her partner and her son's financial independence a year or so after high school helped, too (he joined the military six months into college). Yet after two years, the parish reduced her salary to one-third time. They had expected her to work every Sunday, but Janet's partner is a teacher and she was clear that one-third time meant taking one-third of the Sundays as well, which she did in the summer. The idea of one-third time, or four-fifths time is a convenient fiction for both the parish and the diocese, especially since "full-time" is considered fifty hours a week. In theory, Janet should eliminate one of the three weekly Sunday services, yet each has a steady attendance level and no one is willing to consider combining services.

Role confusion

There is a certain amount of role confusion built into the job descriptions of parish clergy that blurs boundaries between work and home, public and private, on-duty and off-duty. One family is now coming to church because of some informal conversations I had on the soccer field about the parish. I have run into parishioners in the grocery store and started talking about their mother's prognosis until my children remind me they need to get home. I get involved in school board politics because I'm a concerned parent, but as a priest I need not to be seen taking sides. Which pastoral phone calls should I pick up on the evenings I'm home but am putting children to bed or helping with homework? Or, recently, I was asked to come to my eighth grader's health class to talk about the use of condoms in HIV/AIDS prevention. This is right and good in my role as executive director of an HIV/AIDS support program, but I want my daughter to abstain from sex for a while longer (ten years? thirty?) and not have to know about condoms just yet. She and I talked about whether she wanted me to come to her health class in this role; if she hadn't, I wouldn't have done it. They could find another health class, I could find another speaker, but my relationship with my daughter is unique.

Role confusion is often built into the use of "Father" and "Mother" as clergy titles in some parts of the Episcopal Church. When men are called "Father," people's first association is often with their role in the church (even when clergy's own children are present), and sometimes (consciously or not) with God. There may be some association too with "Father knows best," and male authority in home and church. "Mother" is much more ambiguous, often evoking either Mother Superiors, responsible for convents, or someone's biological mother. Whose mother am I? In many contexts I am the mother of the children I am raising, but in the parish I am sometimes seen as the mother of the parish, and often as the one who mediates relationships between parishioners and Mother or Father God. Parental titles often lead to role confusion for men and women. Add to that the tension Jesus highlighted between nuclear families, which sometimes pit loyalty to family above loyalty to God, and the family of God, the church, where loyalty to God can be most faithfully lived out. Then add the expectation, from parish and family, that clergy and parents (especially mothers) should be available to both parishioners and children 24/7. No wonder clergy feel crazy!

Pressure points in church and parish

Schedules

Church schedules designed to accommodate lay people wreak havoc on family time. One single-mother cleric lamented the fact that she felt guilty about not wanting to work on diocesan committees with lay members, because then meetings are held in the evenings and on weekends and that's precious family time. Church schedules designed to accommodate commuters wreak havoc on relationships where the clergy partner is one of the commuters — clergy go off to work when their partners return and vice versa. For single clergy with young children, or clergy parents whose spouses commute, early morning or early evening meetings are a nightmare. It's almost impossible to find a babysitter for 6:00–7:00 on weekday mornings, or to pick up children from activities, feed them, start homework and maybe give the partner a peck on the cheek before heading out again unless the sitter lives in (which is not an option on most clergy salaries) or unless parishioners babysit. The day the senior warden lost my crawling child somewhere in church while I was celebrating a 7:00 a.m. Eucharist was funny only in retrospect!

Then there are the emergencies. Clergy are often able, with planning, to attend children's daytime school activities and to participate in the PTA. But I have learned over time not to make absolute promises. My six-year-old was ecstatic that I was chosen to be class parent for her Halloween party, and looked forward my attendance for a week. Then a very active parishioner suddenly died, the funeral had to be Halloween morning, and she had to be buried in a cemetery two hours away. I had a long conversation with the family, the organist, and the funeral director about other possibilities, to no avail. No parent has yet learned how to be in two places at once, or how not to feel guilty in the face of genuine disappointment.

Then there are continuing education opportunities, some of which are required by denominational officials. Ten-day residential conferences are either out of the question for clergy with young children and working spouses, or require huge amounts of logistical planning and cooperation from the spouse or partner. The director of a highly recommended leadership program was very clear that the program wasn't set up for parents of young children, so no accommodations could be made when my child was born in the middle of a four-year commitment. A female participant of the same program shared a conversation about what each member of the group had to do in order to attend the program. All of the women had made plans for child-care, prepared some meals in advance, arranged car pools, and left detailed instructions for their male spouses. The men were taken aback; they admitted that they had just told their wives that they would be away in enough time for the wives to plan for their absence. Even diocesan clergy conferences often require two or three nights away from family. While the value of time away from the normal routine, of sound programs and of connection with other clergy is undeniable, so is the strain placed on family remaining at home. Clergy with young or school-aged children can only attend if their spouse or partner can care for the children or if they pay for a sitter.

Conflict in parishes

There is conflict in any job — in fact, any time people work together. Yet because of the way family usually participates in the workplace, because the clergy home is often part of the salary package, because clergy are seen as especially holy and powerful because of their institutional authority, conflict in parishes often gets taken out on family. In one household the man was retired after thirty-five years of parish ministry; his wife had moved from stay-at-home mother and active parishioner to student to professional psychotherapist in that same period. The wife observed that one of the biggest tensions in their marriage came from the way her husband dealt (or didn't deal) with parishioners she felt were destructive or dangerous either to her spouse or to the parish. In the course of his ministry, the priest would often feel compelled to make a midnight visit to the alcoholic parishioner who yet again found himself in crisis, while his wife wanted him to establish better pastoral limits. Her husband would complain repeatedly about bad behavior on the part of a lay leader — insults, crises, or threats that jeopardized the parish — without feeling he had the power or ability to change the situation. She would sense his angst and be unable to help. Sometimes she knew her directness and problem-solving actually irritated her husband and increased his misery, and hers, but she couldn't help herself.

Many clergy spouses have been told about their partners' foibles, or about issues they should deal with, and when the spouse has the presence of mind to ask the person to deal directly with the clergy person, he or she is rebuffed angrily. Triangulation with clergy family members is quite common, and can be devastating, especially to children who are told how ineffective or bad their parent is. Matthew Price, in the 2003 "State of the Clergy" report, noted that of Episcopal clergy interviewed in 2001 for a *Pulpit and Pew* study, 50 percent of male clergy and 60 percent of female clergy regularly experience stress due to challenges faced in the parish, and 30 percent of male clergy and 40 percent of female clergy experience stress regularly while dealing with members of the congregation. The conflicts are not about national issues dividing the church but about infrastructure and worship.[85]

Salaries and benefits

Earlier sections have noted that salaries of women clergy are consistently lower than similarly placed and experienced male clergy across all denominations. Becky McMillan and Matthew Price looked at clergy salaries in two types of church polity. In "congregational" polity, including Baptists, Pentecostals, United Church of Christ, and others, congregations have great freedom to determine clergy compensation. In "connectional" polity, denominations have some degree of centralization, and can set minimum salary and benefit requirements. These include most of the clergy included in this book — Episcopalians, Methodists, Lutherans, and Presbyterians. (Connectional polity may help explain the presence, at least at some point, of a research office with some data for all clergy.)

Several of McMillan and Price's findings are relevant here:

- In general, in all but the largest churches, salaries, pension benefits and health care coverage are higher for pastors in connectional than congregational polities.

- Regional differences in compensation are not large, but the difference between small churches and larger, financially stable congregations is huge. Many smaller congregations can barely afford connectional minimums; in both kinds of polity, smaller congregations are moving toward part-time, or less experienced, or less educated clergy. They also devote a disproportionate amount of time to church-growth strategies for the sake of increased operating revenue.

- Clergy with families who are trying first to repay seminary debt, then to support themselves, and then to pay for college must base career moves on economic reasons, rather than on a sense of what God might want or a good match of gifts. Financial dependence on a congregation makes prophetic leadership more difficult.

- Women's upward mobility is still restricted.

- African-American clergy and white female clergy compensation packages are often too low to pay off the theological education debt incurred.

♦ Regardless of polity, only a handful of pastors "earn what most Americans would consider a professional level salary."

♦ Low clergy salaries cause many talented seminary graduates to seek employment outside of parish ministry.[86]

Vashti McKenzie's study of African-American pastors, primarily from Methodist and Baptist traditions in the Northeast corridor of the United States, adds another dimension to the church-family balance. The majority of women she included still work in vocations (McKenzie's word, which fits my understanding of it well) outside of the ministry for economic reasons, because they are either unpaid or salaries are too low to support themselves and their families. "A few women were quick to note that they work full-time in part-time positions in their churches.[87]

Many married women clergy are financially stable because their husbands are the primary breadwinners. This has implications for geographical mobility and sometimes influences lay leaders' willingness to keep raising salaries and women's ability to negotiate higher salaries for themselves. In the Episcopal Diocese of Newark, parishes are required to pay for health insurance for the clergy person and their family *unless the clergy spouse provides such insurance*. That is a huge caveat, given ever-rising health care expenses. Clergy cannot insist on this benefit; the parish becomes accustomed to a lower salary package, the rector leaves, and unless there is enough money in the budget line to offer health insurance to a new rector, the parish either has to choose among candidates who have families who provide insurance or consider reducing other salary or program expenses. If the provider's insurance suddenly ceases, or if clergy become divorced, the parish is hit hard. McMillan and Price suggest that if the church is to be faithful to its mission of preaching the gospel, or empowering members to love God, one another, and their enemies more faithfully, and if denominations expect their clergy to be faithful to God and not only economic needs, some centralized intervention to insure adequate salary and benefit packages is essential.

Church-owned housing

Recently the diocesan council of the Diocese of Newark started a systematic inspection of rectories. Over the years they had found safety issues — falling plaster ceilings, poor electrical work, nonworking windows — that never made it to the "priority list" of repairs paid for by the church. Their preliminary findings were "horrific," sometimes because rectors didn't report issues and sometimes because vestries either didn't respond or used nonprofessional labor to make temporary and substandard repairs. One rector's wife said that after asking for a year for replacement windows (the glass was broken, wind came through in winters, bugs

in summer), she went to a local hardware store, ordered windows, had them in-
stalled, and sent the vestry the bill. The warden's response was, "I didn't know it
was so important to you." Her husband had been reluctant to bring it up again
and again. The triangulation built into the system when clergy spouses aren't
allowed to advocate for themselves to the parish is tremendously disempowering.
Years ago, a clergy spouse came into her kitchen in her nightgown at 7:00 a.m. to
find strange legs protruding from under the kitchen sink. A vestry member was
attempting to do the sink repairs for which her husband had been seeking vestry
approval for months, rather than paying a plumber. When she politely but firmly
asked the vestry member to leave her house, a year-long controversy ensued over
who should have access to the rectory under what circumstances and who de-
termines what repairs are necessary. This became the hook on which all other
parish conflict was hung, at great emotional cost to the rector and his family.

Clergy, their families, and their congregations live and bear witness to God's
love in the midst of social, economic, and political structures that are bigger
than they are. It's easy to let the pushes and pulls of these structures obscure
the good news of the gospel. One of the frequent laments I hear is that the
daily work of institutional church maintenance can intrude on clergy family time
and absorb energy and skill, while all the time a voice in the back of clergy
heads asks, "Is this really what Jesus wants us to do with the resources we have?"
"Are we doing mission work, or are we in maintenance mode, fighting a losing
battle for an increasingly irrelevant museum?" "How much clergy time is spent
teaching, preaching, healing, empowering, and how much is spent ministering to
the boiler?" "Will people please let me stop defending my gender or threatening
my ability to live with the partner God gave me and let me get on with the gospel?"
Many clergy despair when they feel they entered parish ministry to serve God,
and end up serving a dysfunctional church system instead, in a world where basic
gospel priorities (love, justice, inclusion, peace in neighborhoods and the world)
are flouted daily. And yet — and yet. Christians live in a world of "already and not
yet." Nothing is outside the reach of God's love and healing. Jesus was skilled at
naming the "principalities and powers," multiplying resources to fulfill his mission,
and remaining true to his mission in the midst of injustice and oppression. To the
extent that the church can keep its eyes on Jesus, advocate for greater justice
in the world and in the church, and keep on repenting and returning to Jesus
when (not if) we get distracted, clergy and their families will also be more able
to remain true to their vocations.

Chapter Three

Differentiating Service to God and Service to the Church

The tapes running in my head

It was my first day back in the church after my daughter was born. I had enjoyed my work as the curate (or assistant) in this multistaff parish for almost two years. I'd used the diocesan-mandated six weeks of full-time paid leave, plus three weeks of vacation, and it was time to return to work. So I left my nine-week old daughter in her car seat in the home of a woman I'd met for about three hours, cried for a few minutes, and drove to church.

I felt horrible. "Good moms never leave their infants," said old tapes in my head. But lots of good moms do return to full-time work, and their babies grow into fine children and adults. "Good priests care for their parishioners," said other tapes, and priesthood was my vocation. I enjoyed parish work most of the time. "Female priests need to prove that having a baby doesn't change anything" had been a mantra through most of the pregnancy, when I had only missed two days of work and fit doctors' appointments in less-scheduled morning times. The last week of the pregnancy happened to be Holy Week, which put a wrench in scheduling, but Avery, already a good preacher's kid, waited until Easter Monday to be born. It was going to be even more important to show that I was still capable of fulfilling all job responsibilities without slacking.

I was greeted by an office volunteer who was delighted to see me. He'd missed me while I was away. He wanted to talk about an article in the paper that day, about how mothers were leaving their infants with near-strangers and going back to work before the children were even a year old. "Isn't that selfish? Babies need their mothers. If the mothers love work so much they shouldn't have children; they should wait until they have enough money to stay home." The irony of this tirade escaped him completely, but I was floored. The rector rescued me by chiding him that I probably didn't need to hear that today, but it went over his head. He saw me as "Mother," not as *mother.* I went up to my office, all three sets of tapes whirring simultaneously, and before I began to make phone calls and set up meetings and visit folks I hadn't seen for months, I called my husband.

That's the fourth tape, not nearly as loud as the others. The "good marriage" tape, in which the partnership is nurtured in spare time pried from parish commitments or children's activities when sometimes, at least, it should be first. Each of these tapes is about relationships initiated by God and people "for their mutual joy."[1] Each of them also labels a set of attitudes and expectations of clergy parents in committed relationships, attitudes and expectations that sometimes conflict and sometimes enhance each other. While there are individual differences due to upbringing, personality, and situation, there are also some commonalities that can contribute to craziness. This chapter explores some of the expectations in the clergy-parent-life partner constellation and offers some paths to sanity.

Expectations in the ordination process

A call to ministry is really a call to ordained ministry

I first thought seriously about ordination when I realized that I needed to talk to people explicitly about how God was moving in their lives, and create a safe space to know and be nourished by God through word and sacrament. Every clergy person has their story of when they "felt called" to be a deacon, priest, or bishop, in part because discernment processes expect such stories and in part because people are curious about why some of us claim to know what God wants us to do with our lives. I spent the next two years articulating and defending that call in a well-established denominational process. Quotations from Violet Fisher and Susan Wolfe Hassinger in *The Leading Women: Stories of the First Women Bishops of the United Methodist Church* illustrate how these pioneer women felt called to ministry at a time when most other people thought they were crazy.

> I knew, without a doubt, that God had laid God's hands on me. After I started preaching [at 16, in the Methodist Episcopal Church], doors all over [the Western Shore of Maryland] were open to me.[2]
>
> I had this sense of being called to pastoral ministry. And I knew — it was so clear — that my calling was not to be a Christian educator, not to be a missionary, but to be a pastor.... [Her parents'] first reaction was disbelief: "You can't do that." But I remained firm. It wasn't just me saying

this. There was something very deep within me, and I knew I needed to do that.[3]

The sense of God's call to parish ministry has sustained almost all of the clergy I interviewed, when personal or parish circumstances seemed overwhelming.

The institutional understanding of God as the source of authority already differentiates God's invitation to ordained ministry from other careers or from God's invitations to lifetime commitments to a partner or to parenting. Many lay Christians are quite articulate about how their work, paid or volunteer, is vocation, a response to a call from God. The culture, however, has identified vocation with career; some service, usually paid, in the public realm, that provides meaning, value, and status. Christians talk of lay ministry in similar ways, as some sort of service, paid or volunteer, that is doing God's work in the world, but the sense of calling is rarely publicly recognized. The perceived difference between lay people, lay leaders, and ordained clergy varies from denomination to denomination, depending on how distinct the ordained clergy role is. Zikmund et al. divided their sample into three types of denominations — congregational, institutional, and Spirit-led — representing three different understandings of clergy roles.[4]

Many denominations have designated lay ministers such as Presbyterian "lay commissioned pastors" or United Methodist lay pastors and elders. The perceived holiness of ordained ministers is indicated by the attention and denominational regulations dedicated to institutional discernment of calls to lay and ordained ministry. Access to seminary training or other forms of accreditation also differentiate ordained from lay ministry in the mainline Protestant denominations, while preaching ability and functional competence in a congregation are signs of a call in more "Spirit-led" denominations. Perceived holiness is also indicated by the ordained ministers' role in the liturgy: Ordained clergy preside over worship while lay leaders may have more administrative or financial responsibilities. Some denominations (Disciples of Christ, the United Church of Christ, churches in the Pentecostal and Holiness traditions) use personal holiness, the way a clergy person models a life of prayer, "Spirit-filled" preaching, ethical living, and other personal attributes of holiness as a sign of fitness for ordination, while others, including clergy in the Episcopal Church, Evangelical Lutheran Church in America, Roman Catholic Church, and some Methodist and Presbyterian congregations use sacraments, symbols of the office, and clerical attire to differentiate clergy from laity.[5] Ordination vows also convey a "lower" or "higher" doctrine of clergy holiness, moving from a very functional understanding of ordained ministry, as in some Presbyterian sessions or Congregational associations where ordination is dependent on finding a full-time call to clearly recognized congregational ministry, to an ontological understanding of ordination as a specific gift of the Holy Spirit which conveys holiness regardless of whether a clergy person ever functions in an institutional church setting, as in the Episcopal or Roman Catholic denominations. Finally, reflecting the value of money in the culture at large, ordained ministers are generally paid, while the majority of lay leaders serve as volunteers. In combination, these sources of authority either magnify or reduce the perception of holiness of clergy compared to laity.

Even as ministry is understood more broadly in the public realm, Christians rarely talk of the work "at home" of nurturing lifetime commitments or parenting or even caring for aging parents as ministry. The consistent question in discernment toward ordination, asked a hundred and ten ways, is, "How do you know God wants you to be ordained?" Rarely does anyone hear, "How do you know God wants you to start a family?" Most people have stories of how they met their spouse or partner. Gay and lesbian folks have coming out stories, some of which involve a clear sense that God affirmed their sexual orientation. Some parents have stories of when they knew the time was right to begin a family. Many women recount what happened when they discovered they were pregnant, or gave birth, or knew they could not conceive and were open to other options, or when the call came saying "we have a child for you." Very few people ask new parents, as a matter of course, how they knew God wanted them to make a lifetime commitment to another person or start a family. It's either taken for granted or assumed to be private information. The stories are there, but they're not sanctioned by the church as "sacred stories," the way stories of a call to ordained ministry are.

Ordained clergy have an institutional context for the invitation from God to serve the church that is different from marriage and absent for GLBT couples and all parents. Premarital, or precommitment service, counseling in a church usually involves some discussion of how this partnership is of God, but except for the ceremony or renewal of vows, this is a private affair. Most denominations are either questioning whether to publicly bless same-gender unions, or rejecting the possibility out of hand. Many churches have baby-welcoming rituals that include prayers for the parents, but the focus is more the baby than the change in status for the new parents. Baptism is explicitly focused on bringing the baby into the household of God. There aren't ways to recognize parenting as an acceptance of a divine call. Christians don't usually call what goes on in private life "ministry."

Ordained ministry is the most important calling for clergy

As it has nearly from the beginning, the church prioritizes ordination above other invitations from God. Often ordination discernment happens in the context of a marriage or committed relationship, sometimes once children are already a part of the picture. Family members may have listened, sometimes affirmed, and sometimes challenged the desire, but the discernment process emphasizes the individual's reasons, choices, and abilities. Questions about the family and, in some ordination processes, *to* family members, often concern how or whether the family members will support the candidates' choice, not how the family will be affected. This is perhaps especially true for gay and lesbian clergy in denominations or dioceses where "don't ask, don't tell" is the way to avoid controversial issues of sexual orientation in the ordination process. One priest talked about the difficulties of being very honest about his life when he knew that he could only succeed in the process by omitting any reference to his sexual orientation, his partner, or some of his support systems. It's true for married clergy and parents too, in that too much talk of family might make it appear as if ordination isn't the first or most important priority. Yet ordination is a calling, a way of life that encompasses family responsibilities too. One African-American nondenominational pastor said she really appreciated the freedom from any denominational structure, which accentuated the sense of being called, as a couple, to minister as a family, while both also juggled work to pay the bills and raise three children. It was a way of life with ramifications for everything else they did, not just a job. Something is lost when parishes and clergy focus more on career advancement than serving Jesus, but that focus often comes from structures that make salary dependent on the size of church served, not the pastor's needs or gifts.

An Episcopal bishop told a story of mentoring a husband and father of two children toward ordination. The night before ordination, he wanted to spend the night alone in the church in prayer, so that he could really focus on what God was inviting him to do. The bishop asked him instead to spend the night with his family, focusing on the relationships for which he was already responsible. He was astonished, because he didn't think of family life as a place to seek or find God, or that the family and ordination had anything to do with each other. He felt he was embarking on this journey alone, although his family had been intimately involved in the decision to seek ordination, move to a seminary, move again to a field placement, and contemplate yet another move for a first job. There is rarely a place for any candidate to say that ordination is only as holy as commitments to spouse or partner and children, and there isn't the corporate language for that.

Ordained ministers only serve God in and through the church

It would be odd in any job interview for an applicant to tell a prospective employer that their commitment to their job is only as important as their commitment to family. The culture has an expectation that employees separate work from family, and that employees, when on the job, serve only the employer. The question for clergy is, "Who is the employer?" For lay people, "employer" means the person or organization that writes the paychecks. The parallel answer for clergy then would be the parish or church office or institution. Yet too often clergy and lay people alike act as if God is the employer. How many jokes concern clergy reporting to "a higher power?" Jokes reveal implicit expectations. And if God is assumed to be the employer, then a whole host of untenable assumptions follow: How can anyone serve God enough, be good enough, be off duty? In a culture that conveys value by money, serving God as a paid employee in the church is automatically more important than serving God in marriage or commitment vows or parenting, none of which are paid. And whether serving God or the parish, keeping that paid church job is usually important because it pays the bills. In congregations, the responsibility of the clergy to help the parish survive often seems more urgent and of more value to God than meeting the needs of the clergy family. Marlene, working on the staff of the church where her husband was rector, worried that neither she nor her husband were spending enough time with their child, and asked rather wistfully, "How can you say no to God's work?" When asked if caring for her child was also God's work, she agreed, but the assumption that the work of the parish is holier was still operative.

The irony is that of all employers, the church (along with other religious traditions) is the one with the most explicit rhetoric of family values. Many sermons address the hard and joyful work of learning to love family members better. Other sermons challenge the culture's emphasis on materialism and focus on the joys found in relationships rather than possessions. The church is in the business of marrying people, nurturing children and families, counseling families in crisis, praying for family members in trouble, grieving with those who have lost loved ones. Marlene lamented the fact that so many of her days were spent away from her child creating excellent programs for other people's children. A clergy father started a "date night" program in his church that provided a sitter for children at the church while parents went out to dinner. This was a good way to see his wife during "work time." The church's rhetoric is solid, and its practice often good for parishioners, but the clergy family is often left out of consideration.

Most mainline denominations talk about the ministry of the baptized, or the priesthood of all believers. When asked, church members can often eloquently describe how the responsibility of ordained clergy is to provide the resources to help all Christians make God's love known in the world. Nonetheless, in most denominations the implicit and sometimes explicit message is that clergy are the *real* ministers, whose work for God in the church is the holiest form of ministry. Even some of the recent tools for "discernment of gifts" among the laity identify gifts for ministry with work for the church, paid or volunteer.[6] It's easy to understand how clergy and clergy family members can prioritize service to the church over service to God in nurturing marriages, partnerships, children, self-care, or prayer.

Expectations of women in the ordination process

The assumptions above apply to male and female clergy. They become more obvious, though, when women's experiences are considered, especially the experiences of ordained mothers.

Motherhood is the vocation for women

In general, women are expected to be mothers. Social stigmas about women who never had children are fading but still present in the culture. A 2003 United States Census Report found that "[a]bout 18 percent of women ages 40 to 44 in 2002 had never had a child, compared with 10 percent in 1976."[7] Fifty-five percent of mothers of children under twelve months of age were working, as were 72 percent of mothers of children over one year of age.[8] In 2006, approximately 75 percent of all working women were working full-time, and only 25 percent were working part-time.[9] While the majority of mothers now spend significant time in the workplace, the ideal of motherhood as a woman's primary and most fulfilling vocation is found in the media, in parenting literature, in structural realities such as child-care and school schedules, and in religious traditions that promote a gendered division of labor and responsibilities. Poor mothering is often blamed for more social ills than mothers' actual power in social, economic, and religious institutions warrants. Even when not connected by blood or marriage to children, women are often expected to mother those around them, providing physical and emotional support in their careers or as part of their job (and often receiving lower wages than for other types of jobs). Female clergy are often praised for their better pastoral skills because, "being women," they are expected to be more nurturing than men.

For centuries, the vocation of marriage and motherhood has been idealized as the best way for women to serve God unless they joined a religious community. This vocation was proclaimed in the pulpit, in the home, in the media, and in the actual jobs available for women. Other than factory work, most jobs for women until the twentieth century were in education or nursing or in service positions caring for homes, children, the elderly and frail, or fields or gardens. The vocation of wife and mother carried with it expectations of male dominance and female subordination in the home and workplace. The actual experiences of women in marriage or as mothers were rarely considered in writing about religious life, because those experiences occurred in the private sphere and because men were writing about the religious lives of men and women. Even the advice men gave to women about faith outside of a convent either ignored or idealized the roles of wife and mother.

Recently, that has changed. There's an emerging body of literature by and about mothers exploring the spirituality of mothering. While women were expected to be mothers, no one expected mothers to learn new and life-changing things about God. In 1979, Carol Ochs wrote *Women and Spirituality*, comparing the spiritual lessons learned from mothering with the insights of the desert mothers and fathers. For her, taking women's experiences of motherhood seriously changed the focus of spirituality from another world after this one to this world, here and now; from artificial disciplines of sacrifice to actual sacrifices freely offered in the service of greater life for mother and child; from emphasis on experiences of loss, guilt, and suffering to joy, healing, and new life.[10] Margaret Hebblethwaite offered theological reflections on the birth and care of her three young children in *Motherhood and God*.[11] Suzanne Guthrie often incorporates lessons learned from mothering into her sermons and theological reflections.[12] Christians are slowly reclaiming an understanding of the holiness of the family and a spirituality of everyday life that is an essential antidote to implicit assumptions that true holiness can only be found in solitude, away from family, sexuality, or daily events. Celebrating the spirituality of motherhood, however, does not imply that men cannot find holiness in fathering or that women shouldn't look for holiness elsewhere.

In the twentieth century (with some notable exceptions earlier), women began to fight in earnest for the right to serve God as ordained leaders in the church. Women were educating themselves, entering more traditional men's professions, attending to their own experiences and the experiences of other women, and noticing the barriers to women's full participation in the workplace and public life. Many of these women were also mothers; some deliberately rejected marriage and motherhood because they feared those responsibilities would confine them to traditional roles. The church, with centuries of patriarchal tradition, resisted mightily the challenges of women who found themselves called by God into any other role than helpmeet for men or caretaker of home and hearth. Some denominations still refuse to recognize women's ordination or essential equality with men before God.

Two different male rectors of multistaff parishes, both parents whose wives were the primary caretakers of their children, told their female assistants that having children would significantly hamper their ministry and directly interfere with their ability to meet the demands of parish ministry. If the women really wanted to succeed in ministry, these rectors said, they should forego families. One woman seemed to agree with this, and has an enormously successful ministry career as a single woman. The other woman left her parish when her child was still an infant, and is a good single mother and priest. Many clergy parents complained, however, about the tensions of holidays, especially Christmas and Easter, which have such high expectations for family time and in the parish. Families of origin are often impatient with clergy families' reluctance either to travel or to host the family feast.

The irony was that many women found the strength to keep insisting on full inclusion because of their deep conviction that God was inviting them to ordained leadership. The God that they knew in prayer had no qualms about inviting them to serve because they were women or mothers; in their experience, God was no respecter of traditional sex roles. As the barriers came down, more women moved into ordained ministry, many of them bringing with them experiences as wives and mothers. The expectations of motherhood and the reality of the experience of becoming responsible for dependent vulnerable humans shape all mothers' lives.

Women must choose between ordained ministry or motherhood

Which is more important: ordained ministry or motherhood? That's a false dichotomy. Both can be vital for the well-being of the ordained mother, her children, the church, and the world. It's a question that only makes sense in a world where people are categorized by the work they do in the public realm, or in a profession where practitioners have been celibate, or male with other people to care for their children. The church, its clergy, and its clergy families would be healthier if we acknowledged that humans can be parents and priests (not to mention adult children caring for aging parents, another part of many clergy lives) and that it's not only possible, but good to let priesthood and family life enrich each other. A Jewish rabbi talked about the tenet of "shalom bayit," or "peace in the house." One implication is that all family members should choose their work in the world in light of what would best contribute to the well-being of the family. This needs to be interpreted in a truly egalitarian way in the family, but puts the family first in a useful way.

The logistics of honoring both career and parenting are not simple, in the church or in the secular world. I was married for twelve years and ordained for two before my first child was born. Other clergy mothers got married, either started families or other careers, and then some time after their secular job changed, or after the children were out of diapers, or in school, or out of the house, they began to discern a call to ordination. Some women were ordained when they were grandmothers. Once ordained, different options exist (part-time or full-time work, in a parish or in a chaplaincy), depending on family needs. Vocational deacons, people ordained to organize service ministries in the Episcopal Church, usually with no salary, face other challenges: Several women with nearly grown children are working part- or full-time in a salaried position and then volunteering as deacon on Sundays (with additional time required for other meetings). Others can be vocational deacons because they've retired from paid work. Women exemplify a greater variety of paths to ordination than men, and those paths are often more dramatically changed by family needs than those of men. Though they are not yet the mainstream, they may offer new models of balancing home and career.[13]

Honoring commitments to family and to ordained ministry is also shaped by the structures of the church and of child-care institutions. People in any career have to fit into schedules designed for people who have other people taking care of their children — wives (occasionally husbands) or sitters or day-care centers and schools. Ordained women, already fighting some resistance to their mere existence, face both higher expectations and stereotyping of women in the practice of their ministry. There's a sense of needing to prove oneself, to excel, to not give anyone any reason to question either commitment or abilities. A ordained single mother said that she judged her mothering skills by whether she "had a plan" for any particular situation — usually two plans. Her greatest sense of insecurity came when situations changed or plans fell through, and it wasn't clear how she would provide for her child.

Finally, honoring ordained ministry and motherhood is a psychological and spiritual task. For some women it may involve a shift from focus on the child or family to focus on the church. I had to learn to shift away from the intensity of parish life and turn toward my child. I returned to the parish after my first child's birth as a mother clear about my vocation as a priest, but not so clear about my vocation as a mom. The first fifteen months of Avery's life passed in a blur. My intentions to stop by the day-care provider's house every day to nurse her were frustrated by my schedule and by the provider's schedule; soon I was pumping milk in the office instead (and occasionally leaving bottles of breast milk on the roof of the car as I pulled out). Evening meetings, when the sitter was only available from 9:00 to 5:00, meant that I hired high school parishioners to watch Avery in the church in the evening. There wasn't time to drive her home and come back. One day a week I'd stay home with her (except the semester that I tried teaching ethics as an adjunct professor — a short-lived experiment). If I were working in the evenings, I'd try to take her to the park in the morning, or take her along to visit older parishioners who were happy to see a baby. Avery came to more diocesan meetings than she should have, because the diocesan offices were near my home and twenty miles from the sitter, and my husband was not available during the day. Her schedule and my time with her were generally determined by the demands of work.

When Avery was fifteen months old, my husband had a six-month sabbatical across the country in California. His position was in a diocese that was in transition, and I was explicitly forbidden by the bishop to function as a priest. I had always worked full-time, and couldn't imagine what I would do. It never occurred to me that caring full-time for my daughter (in an apartment only blocks from beautiful beaches) could be enough, and I spent much of that period checking academic books out of university libraries with the unfulfilled intention of writing academic articles again. I found the world of mothers' play groups stifling. I volunteered as a lay person in too many parishes until a wise spiritual director suggested that I really look at my child and use the time to delight in her.

This was hard for me. Everything I had lived had been about how important it is that women use their gifts in the world to make a difference for good. It took the full six months of sabbatical for me to realize how much mothering also provided meaning and value for me, and how much mothering put me in touch with aspects of God I hadn't known before. Mothering felt threatening to my dreams of a professional life. There are many psychological dynamics in that resistance (though please don't blame my mother!). I chose to attend Simmons College, in part because the founder had designed the college to prepare women to support themselves economically as professional women. In the late 1970s at Simmons, students didn't talk about motherhood, and talk of marriage also included professional plans. Over time, more of my peers became mothers, but graduate school and teaching, and later directing a social service agency or parish work, absorbed as much energy as I wanted to give, and I loved it. My husband and I were married for twelve years before we even started trying to have children. Other generations of women have come at the career-family issue differently, and it is still a lively topic in higher education and in the work force. Discussion of how men struggle to balance career and family life because of their investment in caring for family members is just beginning.

Honoring both ordained ministry and motherhood can drive women crazy, except when it's bringing sanity instead

A baby is born. Or brought into a family by adoption. Suddenly — or so it seems, no matter how much warning and desire and preparation there has been — parents are wholly responsible for the life and well-being of some squalling creature they never knew they could love so much. Nothing is the same. That's when the deep desire that this new child thrives, and that the family protect and sustain her or him in life-giving ways, comes to the fore. That's also when the tapes of expectations, both realistic and wildly impossible, start playing. Fathers have heard external expectations about providing for the financial well-being of this baby and keeping him or her safe. They may be surprised by the depth of their emotional connection to their child. Yet men are not socialized to believe that fathering is their most important contribution to the world. "Motherhood is a woman's calling," say voices of church, society, and often family, and should be the primary focus of her life. Both external and internal voices conspire to make mothers believe that their tiniest response or lack thereof will have life-changing consequences for their child.

Nothing is enough. In both parish work and motherhood, there's always one more thing that can be done. There are often more truly important things to be done in one day than there are hours to do them. Barbara Brown Taylor talks about working more and more hours to meet more and more needs, only to find that the needs always exceed the time available.[14] I've known mothers who won't let anyone other than a family member care for their child, even if that means days with no break except when the child is asleep. Either of these responsibilities alone can become overwhelming. Combine them in one life and either fireworks or exhaustion follows. There's a fairly extensive body of literature about maternal expectations, but these expectations play out in a unique way for clergy mothers because well-entrenched social expectations for women meet contradictory well-entrenched expectations for clergy.

Because the expectations of motherhood are so firmly a part of the culture and many women's psyche, ordained mothers have the "good priest" and the "good mother" tapes running almost constantly. Married mothers may also have the "good wife" tapes that assign women the responsibility of caring for their husband's emotional needs and nurturing the marriage. Women in committed same-sex relationships may bring some of those tapes into their new context, but they also have the freedom and the struggle of working out new ways to honor their relationship to their life partner. All of these expectations tell women that they are desperately needed at work and home and as volunteers in civic organizations. The emotional demands and real scheduling conflicts pit two loves against each other often. It's no accident that in his 2003 "State of the Clergy" report, Matthew Price found that one-third of women clergy in parish ministry seriously consider leaving the parish so they can better care for their family.[15]

This isn't unique to clergy mothers. Many working mothers say that when they're at home, they're thinking of things undone at work, and when they're at work, they're thinking about home. But the church as an institution preaches the well-being of the family, and on the one hand expects its clergy to model healthy family life, and on the other makes demands that threaten the well-being of marriages, committed relationships, and parenting. Clergy moms are showing the church how the clash of expectations can actually result in healthier choices. Work imposes some boundaries on time and energy given on the child; parenting imposes some boundaries on the time and energy given to the parish. Unrealistic expectations of being the perfect mom or the perfect priest give way to being "good enough" at both, and sometimes actually finding time to read a novel or call a friend.

This seems to be more true for mothers than fathers, because the "good parenting" tapes are louder for moms. A clergy woman married to a priest found that although both she and her husband had some flexibility in daytime scheduling, she was the one who consistently wrote their child's school activities in her calendar and made them her priority. He didn't think of it, even though, when reminded, he found that he indeed had the time and was happy to attend. My husband never feels guilty about missing PTA meetings, which I have somehow come to identify with good mothering, rightly or wrongly. A male priest whose wife had a demanding career in the city found that his wife was really hard on herself because he was doing the afternoon carpool/homework/dinner routine for their two children, getting everything done in time for him to get to evening meetings promptly. Finally talking about this, they realized that unconsciously they both thought the mother should be doing this, and that the father was "extraordinary" for doing what needed to be done. This sentiment had actually been voiced by some of his parishioners, who extolled the husband and criticized his wife for not doing more with the children so that the priest can spend more time in the parish. Mothers who are juggling two sets of responsibilities learn how to prioritize and differentiate between what's really needed, and what could be done with infinite resources but not in the real world. What many ordained mothers demonstrate, despite the guilt and pressures to the contrary, is that both home and family are part of faithful response to God.

Expectations of parish and church for ordained clergy

The presence of ordained women in significant numbers has revealed many formerly implicit expectations about how to serve God and what it is to be holy, and has changed the practice of ministry. Studies have documented the ways women's preaching, leadership, and pastoral care differ from that of their male colleagues, even as people of both genders can use both "male" and "female" styles. I don't want to reinforce stereotypes as I explore some of the differences ordained women may demonstrate in the way they balance parish and family life. I want to find healthier models of how to be faithful, and challenge some of the expectations that make both clergy and the church crazy. Here are some factors that lead people to believe that clergy are somehow holier than lay folks.

Clergy as moral exemplar
Many Christians, clergy and lay, move automatically from the clergy's function of serving God in and through the church to expectations about the character of clergy themselves. In theory, clergy represent the people by offering their worship,

service, and love to God and by living faithfully. In practice, clergy can be seen as representing God instead, especially in denominations with weekly Eucharist where the clergy repeat Christ's words to God and the people. Then, representing God can sometimes get confused with somehow *being* God, or having divine attributes: greater holiness, fewer material or physical needs, omnipresence, and divine authority. Some clergy family members have said that this rubs off on them as well: One teenaged "preacher's kid" wished that when she slammed her finger in a door her friends would bring her ice or offer sympathy rather than express surprise that she cursed.

In *Leaving Church*, Barbara Brown Taylor describes the role of professional Christian. "Being ordained is not about serving God perfectly but about serving God visibly, allowing other people to learn whatever they can from watching you rise and fall."[16] That is a very healthy description about the role of ordained clergy in the church and world. But neither clergy nor people watching them want to see clergy fall. In an earlier chapter, I talked about how many clergy strive for perfection. Clergy aren't the only ones who expect perfection. Many lay people expect clergy to exemplify all the Christian virtues all the time: to be more moral, nicer, more compassionate, less angry or tired. I'd like these virtues, both in the parish and at home, but I guess I haven't prayed enough!

As in any helping profession, clergy learn more or less well how to manage their emotions in dealing with people who are hurt, angry, needy, or destructive. The façade doesn't always stay in place, however. There are countless stories of people being surprised when clergy know more obscenities than they do, or curse at the driver who just cut them off. Or when clergy cry at funerals or in hospital rooms, or become angry when the bridal party shows up drunk for the rehearsal. I remember angrily carrying my screaming five-year-old home from the playground when all reasonable (and some unreasonable) entreaties had failed. I'd come from church and was still wearing a collar. I half-expected either the police to come arrest me for child abuse or some reporter to take pictures of the "mean priest" — it wouldn't do for a clergy mom to be angry with her child, especially in public. (The "mom" tape was also running: A good mother always knows how to avoid public scenes!) And when the façade does stay in place, so that clergy only express acceptable emotions or pious thoughts, the clergy person has traded authenticity for sanctimonious appearances that eat away at her or his soul, another danger of confusing clergy with God. Clergy families have been sorely hurt by the pastor who wants to hold the façade of family peace in place, when spouse and children feel the clergy's insistence on secrecy and denial is a refusal to deal with real problems at home.

There's another dangerous corollary of the expectation that clergy lead morally exemplary lives: Clergy don't need structures of accountability to keep them honest. The exposure in the past twenty years of clergy sexual misconduct and financial misconduct demonstrates the costs of corporate denial for victims, the perpetrator's family, and for the church. A decade ago an analysis of the professions of domestic violence offenders found that the "top five" professions were military men, doctors, lawyers, police officers, and pastors, in that order.[17] When male clergy abuse their wives, the wives often say either that they could find no one in the church or community to believe them, or that people in their congregations wanted the women to keep silent and endure the abuse in order to protect the reputation of the clergy and congregation.[18] As procedures have been developed across mainline denominations to address the problem of sexual exploitation by clergy of parishioners, attention to the needs of the family members of clergy has grown in sophistication from basically ignoring family member needs (even at times blaming wives for their husband's sins) to offering appropriate emotional, financial, and pastoral support.[19] Clergy need to be held as accountable as anyone else who is charged with the care of vulnerable people, precisely because they are seen as moral exemplars.

Revising Christian sexual ethics

The changing understanding of clergy as sexual beings has another ramification that is not necessarily gendered. For centuries, Christians have defined "appropriate sexual expression" in terms of the institution of marriage. Sex outside of marriage was always wrong; marriage was always right. Accessibility of birth control, the "sexual revolution" of the 1960s and 1970s, the recognition that sexual attraction to people of the same sex is a normal and healthy expression of sexuality, and the acknowledgement in the 1980s and 1990s of the prevalence of violence within marriage, has led many Christian ethicists[20] to reframe sexual ethics in terms of the quality of relationships: Are they loving, just, respectful, responsible, and faithful? If so, they are morally right and holy both within and outside of the context of marriage. If not, marriage alone will not make them so. Much mainline Protestant pastoral counseling acknowledges not just the reality but in many cases the moral rightness of sexual relationships before marriage, after marriage, or "without benefit of clergy" when the laws and the church don't allow marriage as an option. Pastoral counselors help people in abusive or emotionally crippling marriages discern when divorce may be the most life-giving option. Yet the public rhetoric about "Christian marriage" still largely focuses on the institution of marriage itself.

Carla, a young single rector, living in a rectory adjoining the church, dated several men during her tenure as rector. When things got serious, she was uncomfortable less with the idea of making love than with the thought that dates would park their car in front of the rectory overnight. Not until she announced her engagement did she let her fiancé spend the night at her house, and then she heard about it from parishioners — teasing, not complaints, but comments that nonetheless showed that people were watching. Carla was well aware of her role as moral exemplar, equally aware of her own belief in the moral rightness of her actions, but uncomfortable because the rhetoric of the church proscribes sexual relations outside of marriage. The idea of an adult forum discussion of where her fiancé sleeps felt much too personal. The church's hesitancy to discuss sexual ethics openly and honestly hurts clergy and laity alike.

The ghost of celibacy or asexuality

The Christian tradition has always been more suspicious of family life than the Jewish tradition. One source of suspicion goes back to the first centuries of Christian existence, when desert mothers and fathers sought in the desert a single-minded focus that would help them experience God and develop a particular way of becoming holy. Even within marriage, sexual intercourse was understood as sinful unless its purpose was to conceive children or "render one's debt to a spouse."[21] Another comes from Christian suspicion of bodily needs in general, building on Platonic dichotomies of soul and body, intellect and instinct, rationality and desire. Sexuality seems overwhelming and irrational, something to be repressed rather than integrated into a healthy Christian life. Attempts by the church to control women's sexuality helped protect patrimony and offered yet another image of especially holy people as celibate or virgins. Scriptural descriptions of Jesus as asexual and independent of family, and his condemnation at times of family ties, provide a third source of suspicion. Beginning in the eleventh century, the Roman Catholic Church began to require celibacy of its clergy in part to keep church property from being dissipated through claims of family members. All of these factors combine to support expectations of celibacy or asexuality as a sign of holy clergy life, despite a healthy rhetoric in the Protestant tradition affirming both the goodness of sex in appropriate contexts and the goodness of family life.

Ordained women make the affirmation of sexuality explicit because of the gendered ways women's bodies are seen. One of the arguments against women's ordination was that female bodies were a source of temptation to lust for men. Women's bodies were by nature dirty, impure, and dangerous, said strands of Christian tradition from the church fathers to the present. Women's bodies are also sexualized in media and culture, and used as sex objects to sell almost anything. So imagining or seeing women as clergy highlights a disconcerting contrast between sex object and person of respect. Conversely, one of the implicit privileges of being male is the recognition of sexual desire and the access to willing (more or less) women. For years, clergy men were excused for their sexual affairs with women in their parish because "the woman must have invited him" and "boys will be boys." The recent exposure of the problem of clergy sexual misconduct is partly due to growing numbers of women in ministry. Another vital factor was the presence of women high enough in the hierarchy who were willing to listen and believe female victims. Just by being women, women challenge some notions of what it is to be holy.

When I announced that I was pregnant with my first child, a parishioner said that she had thought I looked pregnant but didn't think that female clergy could get pregnant, because, she said in a whisper, that would mean that I had made love. She knew I'd been married for years. She said that the idea of priests having sex was odd to her, even though the male married rector had two children. Someone overhearing this said jokingly, "Well, at least she only made love once!" But the first parishioner's surprise and discomfort were real. The idea that "priests don't get pregnant" reveals some discomfort with the idea that someone supposedly "spiritual" could also be sexual, or if they are, they shouldn't let it show.

A woman whose husband had become a priest after their marriage confessed that she was initially uncomfortable about the idea of making love with her husband once he had become a priest. She had to expand her understanding both of her husband and of priesthood. But sharing a bedroom is considered normative for heterosexual couples. A gay rector and his partner have found more than one parishioner looking for their bedrooms during parish events at the rectory, or asking where the partner sleeps. The parishioners aren't shy about wanting to know whether they use one bedroom or two. That is an enormous invasion of privacy, but the fact that homosexuality is "different" means that some parishioners don't experience their questions as intrusive.

Inherent tensions between the institution of the church and clergy family needs

Parishioners are also often bold to comment on the perceived quality of relationships between the clergy person and her or his spouse or partner. One of Martin Luther's arguments supporting clergy marriage was that clergy and their wives could model a healthy marriage and Christian family life for the congregation. Maybe we could, if we weren't working every evening and weekend when most spouses or partners are expecting family time! Some clergy are really good about protecting a date night with their spouse or partner. One male partner got tired of eating alone and insisted that his partner join him for every dinner, no matter what time they ate; they both came to appreciate this "enforced intimacy." A parishioner said that under one rector, parishioners knew better than to get sick or die on a Friday night, because the rector was simply not available. In an increasingly frenetic culture, this can be useful modeling.

Nurturing a relationship isn't easy in the best of circumstances. Parishes and infants make their needs known loudly and insistently; the needs of spouses or partners and older children are often much more subtle and easy to miss. Before we had children, my husband and I both worked long hours to establish our careers, and supported each other in that. Before I was ordained, we bought a house in the country, and we would spend weekends refurbishing it together. Once I was ordained, it was harder to get there on weekends because of the distance, but we still made time for each other. In the first year of Avery's life, there were huge changes in the marriage. By choice and circumstance, I was with Avery the vast majority of the time; there were days when my husband didn't see his daughter awake. Neither of us made the time to nurture our relationship except through parenting. Work on the quality of relationships, whether intimate commitments or friendships, all too often seems like a luxury, when it's actually a necessity for the sake of the marriage and for God. Once again the Jewish tradition, which spells out the holy obligations of how husbands and wives should treat each other, find pleasure in each other, and work to establish and maintain peace in the home, can remind Christian families that marriage vows are at least as important as ordination vows. Same-sex couples may also offer models for more egalitarian relationships and sharing of responsibilities in a life-long partnership.

Expectations of clergy spouses

There is an entire body of literature devoted to expectations of clergy wives, from Martin Luther to the present. In 1983, sociologist Leonard Sweet wrote *The Minister's Wife: Her Role in 19th Century American Evangelicalism,* using advice for clergy wives to identify changing understandings of women's roles in society.[22] Evelyn Kirkley's dissertation, discussed in the previous chapter, continued Sweet's method of analysis. Kirkley concludes that even into the 1980s, when her dissertation was completed, the roles of clergy wives were still largely determined by the prevailing view of women held in American culture. Individual personalities were seldom considered when forming the ideal role of a minister's wife, while the expectations of her husband, her husband's parish, and prevailing social norms for femininity were central.[23]

No similar literature exists for husbands or male partners of clergy. Dr. Richard Schori said it well: "I know how to be the *spouse* of the Presiding Bishop; I don't know how to be the *wife* of the Presiding Bishop."[24] As spouse of the Episcopal Church's Presiding Bishop, Katharine Jefferts Schori, he expected to determine for himself and in consultation with his wife what role to play in his wife's career. Wives presumably are expected to conform to gender-stereotyped roles of hostess, caretaker, and social secretary. Many church members laugh or remark on their own different expectations of a clergy woman's husband, as if they know they would never ask of a husband what they would of a wife. The culture hasn't developed similar expectations for members of same-gender couples. The confusion over expectations often gives male spouses and partners freedom to determine for themselves, without being asked, how or whether they will be involved. I expect that female spouses and partners, especially those with well-defined careers, will also make their own choices, but that there may be more "muttering" in the congregation. Some members of a United Methodist congregation where the pastor's wife is a very successful surgeon were quite upset at the wife when the clergy family bought a very expensive home and moved out of the parsonage — "Who does she think she is?" They also resent her rather limited participation in church meetings, although they were not at all upset when their previous pastor's husband also limited his participation because of his career. Conscious and unconscious expectations of what it is to be male in the culture clash with expectations of being a clergy spouse, because the image of clergy spouse is still female.

Richard and Brad are, in some ways, the most traditional clergy couple in my interviews. Richard has been rector of a medium-sized parish in the Episcopal Diocese of Newark for eight years. For most of that time, Brad has happily fulfilled the role of pastor's wife, working practically full-time at tasks around the church that fit his personality and gifts and supporting Richard in his vocation.

When he and Richard were first called to the parish, Brad was working as an accountant for a media company, but was unhappy in that job. Brad had always admired his mother, who had been a very successful socialite, organizing major fundraisers for several nonprofit organizations and entertaining to support her husband's career and her own social ambitions. Brad's family attended church every Sunday, without fail, as did Brad once he was on his own. But his family was never involved in any church activity outside of Sunday attendance; church was a weekly hour-long obligation. When he arrived at St. Matthew's, he found himself busy entertaining in the church and the rectory, and he loved it. Brad's family, in life and after his parents' deaths while he was at St. Matthew's, provided the financial resources for him to stop paid work and devote his energy to the parish, the golf course, the beach, and the relationship. Every inch of the parish reflects Brad's touch, in decorating details and hospitality, and the parish delights in these small but vitally important signs that they are loved, appreciated, and made to feel comfortable in their parish.

Family dynamics

God the Father. As noted in chapter 2, in the Episcopal Church, many priests are called "Father" or "Mother." In other Protestant denominations, the titles may be different, but the dynamic of clergy as patriarch or matriarch of the parish family is still strong. People transfer their images of God the parent and/or their own parents onto clergy people unconsciously but with sometimes dramatic effects. Language in worship that consistently refers to God as Father makes this transference more automatic for male clergy, and has made it harder for women to be accepted as clergy, especially when coupled with the fact of Jesus' maleness and the scriptural naming of twelve male apostles. Adding references to God as "Mother" might help female clergy be accepted more easily but doesn't help change the dynamic of transference. Men seem to be more comfortable with the title "Father" than women are with "Mother," because of tradition (some women want to be called "Father" since it is one traditional title for a priest) but perhaps also because "Mother" evokes as many family images as church images for women. I often come home wishing I could tell certain parishioners that I am my children's mother but not theirs; their expectations that I will clean up the church, or find and then deliver items left in church, or grant or withhold permission for them to do something can be unreasonable.

One of the more dramatic examples of the clash of internal images of God with the appearance of actual clergy came when I baptized a baby when I was seven months pregnant. The baptismal formula used in that parish for at least a year, by male and female celebrants alike, was "I baptize you in the name of the Father and of the Son and of the Holy Spirit, one God and Mother of us all." I held the baby, pronounced the words, and heard a huge crash from the choir loft. A man flew down the stairs and out the door, yelling, "She's emasculating God!" I never had the chance to talk with him about what led to his outburst, but my sense was that my gender and my pregnancy in a very holy moment contradicted many of his unconscious assumptions about God, priesthood, and holiness.

Father knows best. Lay people sometimes put off making decisions, or wait until they know what "Father" or "Mother" wants, because implicitly or explicitly "Father knows best" or they seek "Mother's" approval. Clergy often work hard to counter this unconscious expectation, but it is a shift in the way authority has been exercised in many parishes that keeps creeping into parish life. It creates a false sense of dependency that can increase expectations of what clergy should be doing.

Clergy are expected to be available all the time. This is a reasonable expectation for real emergencies — births, deaths, accidents, sudden illness or catastrophe — although expecting clergy (or God) to fix everything as they would like is not reasonable. It's often in emergencies that God feels absent, and also when adults and children both crave parental protection and support, and the clergy are expected to stand in for God and parents. Yet what can feel like an emergency to someone in trouble may not objectively be an emergency. Is it an emergency when a parishioner asks for an hour or so of time on Christmas Eve day to talk about her father's diagnosis of terminal cancer because she's leaving to see her father on Christmas Day, but she's known about this for weeks? When should rectors either cut a family vacation short to comfort a family facing a sudden death, or make phone time during the vacation, or refer the family to the clergy on call? Establishing guidelines in a parish about what constitutes a real emergency is important boundary work for clergy and church leaders alike.

The expectation of clergy presence is a little less reasonable for parish meetings. An ordained psychotherapist, currently serving as a part-time associate, talked about how parishioners are often disappointed when there's no clergy presence at a church meeting, even when the clergy person has no particular expertise or authority on the subject. People in his parish measure the real importance of their work by whether the rector, not just any clergy, are present. Clergy presence conveys respect and value. The rector's presence conveys the additional feeling of parental concern. Clergy absence can consciously or unconsciously trigger feelings of worthlessness or abandonment. One rector deals with this by making clear his "three-meetings-a-week limit" often and then, when a lay leader insists that the rector's presence is essential, he asks them which other meeting they would like him to sacrifice. In the past twenty years, the ministry of lay visiting has expanded tremendously, yet many parishioners still value the visit of a clergy person over a lay person, sometimes despite the greater pastoral skills of the lay person. "I want Daddy/Mommy/the 'real' representative of the church," not a lay person, however duly commissioned and trained to bring sacrament and comfort in the name of God and the church.

Least reasonable of all are the expectations that clergy should be available for parishioners who call at dinner time because they "just want to talk," or building users who need the key to the church, or strangers who have been referred to the rectory by the police at midnight because the police can't or won't make the necessary social service referrals. Yet those are the situations that evoke both the "Hooray, I'm needed" response and the "How can I say no without appearing uncaring?" response. When I called the police station to ask for help in finding a place to stay for the night for the person they sent me at midnight, the officer said, "Isn't that your job?"

Sibling rivalry. A dynamic of "sibling rivalry" between parishioners and the clergy members' actual children has become especially visible since men have become more involved in parenting and since women have been ordained. I've had homebound parishioners express disappointment that I won't bring them communion on Christmas Day. I make hospital visits on Christmas Eve day, and schedule other visits for a day or two after Christmas, but keep Christmas Day, except for worship, for my family. One of them offered to let me bring the children if I'd like. Another parishioner was upset when I ended a hospital visit after forty minutes because I had to pick up my children — she said she was disappointed that I couldn't give my ministry the priority it deserved. When the clergy man's wife's care for their children was largely invisible to the parish, the competition between "parish children" and the clergy person's children was also invisible — the clergy man's allegiance to parish first was assumed, or his acceptance of parenting is praised. A male rector was surprised that a committee accepted his request to reschedule a meeting so he could pick up his children — they praised him for being a good father (and resented his working wife for not joining the women's group that meets during the day).

A rector prohibited his associate's infant son from being baby Jesus in the Christmas pageant, despite the tradition that the youngest baby would play Jesus and his own children's repeated appearances in the pageant. He cited his need for her to keep the fact that she was a mother out of the limelight, especially because the mother had been artificially inseminated, so she was a single mom. The irony of forbidding an unmarried woman's baby son from representing Jesus was lost on him. An associate's three-year-old son greeted her at the back of the church and immediately started tugging on her alb, wanting her to take it off "so you can be *my* mommy again." When other children or adults approached her, he grabbed her legs and insisted, "My mommy. My mommy." These children know they have to share their mommy with others and they're not always happy about it.

My second child was born after I had been rector for a few years. Response to the pregnancy was generally supportive, although working out the logistics of family leave in a small parish was hard for everyone. But real tensions developed after Marin was born, and deepened for a few years. I heard many complaints, in one-on-one conversations and in meetings, about her behavior in church when she was about eighteen months old. I blamed myself first, thinking that I hadn't trained her well enough. Then I blamed my husband because he didn't keep her quiet enough. She was probably more disruptive than my husband and I wanted to acknowledge; parents do often minimize the effects of their children's behavior on others. But jealousy also played a role, as I discovered as I processed the ongoing parish angst through conversations with other clergy mothers. A real infant, who needs to be fed, or changed, or sometimes just held for a few minutes by the mother she sees taking care of others, demonstrates a lapse in parish work. People were feeling jealous because I seemed to put Marin's needs first even if I thought I was giving the parishioner enough time and attention. It felt like sibling rivalry, and the parish "children" needed to know that Mom had enough love for everyone.

Church as mistress. In some clergy marriages, the family jealousy dynamic played out differently. Several wives of clergy now in their sixties and seventies talked about feeling that the parish was their husband's "other woman," one that was known, and whose needs often came before the wife's. In these marriages, the wives were primarily responsible for caring for husband, children, and home, even if the women also developed their own careers. Spending time with the church mistress might be resented, but it was expected. This may not be so different for men in any other career, or in relationships where the husband's primary responsibility is to bring in money in exchange for care of self, children, and home. Yet other careers don't expect the kind of emotional bonding that parishioners want from their clergy — time, energy, and priority of commitment, perhaps, but not love. The irony of clergy who use the excuse of "couple needing counseling" to either put off or avoid an unresolved issue in their own homes is rarely lost on the spouse or partner at home. Descriptions of the relationship between a clergy person and parish as a marriage, or the search process as a courtship, or even acceptance of the language of "mistress" which in any other context is seen as a violation of the marriage vow, exacerbate this dynamic. Love may be in fact what's needed in a parish-clergy relationship, as in therapy or other healing ministries. But then the understanding of how to use love appropriately in professional work, including boundaries that protect the clergy person, her or his family, and the parishioners, needs to be explicit in both parish and home.

The vow — or expectation — of poverty

Where did the expectation of clergy poverty come from? One answer is in the vows taken by men and women joining religious communities that shape general notions of holiness. Clergy may be holy, but really holy people join a monastery and give up everything for Jesus. Jesus' persistent warnings about how money can keep people from knowing some aspects of God also play their part, though many people are more eager for the clergy they pay to adopt a life of relative poverty than they are eager to adopt it for themselves. Lay people, however, donate considerable amounts of time and labor to sustain parishes, usually in addition to their own paid careers. Most churches depend on an ethos of volunteer service that colors expectations of clergy work and compensation. Another answer is in the reality of the disparity of salaries for clergy and similarly educated people in other professions, although that disparity has decreased to some extent in the past generation. Clergy are often expected to sacrifice financial support for the sake of doing God's will, on the theory that God will provide. That theory is fine; it is an axiom of faith. Too often it has been interpreted to mean that the institution doesn't have to provide support, leaving clergy to find funding elsewhere. Sometimes God may want to provide by asking the institution to pay its fair share.

For instance, a bilingual and bicultural woman graduated from seminary and was eager to minister with Hispanic congregations. Two nearby towns had growing Hispanic populations, but there was no parish or diocesan support to start an Episcopal Hispanic ministry there. A wealthy Anglo church in another diocese offered her $20,000 to cover a half-time salary and all program expenses, so she could start Hispanic ministry in their basement. Benefits were not even mentioned. Another half-time position was not much more generously compensated, and a third part-time position had so many potential conflicts that it seemed a sure set-up for failure. Is this a reflection of the way Hispanic ministry is valued? Is it because she is female, or because she has a working spouse? There is still a disparity between salaries of male and female clergy in mainline denominations, even when years of service and types of experience are considered.[25] Was she supposed to ignore her real financial needs for the greater cause of ministry? She felt insulted, but no one offering these positions seemed embarrassed or even aware that their offers were untenable.

"Here is your wife, and here are your sons"

Exodus 18 includes a useful story for clergy with families. Moses has returned to Midian, to the house of his father-in-law, Jethro. He had sent his wife and sons to Jethro's while he led the people of Israel through the plagues and out of Egypt, ostensibly to keep them from danger. But Jethro is genuinely delighted to hear how Moses and Moses' God delivered the people. The next day Moses takes his place among the Israelites to judge them, working from morning to night. And Jethro watches, taken aback. "What's going on here? Why are you doing all this, and all by yourself, letting everybody line up before you from morning to night?"[26] Moses defends himself; he's doing God's work, and instructing people about God. Jethro suggests rather pointedly that he delegate some of this work to many others, for Moses' sake and for the sake of the people.[27]

This story is often preached as a way to encourage clergy to delegate, and sometimes to encourage lay leaders to assume greater responsibility. For the first time, I also heard Jethro implying that Moses needed to spend more time with his wife and sons. Is this an overzealous father-in-law, or the voice of God speaking in and through family relations? There is a time to sit and judge the people, to care for the people of God as faithfully, lovingly, justly as possible. And there's a time to sit with a child reading, or get to a basketball game, or go out to dinner with a spouse or partner alone. What demands lead to sanity, to responsiveness to the work God really has given us to do, and what demands lead to confusion, overwork, and neglect of home or parish or world? Jethro offers one clue: If you delegate, "you'll have strength enough to carry out whatever God commands you, and the people in their settings will flourish also." (The New Revised Standard Version says "all the people will go to their home in peace.")[28] Expectations which lead to exhaustion and dependency are not of God: The flourishing of all people, in the clergy home and in the congregation, and the presence of enough energy to do God's work at home and in the parish, is of God.

Chapter Four

Life on the Tightrope

When Avery was born, we were living about a half-hour away from the parish I served. I chose day-care near the church, because I had intended to stop by the sitter's once or twice a day and nurse the baby. That quickly proved to be impossible for many reasons, so I would nurse her upon waking, add filling the diaper bag to the morning routine of gathering whatever I'd need during the day, trying not to forget anything because there was rarely time to go home and retrieve anything. Then I'd get in the car, usually later than I had intended, and pray that traffic would move swiftly or that I could pass one car or another as I barreled up the parkway. But enough time had passed that she would need another snack before I left her for the day. I found an abandoned gas station and I would literally pull out of the fast lane, slow the adrenaline, and let her nurse while I watched a bit of a waterfall as the seasons rolled by. I had to add another half-hour to the expected commute time, but I found it became invaluable time to pray, to appreciate Avery and nature, to collect myself before entering into the flurry of parish activities. That experience of pulling out of the fast lane to attend to a child before returning to work became a metaphor for how parenting changed my approach to work. The "fast lane" represented economic and social structures, expectations of clergy and the nature of parish work; pulling over to nurture a child and, by extension, myself and my relationship to God, represented all the important but not urgent, nonproductive but life-giving opportunities that are all too easy to miss.

Social, economic, and religious structures shape some of the choices open to people. Those who become clergy face powerful external expectations of how clergy and their families ought to behave. Ultimately it is each person's decisions about how they will respond to God's invitations, how they use their strengths and weaknesses in ordination or parenting or committed relationships that shape

74

the direction of their lives. When it comes time to choose a way to earn a living, people can prayerfully consider how their unique personality traits, given by God, can be best used to further God's work in the world. When people fall in love, the growth of trust, respect, love, and intimacy is also a gift of God, as is the other person. The intimate love between two people, and the commitment to nurture that love in marriage or union, both comes from and deepens their relationship with God. When people decide to become parents, the miracle of birth or the joy of adoption is a gift, as is the willingness to take on the responsibility of nurturing another life. Each of these commitments is rooted in God, the source of life, and can teach people more about how to love and be loved by God, just as deepening a relationship with God enhances one's abilities to work, love, and nurture children.

Invitations to work (defined as both a source of income and a source of meaning, identification, and value), to marriage or committed partnerships, and to parenting can happen to anyone. People in familial relationships juggle tensions between commitments to work and family and self regardless of the profession. Acknowledging that God is the source of the commitments that sometimes compete against each other in real life can help restore sanity and perspective for all Christians. Remembering that human institutions, not God, established requirements for work schedules, sick leave, health benefits, traffic time, and other frequent "glitches" in the home-work blend, and that God isn't (usually) responsible for family crises that disrupt work also can redirect anger at the source, not life in general. Lisa, a Lutheran woman, wasn't so sure — she wondered, only half-laughingly, what she did to deserve her dog's developing a medical condition that required almost daily treatments at the vet's within the first two weeks of her maternity leave!

When one or more members of the family are ordained, however, the general idea that work, love, and nurture of children are all of God runs headlong into the expectation that ordained ministry is holier than any other occupation. Responsibilities to family, community, and self are all paths to holiness which are as important as responsibilities to the church, but clergy, clergy families, and the institutional church often function as if the church's needs should come first. The needs of the church are infinite, urgent, and relentless at times, so it is ultimately up to clergy to prioritize needs and set their own boundaries even when other parish leaders, family members, and the institutional church can play a role. Choices can and do have to be made, and even Jesus refused some of the pleas for help addressed to him. This chapter offers examples of some of the dynamics that emerge as life as partner or spouse, parent, and clergy person unfolds. It offers several perspectives on various decisions along the way, and the tensions or joys experienced as commitments multiply and vocation expands.

Dating

Ordination makes a difference in dating, straight or gay. Sexuality and ordination don't go together in many people's minds, because of higher standards held for clergy (somehow clergy aren't supposed to be interested in sex or romance), the psychological and social power of both spirituality and sexuality as demonstrated by the existence of special rules for holy people and sex in all religious traditions, and heterosexism. Several single female priests laugh and cry about how to tell a date what they do for a living. When they say that they're clergy, they're met with incomprehension, rejection, confusion, expectations of prudery, or the need to "behave" in the presence of a moral exemplar. I'm not sure about men's experiences, but male clergy are certainly more familiar in the culture and less likely to be seen, consciously or not, as sex objects. For single ordained women, dating can be especially awkward. Ordination often connotes either celibate religious life, or the breaking of gender stereotypes, or the exercise of power and authority that was formerly reserved for men. For straight ordained men seeking a partner, a collar is usually either neutral or positive. Some women may want to share ministry with their husband; in previous generations the unmarried male cleric was sometimes seen as a real catch for young single women in the congregation. Others feel that ordination indicates a man who has done some psychological work and is more able to be sensitive and caring. For gay and lesbian clergy seeking partners, the situation is often more complicated. Some potential partners are suspicious of any church involvement because the church has done so much harm to GLBT people.

Young, single, straight, and dating

Blair was ordained in the United Methodist Church when she was twenty-four, part of a denominational drive for younger clergy. Many of her seminary classmates were also single young people, and both the seminary and the denomination offered support for them. Methodist clergy are assigned to congregations by their district superintendents or bishops. The administrators know the parishes' needs and the gifts of the clergy, and make matches accordingly. But Blair's first assignment was not a good match. She was twenty-four, single, in a rural parish where she was related to many members of the congregation and was seen as their daughter or sister or friend, but not pastor. After a year, she was moved to another large suburban parish as an associate, and that's where she met and married her husband. Although her husband was not from the parish, she did date some parishioners, with the approval of the senior pastor and the understanding of the parish.

Dating while gay and closeted, and then coming out

In a culture of secrecy and conflict around sexual orientation, the dynamics of dating change. Sean was out to the search committee and vestry when he was called to this parish. Their implicit agreement was "don't ask, don't tell," which felt like progress after coming from a diocese in which being closeted was the only way to be in parish ministry. This meant, however, that Sean couldn't talk about dating, which in turn created an odd bifurcation of personal and parish life.

Within Sean's first year at the parish, he met Charlie in a social context outside of the parish. When their relationship got serious, Sean wanted Charlie to come to some parish events, and to introduce him as his partner, but he was hesitant. Charlie didn't understand why Sean had to lie or hide the relationship. As the relationship developed, the sense of hypocrisy grew — the idea of "don't ask, don't tell" became challenged by the reality of growing commitment and joy. So Sean started being honest about his sexual orientation and his relationship with Charlie, at about the same time that Sean officiated at a same-sex blessing in the parish. Both moves had the unanimous support of the vestry, but both also evoked unhealthy muttering among members of the congregation. Some people left the parish when Charlie moved in. Which raises an interesting question: What do you do when your partner wants to move into the rectory, when a straight couple would be married before moving in officially, but when marriage isn't permitted for GLBT persons?

Sean said that "in hindsight, [coming out to the parish] looked pretty good, but at the time it felt absolutely awful. Would being honest about one part of my life jeopardize not just my career but relationships within the parish? And what would the toll of that strain be on the relationship?" But acceptance came over time. One of the most effective ways to combat homophobia is to let people discover that someone they respect is gay or lesbian. So in some ways the gradual coming-out process was a gift to the parish of another level of exposure to gay people. Eventually Charlie was expected to become part of the parish family, and he did so as he felt comfortable, rarely attending church but hosting great parish events at the rectory.

Dating, same-sex commitments, and civil unions

There are as many stories of dating and commitment as there are couples. Yet one more story illustrates additional dynamics that shape the lives of clergy. Marie had been married for several years, and taught school when her son was born. She divorced when she acknowledged her sexual orientation; the issues of self-awareness led to a recognition of a call to ordained ministry. Marie attended seminary as a single lesbian woman, and found great support professionally and as a single mom. There was good child-care on campus and other parents to share responsibilities and stories. She worked in a urban parish as an associate for years while her son was in elementary school, and when he was in junior high, she moved to a different diocese to become part-time priest-in-charge of a struggling congregation. She needed another part-time job to make ends meet financially, which limited her time with her son, but they were managing.

When her son was in high school, Marie met Janet. The wardens and vestry knew of her sexual orientation when she was hired, and while she made no announcements to the parish, she didn't hide the fact from anyone who asked. Janet was a musician and elementary school teacher. In time, she began playing for the parish worship, and the two enjoyed planning liturgy and getting to know each other. When it was clear that this relationship was for life, they went to the bishop, as would any straight clergy couple, and arranged precommitment counseling. They decided, however, to hold their commitment ceremony, at which the bishop officiated, in a neighboring parish. The vestry agreed, both because the other church was bigger and because the parish as a whole was not ready to embrace such a public celebration of same-sex commitment. No one raised an eyebrow when Janet moved into the rectory. She continues to participate in liturgy planning and music and has become increasingly committed to nurturing her own spiritual journey. When civil unions became legal in New Jersey, Janet and Marie had a smaller celebration with family and friends, also away from the parish.

Gay and lesbian dating in denominations where it's forbidden

When ordained clergy try to be faithful to all of who God is calling them to be, obviously conflict happens in denominations where gay and lesbian clergy must be celibate or cannot share their sexual orientation. Equally obviously, each person handles this differently, yet the psychological, spiritual, and professional costs are high. One man said that closeted pastors he knew could easily hide one-night stands or short flings and remain in ministry, whereas he felt he couldn't hide life with a partner that he intended to be lifelong.[1] Hoge and Wenger's study of why clergy leave parish ministry included twenty-one gay men and six lesbians from four denominations: the Evangelical Lutheran Church in America (ELCA), Presbyterian Church USA, Lutheran Church–Missouri Synod, and United Methodist Church. These ministers were deeply fulfilled by and successful in parish ministry. They were either forced out by their denominations or left because of personal circumstances, including depression, a sense of hypocrisy that conflicted with the gospel call to truth, or disillusionment with the institutional church. Their anger at their denomination and the wider church is fierce; most would come back to parish ministry in a heartbeat if they could be open and accepted for all of who they are.[2]

While a Presbyterian study of 1,404 female clergy found that only 1 percent of their responders faced discrimination because of their sexual orientation, these women were clear that it was due to denominational positions. Said one respondent, "The only reason I left was the church's position/policy on the ordination of gays/lesbians. Especially miss preaching."[3] Among my own colleagues is a lesbian couple, in which both partners are ordained in different denominations (Disciples of Christ and Presbyterian). They lived in the manse of Cynthia's Presbyterian congregation for a while, although Cynthia was not out to her congregation. She said that several parishioners thought it was "nice for Cynthia to have a roommate; she must be lonely at times." Others seemed to know, but "roommate" was a convenient fiction for everyone. Cynthia said it was awkward at times when she wanted to celebrate her relationship or when people in the parish would want to set up a date for her with a man because "it was time she settled down." Eventually they both moved into college chaplaincy positions as openly lesbian pastors.

Where will we live?

In my informal interviews with clergy and spouses, I found that in both the church and secular positions, the husband's careers seemed to determine family moves and opportunities, especially when the man is the primary breadwinner. Denominational statistics from the Presbyterian and Lutheran Churches support this. A 2003 study of clergy women's experiences in the Presbyterian Church found that 62 percent of the respondents felt geographically bound to a particular region. They cited family considerations, such as proximity to extended family or shared custody of a child, most frequently, followed by spouse's employment, and then general preference for culture, climate, sense of roots, or (in some overlap with the first category) because it was near family.[4] A Lutheran study which compared male and female "rostered leaders" revealed more detail in a similar pattern. In general, "white men are more likely than all other clergy to indicate their call had an impact on deciding whether or when to move," yet they are also more likely to say that their family had an impact on their decision to accept a new call or not.[5] For a first call, women are more likely than men to name a geographic limitation (30 percent vs. 18 percent). For subsequent calls, white females were "somewhat more likely" than other clergy to place either geographic or familial limitations on their most recent calls, as are women (white and women of color) under fifty years of age.[6]

Sometimes, as in the case of Roger and Roberta, moving depends on the special needs of a child. When the secular partner has particular geographic limits, there are usually ways to find churches within those parameters, although this may not be the case for same-sex couples, since fewer dioceses are open to them. For some families, the family moved because the priest's job provided housing, but the husband's workplace didn't change. One clergy woman needed to find a church within commuting distance of her partner's teaching job, because her partner only had a few years left until retirement with full pension benefits. Another limited her geographic search to cities where her husband, in a specialized career, would have at least some opportunities. Another male cleric stayed in one parish long past the time he expected to do so, in large part to let his third child (who arrived twelve years after the first two) benefit from an excellent school district. Often clergy can find church-owned housing in neighborhoods where they could not afford to buy a home. Another male cleric followed his wife's moves because she was in the Army, and they were often living on military bases. He talks of parallels between being an officer's husband and his wife being a rector's wife. Couples nearing or past retirement often recounted their lives in terms of the parish the man had served, and the opportunities for work or child-rearing found by the wife once they settled into his parish.

Sarah and Don were also married shortly after their college graduations, and they moved to New York because they were both interested in opportunities there in public relations and video production. They each pursued secular jobs until their second child was born and the cost of day-care for two children was greater than Sarah's freelance salary. That break in career freed Sarah to go through the ordination process. Sarah chose not to live at seminary, because her family was well established in schools and jobs in a town within commuting distance of seminary. This was in the late 1980s and was still fairly rare, but she was clear with her bishop and the seminary that her family's needs came first, and they accommodated her. Her family has followed her to two different positions within about five years, not always happily. Both positions were within commuting distance of her husband's work, although one was far enough away that they seriously considered relocating the business he owned. It was fortunate that they did not relocate, for that position ended within six months because of financial mismanagement, and she was once again on the market, and the family made one more move.

Church-owned housing

Life in church-owned housing has its own advantages and disadvantages. A 2001 study of Presbyterian clergy found that only 20 percent of clergy live in church-owned housing. While there are no exact statistics for the Episcopal Church, the trend is toward having clergy own their own home except on the coasts, where the price of housing exceeds most clergy family incomes. Yet life in rectories brings its own challenges and joys.

Regina's rectory had been in need of major repair at least throughout her own tenure and that of the past two rectors. Plaster was literally falling from the ceiling. Windows wouldn't close. Kitchen cabinets were sagging, so the doors wouldn't close. Regina painted all the rooms herself, and did small repairs. Parishioners frequently complimented her on the good things she has done with the rectory, but the vestry kept putting off major repairs. When she "threw a temper tantrum," as she put it, they let her arrange for workers in a local prison work-release program to come for three days of work. The crew was supervised by a lay person who changed Regina's work request for the rectory and then moved the crew to the church for the third day, so that some of the most pressing rectory needs were unfinished. "It's really hard at the end of a lousy day to come to a rectory where everything is literally falling apart," she said. "It's not a sanctuary." Regina would be happy to buy her own home, but the parish couldn't rent the rectory in its current condition and cannot afford to give her a housing allowance. As Regina said, "They realize it's not acceptable for tenants, but still think its fine for the priest!" There often seems to be a tension built into an arrangement where housing is part of the salary, because perceptions of housing needs (i.e., what's a basic repair and what's a luxury) are often subjective. Issues of taste and control arise; one clergy wife complained that when her husband asked the vestry to dedicate a work day to repainting the rectory interior, after only fifteen years since the last painting, the vestry asked members of the congregation to bring in any leftover paint, regardless of color, to save money. One warden, during salary negotiations with a priest she liked and respected, made a comment about "how cushy a job it was to have utilities included," as if this were not part of the total salary package. In every family, housing is determined by the family income, but in church-owned housing the family's choices become much more limited. More denominations are moving away from church-owned housing because of the financial liabilities inherent in the lack of the ability to build up equity, except in geographic areas where the cost of housing is higher than many clergy families can afford (even with two incomes).

Stories like this abound; so, mercifully, do stories of proactive vestries and dioceses who work to ensure their rectories are livable. When I was pregnant, the wardens offered to have the basement refinished so that there would be room for the new child. My family did some of the painting and finishing work. Several parishes set aside a budget line for rectory maintenance that can be used as the clergy family desires. Many clergy families live in houses they otherwise couldn't afford, with access to schools and amenities for children that might otherwise be beyond their means.

Marriage and pregnancy in the parish

When Barbara first began to serve a small urban parish, she was single. Shortly after she arrived, one of the members of the search committee, who had been hospitalized during the final interview and decision to call her, rang the doorbell to announce that "if he had been well, the parish would never have hired her." Barbara attributed that to sexism and lack of familiarity with women in the pulpit, but much later people in the congregation shared with her that his worry was that she was lesbian. Guesses about sexuality happen to any single clergy person, male or female, gay or straight. It happens in secular workplaces too, but in the secular world private behavior is expected to take place after-hours and off-site. In a job with expectations of constant availability, leadership through personal example, and higher ethical standards, the dynamics of dating, rejection, acceptance, sexuality, and other life changes necessarily have a public dimension.

Yet Barbara continued to build a ministry in the parish, with the usual struggles — including this man's refusal to receive communion from her — and joys. One day an old flame appeared in the congregation. Barbara had dated him many years before, and he wanted to reconnect. The romance flourished, to the congregation's delight, and after a few years the entire congregation was invited to the wedding. The women of the parish held a bridal shower for Barbara, and with great joy recounted how they told the sales clerk that the sexy underwear they were buying was for their priest! There was a sense of camaraderie in being women, celebrating a transition together, which reduced some of the distance between clergy and laity. A few years later, Barbara's daughter was born, amidst jokes about needing to move the altar to accommodate her growing girth and how vestments really do make good maternity clothes. After the birth, one of the wardens called the bishop and announced, as proudly as any grandfather, "Barbara had a girl!"

Pregnancy, and the conflicts and joys it raises

Women clergy becoming pregnant and raising children was fairly rare until the 1990s, when a critical mass of women of child-bearing age became ordained. Several second-career women with whom I have spoken couldn't imagine being ordained while their children were young. Some stayed home to raise children, or worked part-time or full-time in secular jobs with more regular hours and firmer boundaries between work and home. Reasons differed, but one consistent theme was the feeling that they didn't have enough emotional energy to share with their children and the parish at the same time. Children's and parishioners' needs are often ongoing, constantly changing, requiring quick responses that can have a long-term effect.

When women are ordained first, before they decide to have a child, the "biological clock" seems to take precedence over perceived or real issues that might arise from a pregnancy. For many women, pregnancy happens while they are serving a church, and they do whatever pregnant women do in workplaces — decide when to announce the pregnancy, arrange maternity leave, schedule doctors' visits around parishioner visits, and go about their lives. Several women I interviewed were either pregnant or close to finalizing an adoption when they were either moved by a bishop (in the United Methodist Church) to a new parish, when a parish closed, or when another opportunity arose. One associate's position lost its funding, and she knew she only had a few months to find another position. She and her husband decided she should try to become pregnant anyway, saying, "If we waited to find a church for me, a job for him, schools for the children, and a normal routine, we'd never have another child." Her baby was three months old when she started a new position.

Once pregnant, however, sometimes parish needs become primary again. Someone should do a study of due dates of clergy women's babies, because it seems that a disproportionate number of babies (even adopted ones) arrive too close to Easter or Christmas! At least five women I talked to had to cut maternity leave short to return for major feasts of the church, both as associates or solo pastors. There's both a psychological pull, because clergy are living the drama of the church year with their communities and want to lead, and firm expectations — if not orders — from senior pastors or lay leaders, whether women want to return then or not.

Nothing surfaces issues of gender in ministry more than pregnancy. Many women are still serving parishes as "the first woman," and all the fears of whether women can lead are now magnified by the question of "can pregnant women lead." Implicit bargains about accepting a woman because they can indeed perform as well as men are betrayed by physical proof that women are different, even if not in matters of leadership style. What about hormones, fatigue, physical symptoms? Those can usually be addressed directly. I was first pregnant in August, in a church with no air conditioning, and I was constantly vaguely nauseous but soldiered on valiantly most of the time. When I gave in for a time and collapsed on a couch in the church office for twenty minutes, the secretary proudly announced to several callers that "Allison was taking a nap." So much for privacy! Several other women clergy found that lay women would try to make them slow down, or choose among events rather than trying to do them all, or just eat after church. Sometimes the offer was gratefully accepted; sometimes the suspicion of looking lazy or no longer up to responsibilities pushed women almost past their limits. "I had so much that I wanted to do and accomplish personally and professionally . . . it was just crushing to realized that I couldn't do it all. . . . And I crashed . . . I actually called in sick on Mother's Day. It just seemed totally symbolic."[7]

Deeper and less conscious issues of sibling rivalry, or sexuality, or women's power, also swirl around a pregnant leader and her parish. A Presbyterian woman gave an extreme example: "I left a position after two and a half years. I followed a thirty-eight-year pastorate. The church was growing financially, numerically, and structurally. The growth was causing growing pains. When I got pregnant, it was more than they could take, and conflict erupted everywhere."[8] A much more positive story comes from one of the first female bishops in the United Methodist Church. Bishop Susan Wolfe Hassinger described her first pregnancy, in a suburban congregation who had had serious questions about having a woman appointed as their leader:

> When a male pastor has a child born in the family, it's great but not such a big deal. But when the chair of the parish staff would say "My pastor's pregnant," you get an incredulous and mystified reaction. Yet, by that time, he was proud to say it. And the church members were willing eventually — at least some of them — to go talk to other churches that were having difficulty with the idea of women pastors. Just imagine![9]

Another of the first women bishops told another story of affirmation from her family of origin. Her story reminds me that resistance to what God seems to be insisting is right sometimes comes from other sources than the church, and yet is a factor in showing up every Sunday and trying to be faithful. "I think my parents had hopes that I'd come to my senses, or that once I had a baby I'd settle down. It was after Matt was born that my parents came and I preached and Daddy said, 'You know, Janice, when I see you up there, it's almost like you're a different person. This must be what God wants you to do.' Oh, it was wonderful."[10]

Regina was unmarried and turning thirty-five when she decided she would become artificially inseminated so she could have a child. At the time she was the associate rector for children and families in a multistaff parish. When she spoke with her rector about her plan and asked if she should leave the parish before beginning her family, he said no, but as the pregnancy went on, his concerns grew. He lamented the ministry she would never be able to accomplish because of her child, and the negative effects he feared in the parish. Regina noted that this was a father who rarely took time for his own children's activities — at one point he asked his daughter to drive by the church on prom night so he could see her before she went out, because he couldn't make it home. Yet she persisted, because the chance of finding another position while pregnant seemed remote.

When Regina announced her pregnancy, reactions were mixed. Many parishioners, especially parents, welcomed the news. A few sent hurtful anonymous letters condemning single motherhood in general, and the pregnancy of an "unmarried priest who must have had sex" in particular. (Regina commented that "obviously that person was not familiar with the technology of artificial insemination, which could never be confused with sex!") When her child was born, however, everyone wanted to see the baby. The hospital and then the rectory were swamped with visitors. "I was glad to see them, just not *all* of them *all* at once!" Others have echoed this sentiment, though living at some distance from the church mitigates that happy problem. A more serious issue arose the year after her child was born when her staff position was eliminated, although she was the associate with the most seniority and the most demonstrated success in ministry. The rector still seemed uncomfortable with the way Regina was letting her child be seen at the workplace.

Once the baby comes...

Blair, a United Methodist pastor, was pregnant when she was moved by her bishop to her fifth congregation, as solo pastor of a small inner-city parish. After only ten weeks there, her son was born extremely prematurely. Her next months were spent shuttling between the neonatal intensive care unit and the parish. The congregation was very supportive of her needs as a new mom of a child with multiple special needs, and in many ways the situation was ideal for her. Blair was close to the specialized hospitals and doctors in the big city that she needed. She wasn't working eighty hours a week, as she had sometimes as an associate with many programs to oversee. The first time she brought her son to church it was Ash Wednesday. He was six months old, five pounds, situated in a bouncy chair with oxygen attached, and he sat quietly until the dismissal "Let us depart in silence." Then he screamed, and she processed out, around, and back to scoop him up, to the approbation of the congregation. Blair used child-care sometimes, worked from home sometimes, brought him to work at other times, and found a rhythm that worked for her and the parish.

Part of her work for the parish, however, was discernment that it was time for this parish to close. There were three other struggling parishes nearby, and no interest in combining ministry. Blair attributes that in part to a "lone ranger" competitive attitude among clergy that reduces possibilities for creative cooperation. At an all-parish retreat everyone agreed it was time, and that they would spend the next year finding new places to worship and distributing assets. Blair and the congregation assumed that she would be with them in that final year, but her district superintendent had other ideas, and someone else was brought in to close the parish. Blair needed to stay in the metropolitan area, close to the specialists her son needed. She had enjoyed working as an associate, doing program ministry that suited her gifts. Yet the demands of that position — seventy-hour weeks and work every Saturday — were too great for a woman with a special-needs child and a husband who worked in retail, for whom Saturday work was also required.

This left only one other option, a small parish two hours from the city, twenty minutes from a pediatric ICU unit, at the outside of her parameters for acceptable distance. Blair followed a well-beloved male pastor, whose child was born while he was serving that parish with no disruption in his schedule of parish work. The parish did not want to lose him, and they really did not want a woman with a special-needs four-year-old, but in the Methodist system the male pastor was needed elsewhere and Blair was appointed. The first six months were spent addressing their grief at losing a pastor they loved and adjusting to a new personality and leadership style. Just when Blair felt that she and the congregation were beginning to work together well, she discovered she was pregnant again. Doctors had said this would be impossible, so first she dealt with her surprise and her husband's. Then they sat down with doctors to see what would be required for this pregnancy, also expected to be high-risk. Then she went to the district superintendent, and laid out a scenario that included surgery for her during the pregnancy and possible bed rest. The district superintendent was supportive, suggesting they take things "one day at a time," and they made a plan to tell the parish everything they knew about what they could expect. All hell broke loose. The parish went to the district superintendent and then to the bishop, saying they didn't want her, they wanted a man. The district superintendent would not remove Blair, who by now was on limited bed rest, working from home to make calls, hold meetings, plan programs, and find child-care for the baby-to-be. She is expected to return a month after the baby is born, and work from 8:30 to 4:00 every day but Saturday, and three evenings a week, because she will have used more than the disability time allotted to her and the parish wants to make sure that she will give them their due.

Blair says that for her it makes most sense to find a part-time call, but she can't because she provides the medical benefits for her family, and new insurance plans would not provide the services her son requires. She laments the expectations placed on full-time clergy that seem more than full-time in either associate or solo positions, longs for a staff position where she could use her gifts for program ministry, and feels trapped by her parish's obvious resistance to her even when she can show them how hard and effectively and faithfully she can work once her baby is born.

On the other hand, the United Methodist Church has guidelines for maternity and parental leave, and denominational officials to help Blair and others negotiate leave when necessary. Vashti McKenzie, an African Methodist Episcopal presiding prelate, tells the story of her third child's birth in a context without external provisions for maternity leave. She maintained a full teaching and preaching schedule in the two congregations in her circuit, nine hours of seminary courses, duties at home, and her sanity, up to the day of her daughter's birth. (Her daughter conveniently waited until after Sunday morning worship to be born.) Two weeks later she was back in church, three weeks later preaching again, with an associate to fulfill other responsibilities until she "was at full strength."[11]

The parish as extended family

Other stories are more hopeful. Once a mother or father returns to the parish, babies can bring unique joys. Several clergy, men and women, talked about how they brought their baby to homebound or nursing home visits, to the great joy of the people they saw. (It is important to ask first, however, since not everyone is so pleased.) When babies come to church, the parish often assumes the baby is theirs. This can be good. Donald and Marlene are white parents who adopted an African-American baby. They get lots of advice from African-American parents about skin and hair care. I was pleased to see that when my husband was away on Sundays, my children felt comfortable finding any number of adults to sit with even at age two or three. (For years they were almost the only young children in the parish.) But parents also lose control over who holds the baby how and when; in the early days of a first baby, this can be especially harrowing! And later, their discipline style and standards of church behavior may be different than that of the parents. Regina remembers preaching while her two-year-old started noisily banging books; the parent he was with allowed him to do this, but one look from Regina made him stop quickly and find a quieter activity.

In an article published on the Episcopal Church's website, Kate Moorehead articulated what many of the women I spoke with found: that "the more that I include my children in the life of the parish, the more young families come to the church."[12] New parenting groups spring up, the "mommy and me" group takes on new life, Sunday School is started first to care for the priest's child and then for the new infants who arrive, there's new emphasis on intergenerational programming or family worship services. The clergy fathers I spoke with didn't talk about this phenomenon, nor do they (in my unscientific poll) seem to come to church as often without their spouse present to care for children. For various reasons (work schedules, lack of interest in church, attending another parish as clergy or lay), many of the spouses of clergy mothers I know don't attend church. Some of the women and I suspect that female clergy are more obvious in their parenting role, even when they are fully vested and leading worship without their children around. One clergy couple with young children sharing one full-time position alternated Sunday leadership. They wanted their parish to understand that because they were sharing the position only one of them was "on duty" each Sunday. They addressed this issue by having the presiding pastor wear a collar so that all pastoral questions were addressed to him or her, and all parental questions referred to the "collarless" parent. It worked "fabulously" in one parish, but in two others, both of which had other conflicts, this arrangement was not as well received.

One of the more dramatic examples of mother/clergy melding came in an informal Eucharist I was co-leading with a Roman Catholic priest at a meeting of the Society for Values in Higher Education. The group offers worship from a variety of traditions and is a fertile ground for trying new things. My colleague and I were vested; I'd led the initial part of the service, he was preaching, and my child, fifteen months old and previously happy in a friend's arms, was hungry. And noisy. And inconsolable after a while. So my friend brought Avery to me and, without really thinking about what I was doing, I nursed her for the rest of the sermon and the prayers, until she fell asleep. I set her down and we proceeded to celebrate Eucharist together. Afterward, people said that the image of a female, obviously a priest and obviously a mom, at the altar literally offering food for body and soul would remain with them forever. (The story has circulated in the group for at least the past decade, at times to my chagrin). It's certainly an example of solving problems as they arise, a theme of many stories of clergy moms, though I'm not sure I'd recommend or repeat it.

Couples juggling work and children

Babies grow, and needs change. Lisa, a Lutheran woman, has two children, two-and-a-half years old and six months old. Her husband is a busy physician. Before children, she had worked three-fourths time in a parish and half-time in the denominational offices. After her first child's birth, she reduced hours in the parish to half-time; with the second child and a change in parish leadership she preaches and presides once a month in the parish while continuing half-time for the denomination. Lisa's work schedule is now fairly stable with some work that can be done at home, but with an infant, every time she works out a balance of work and parenting that makes sense, the infant's schedule and needs change — afternoon time that was perfect for writing while the baby slept becomes late nighttime when the baby decides to nap at dinner time instead. When she makes that change, the toddler moves to a new developmental stage or a different day-care schedule, and when equilibrium is restored again, it's the dog's turn to have a crisis. It's exhausting. Shortly after Lisa became pregnant with her second child, her "ideal full-time job" opened. She considered its cycles of intense work and many weekend commitments, and didn't apply. The timing just was not right.

As children grow, the changes come less frequently, but they still come, and cause ripples in the parents' psyches, the family schedules, and sometimes the parish life. Infants are fairly portable, and several women talked about bringing their baby to meetings until they were about six months old and suddenly not content just to eat and sleep. Full-day school means that mornings or afternoons that used to be for children's activities, to make up for so many evenings out, are gone. As children get older and the number of after-school activities increases, time with children other than evenings is even more scarce. Having children of different ages often means that parents play "tag-team," one with one child and the other with the other, and family time and marriages can suffer. Consider the life of Karen and her husband Bill, both Lutheran pastors serving different churches, and their three children. They met in seminary, got married, and were ordained in a joint service in 1996. They chose to serve different congregations, however, because their skills were different. Karen's first position was solo pastor of a small suburban congregation. In the six and a half years she was there, all three of her adopted children arrived, the last just as they were moving to her next call. Her husband served a parish for a year or so, then spent some time at home full-time with two children, had a secular job, and then was interim in a parish. He does wonder if this sequence of jobs, or the lack thereof, has something to do with the fact that he is African-American, serving in a predominantly white denomination where typically it takes longer for African-Americans to find jobs than Anglos.[13]

After six years or so, Karen took a half-time position as camp director. Knowing that three months of the year would be very intense (eighty to a hundred hours a week), she worked out a detailed pro-rated schedule of part-time hours off-season that startled her superiors. She said that by being very proactive and very clear about her limits, she could actually maintain her schedule and accomplish the necessary work. Her husband, in the meantime, took a half-time call to a parish that closed after a year or so; they lived with three children on a part-time salary, but felt the financial losses were compensated by time with children. Then they both received full-time calls, she as an associate, he as a solo pastor, when their children were ten, seven, and five years old. They own a house midway between the two jobs and have developed an admirable system for scheduling child-care amidst two parishes' worth of activities. "The Palm Pilot has been our salvation — we communicate every schedule change as soon as it happens. When obligations conflict, whoever scheduled the meeting second is responsible for arranging child-care." They always took Friday off as a dedicated family day. Emergencies that challenged that commitment happened perhaps four to six times a year. Once the children were in school, Karen and her husband kept Friday as a "couples day," going to museums or movies or activities "that were fun and didn't require too much thinking." One Saturday a month became a tightly guarded family day, though, as Karen says, "there's usually a sermon hovering over one of us." Organization, clear boundaries, and "communication, communication, communication" help them maintain sanity.

Sometimes things happen — two clergy serving two parishes on Christmas Eve don't need a child violently throwing up. When this happened to Karen and Bill, they quickly figured out which parish had an adult that would be willing to stay with the child, and passed him back and forth as they led early and late services. Karen also told of "her worst mothering nightmare." Her son John was nineteen months old and in the nursery while she was in the sanctuary one Sunday morning. While she was preaching, she noticed someone from the nursery summon Corine, a parishioner who has served as a surrogate mom for John. At the peace, the woman said, "John had a pretty bad fall, his mouth is bleeding, but he seems to be ok with Corine." "Are you sure he's ok?" Karen asked. "Yes, he seems fine." "OK, so I'll go do the offering now." After church she picked up her other two children, dropped them off at her husband's parish, and took John to Urgent Care, just to make sure he was all right. The staff at Urgent Care took one look at John and sent him to the emergency room, because he was young and needed stitches in his mouth. Her husband found care for the other two children and joined her at the emergency room, where they tried to comfort John, who was screaming bloody murder at the sight of instruments, the local anesthetic, and the doctors. The parents looked at each other and, as they held either end of their distressed child, remembered Mary at the cross, watching helplessly as her child suffers. "Save this story for a sermon sometime," thought the clergy parents.

June, a second-career cleric and mother who stayed home with her children until they were in elementary school and then worked as a teacher, started seminary when her children were in junior high and high school. Her children, now in their late teens, still have a hard time "sharing her [with the church], especially when there is a conflict between church functions and their functions or when they feel that 'I love Jesus best' and tell me so."

Pat's children were seven, nine, and eleven when she was ordained, after years of part-time work and five years of seminary. She needed to work full-time for financial reasons and because of her desire to minister. Yet for her there's a sense of wishing things could be different: "I prayed that God would be a presence in my children's lives when I could not be there." She regrets not spending more time helping children with schoolwork. One of them had a learning disability that was not diagnosed until middle school, and another had a behavioral problem "which was probably exacerbated by my not being around."

Sometimes seminary and ordained ministry is taken on after marriage and parenting. When Sarah decided to commute to seminary, her husband was very supportive. He took responsibility for getting their children off to school, and they accepted the financial ramifications of seminary. Sarah was proud of the fact that she has never missed any of her children's events. She admits that she may have slept through some, but at least she was physically present!

Vanessa worked full-time teaching school until her children were born. Then she worked part-time and went to graduate school for three years, worked part-time with young children for five years, and then spent five years in seminary instead of the typical three before becoming ordained. Yet once she was ordained, she worked in parish ministry full-time, through three churches, for a total of thirteen years so far. Vanessa said she might have wanted to take a break for a while between parish positions but didn't want a break in pension, and she couldn't afford to pay pension benefits out of her own pocket. Part of what made this work was that Vanessa was clear about her own boundaries. In her first parish as an assistant, she protected her need to be home by 3:00 p.m. for after school activities; she balanced work requirements with evening meeting times. She said, however, that she was required to be in the office every Saturday from 9:00 a.m. to 1:00 p.m., regardless of whether there were any scheduled activities (as was the rector). That was hard; her husband did most of the Saturday sports and activities. "Once I was in charge of a parish, I changed that — I work plenty of Saturdays, but only when I need to." Work sometimes interfered with her ability to spend the kind of time she wanted with her growing children, and yet the "middle of the day flexibility" made it possible to do some things that a more nine-to-five schedule would not permit. Now her children are three to five hours away in college, and while daily work is much easier without constantly negotiating child-care or carpools, weekend work makes it harder travel to visit them or enjoy them if they come home unexpectedly.

Vanessa's reflections are poignant, and convey well what many other women have said.

> All of my work decisions have been made in light of what the family could bear, though (unfortunately) not what might have been best for them. The main question is the ratio between kid/family time::marriage time::work time in a job that just never quits. Some of that is pastoral emergencies, some of that is what is "good" for parish development, and some of it is my own love of the job. Being a married woman with children and being a rector has been hard, with all of the societal (and personal) expectations about the first half of that equation. But despite the difficulty and heartache, it has also been a joy.[14]

United Methodist Bishop Susan Wolfe Hassinger was ordained before marriage or children. Her first call as a pastor was to a struggling suburban congregation that couldn't afford a full-time pastor, although the Methodist *Discipline* technically didn't allow part-time calls at that time. She was there for a year, moved into full-time work and full-time salary, and became pregnant before there were guidelines for maternity leave in the *Discipline*. When her second child was born, she wanted to work only part-time hours, which worked because another lay woman in the parish was willing to do much of the administration and program as she discerned her own call to ordained ministry. Then she and her husband, also ordained, each worked three-quarters time on the staff of a large church. "How we got away with doing some of that, I don't know. Quietly devious. I'm still doing that."[15] "Quietly devious" is an apt description for some of the path-setting that pioneer women in any denomination did for the next generation. Needs come up, in the parish or at home, and because the situation is unique, there is both the difficulty of no models and the freedom of no precedents.

Other parents found the juggling act was not right for them. Evening and weekend hours for clergy and Monday through Friday work for spouses or partners can wreak havoc on marriages and committed relationships. Each couple handles this differently — some clergy spouses have more flexibility in scheduling their hours — but this was the number one issue in the Newark survey and comes up in every interview. A Lutheran couple, Martha and Mark, were both ordained clergy. Their twins were conceived when Martha was in her internship, in her third year of seminary, and the one final year of on-campus study became two. Her husband had already graduated and was working full-time in a parish. Another child was born three years later. She took primary care of the children until she graduated, and then she and her husband shared his position until their children were in school. Then they left the parish setting, and Martha worked full-time at denominational headquarters while her husband worked part-time. Once the children were in school all day, he became a full-time chaplain. As she said, "We've both worked full-time since then, though neither in a parish setting, which has been much better for our parenting. We are both PKs and realized that we would always be busiest and most distracted when our children were the least (evenings, weekends, and holidays)." Another woman, part of a married couple of PKs who were in parish ministry, described how she and her husband "resolutely stuck with fifty hours or less a week as full-time. . . . How can you do a decent job of parenting or 'spous-ing' if you are working more than six eight-hour days a week? We don't know our fathers because they were always at church. We don't want to do that to our kids."[16] They're wise to consider this: A study of Baptist clergy children found that 84 percent complained of not having enough time with a clergy parent. "Even when Dad is home, he works on his sermon," lamented one child.[17]

Most of the research available on women in parish ministry suggests that more women than men leave parish ministry after being ordained and working in a parish for a while. Researchers are less clear about why. Barbara Brown Zikmund evaluated several findings of previous studies and found seven factors that make it *unlikely* for women or men to leave parish ministry: strong professional self-concept, good health, ability to set boundaries between church work and private life, fair compensation, respect from denominational officials, belief that a better church position will be somewhat easy to find, and participation in a clergy support group.[18] There are some denominational characteristics that make life more difficult for women: Southern Baptist clergy women face severe resistance from other clergy and laity, and often have real difficulty finding a second call. United Methodist clergy women with families have trouble balancing family and career needs with the expectations that they will move to a new congregation every three or four years.[19] Matthew Price found a large pay gap between male and female Episcopal clergy: Full-time male clergy earn 7.5 percent more than full-time women clergy, even when comparing men and women in the same relative positions and with the same number of years of credited service.[20] He attributes this in part to three factors. First, more women than men begin in assisting clergy positions (59 percent of women vs. 42 percent of men). Second, the percentage of women clergy in senior rector position grows more slowly than the rate for men; after ten years of credited service, almost 25 percent of male clergy are senior rectors, while only 13 percent of women are. Third, the parishes where women are solo pastors have lower average Sunday attendance (ASA) and operating revenue than those with male solo pastors with the same years of service.[21] All of these factors contribute to greater stress for women clergy.

Zikmund et al. approached the question of impact of children on clergy career paths from a different perspective. First, they looked at career histories of women and men who had children within five years of ordination. They found that many more clergy men than women had children within this period. Men were much more likely to move from college to seminary to marriage and ordination and children, while women were more likely to be single — either never married or married and divorced — prior to ordination. Many women started seminary after children, or, if ordained first, delayed child-rearing for more than five years. Then Zikmund et al. looked at second jobs, or jobs after children were born. Clergy men with children are more likely to be in senior or sole pastorates than clergy men without children, so fatherhood seems to be an advantage. This may be because more married clergy men have stay-at-home wives who assist their husbands in their jobs, or because denominational officials take some care to make sure that clergy men with families serve in churches where salaries are higher.

But for clergy women, there is either no impact or the impact is negative. Similar findings obtain in studies of female executives and professionals in secular organizations. "There is a perception in church and society that women have a disproportionate role (compared with men) in caring for children and that there-fore they will not give as much energy to their careers as will men with children."[22] Zikmund et al. also found that lay people are consistently more concerned about the family responsibilities of clergy mothers than of clergy fathers. For women, comments consistently include the theme that "raising children is the most im-portant work anyone can do," or "in God's wisdom, a woman should care for her children." In contrast, lay people, male or female, never mention the issue of child-care if their pastor is male, unless he is a single parent, when they are almost universally positive.[23]

And what about the children?

There are advantages and disadvantages in the life of a "PK" just as there are for children of children in any other profession, and as many different interpretations as children. Nonetheless, some common themes emerge as parents reflect on their experiences, hopes, and regrets.[24]

Laurie puts on her collar and her three-year-old says: "You sit down, Mom. Don't go out." Lots of clergy children don't like to see their parents putting on clericals, because it means they're going to their other family. I'll say, "I'm just going to church for a minute," and the children respond, "Don't talk to anyone!" A clergy spouse complains that with the rectory next door, when her husband says "I'm just going to church for a minute," it's at least fifteen minutes and often means delayed meals or skipped conversations as parish work comes into the home again.

Sometimes I try to multitask by having meetings in the rectory when the babysitter cancels, having one child come to the first twenty minutes of a meeting so my husband can pick up the other one, putting an acolyte robe on a four-year-old to keep her close to me for an early service and there's no sitter or spouse available. I'm used to juggling attention, and although it violates both the "good mom" and the "good priest" tapes, it feels as if I'm accommodating both needs. But sometimes I'm not. In retrospect, there have been times when parishioner needs really have been slighted, and I wasn't able to be fully available. Or when my children really wanted a parent to put them to bed, and my husband was living in another city during the week, and I had yet another meeting, and the plea is "Mommy, are you going to put me to bed tonight PLEASE?"

Regina, as a single mother, faces the same question from her son. How many nights can a sitter or an aunt put your child to bed before you both lose the closeness that can come from that time? Regina also wonders, as do I and many other clergy mothers and fathers I spoke with, whether, if our children are bright and compliant, we often ask them to do things (acolyte, read, visit, behave) well beyond their years. Regina's son could sit in a pew by himself and walk himself up to the rail for communion and back before he was three. Karen finds that her children are with her husband, also a pastor, more often than with her because his parish is more accommodating of children. But as an associate, there are times when they are with her and she actually gets to sit with her children during worship — a rare privilege for all of them! One woman said that "[her] children know [her] ministry is important, and they want to share it with [her], just not all the time." Fair enough.

Then there are the virtues of knowing themselves to have a place in an extended family. Peter's children are comfortable in church, and feel safe; the children's best friends are in church. Les and Pam, now in active retirement, remember their first parish fondly. Les was the curate; their first child was born there and welcomed, and the curate could do no wrong. Pam felt loved and supported, and there was lots of support for the young family. Many parents said that sometimes parishioners offer to babysit when child-care plans fall through. My children each have their favorite adults with whom they have special relationships. My children will sometimes ask to visit "so-and-so" in the hospital because they want to encourage her to get well, and the affection between parishioner and child is obvious. Barbara's daughter has been part of the Women's Group since she was two years old, and now as a teenager still attends meetings every once in a while, or seeks out women her grandmother's age just to say hello. One teenager in a survey wrote, "When [she] was younger, the extra Christmas presents from parishioners made up for [her] having everyone's eyes on [her], but now [she wasn't] sure."

There are benefits, too, especially if the clergy child *likes* to acolyte all the time. Children can feel proud of how they participate in their parent's work. Many clergy spouses or partners talk about enjoying family participation in a life of faith, about being able to support the spouse's vocation and work together in ministry, and about being able to use church facilities for family activities. One teenaged child created a "hide-out" in a remote part of the church, undiscovered for several years until the sexton found it, complete with cigarettes, ash trays, and a few scorch marks in the wood. Another created a darkroom in part of the church basement. The basement of one of the rectories we used had been turned into a stage, with lights and a platform, for a band organized by a child of the previous rector but ultimately used by the whole youth group for small rock concerts.

There are also significant differences among parishes in the degree of welcome, for clergy children and all children. When Karen, a Lutheran pastor married to a pastor, was in charge of a small suburban parish, she found parishioners completely understanding about her young children's presence at Bible studies and worship. They seemed anxious about helping her make arrangements for three toddlers, sharing sitting responsibilities or passing babies around. Now as an associate in an urban parish, the expectations are different. Parishioners travel from farther distances and have more obligations outside church. Karen was surprised to hear complaints when she brought her children to what she thought was an informal worship committee meeting, scheduled immediately before a family event where her children were expected. They were school-aged by then, and were taking care of each other in an adjoining room, but there were interruptions for bathrooms and a tantrum. Committee members were not pleased, even though on other occasions lay people had brought their children and even a dog. Interruptions divided her attention, when the committee members expected her to be fully present. Karen could see both sides. No one would bring three children to a corporate business meeting, but a corporation wouldn't expect her children to participate at all.

When I was an assistant in a medium-sized urban parish with lots of families, my baby was welcome, I received lots of advice, and there was even a high tolerance for nursing. (On Sunday mornings, one corner of the church had become the de facto nursing corner for lay women). Seven years later, the small congregation I served as rector had no children under the age of five. They accepted my older daughter, who by nature was quiet and reserved, but had much more trouble with her infant sister who was active, noisy, and clearly needy. The good news was that my husband revived the Sunday School, and the following year there were three new families; a year later, there were monthly youth services, and the parish had new energy from the critical mass of children.

And then there is the public dimension of parenting. Peter finds that the congregation assumes they can say anything they'd like about his children, no matter how critical, and Peter has to remain calm and professional. This seems to come up especially when there are other conflicts in the parish, and criticizing a child feels sometimes like a way to express anger about a decision Peter has made about parish life. Peter says that he has been ordained for fourteen years and still hasn't developed thick enough skin to deal with all of the criticisms, even when he knows intellectually that it's not about him. In another parish, one of the congregation's "most proper people" came to the rectory door one day to find the three-year-old, completely naked, running delightedly away from her clergy mom. Les and Pam's parenting style was "on the extreme edge of permissiveness" in the 1960s, when conflict about authority was running high throughout the culture.

Sometimes parishioners would complain about their son's long hair — one family gave that as the reason they left the parish — or the fact that Les and Pam didn't expect the children to be in church every Sunday. The parents weren't going to force the children to be model clergy children, and they weren't.

I live next to the church. One morning during school vacation, I wanted to make a hospital visit early. We discussed the plan the night before, so both children knew I would be gone in the morning but would come back soon. In the morning I woke the twelve-year-old, told her I was leaving, and let the five-year-old sleep. But the twelve-year-old went back to sleep, the five-year-old forgot the plan, panicked when she couldn't find me, went to the church in her nightgown, hysterically crying that I'd abandoned her, and locked herself out of the rectory. The staff at the church tried to call my cell phone, which of course didn't work in the hospital, and their messages over the next thirty minutes became increasingly concerned that something really was wrong. Mercifully, I picked up messages before they called the police. How many people should know that I left my children alone?

Bruce Hardy found another dynamic unmentioned by the clergy parents in my research. He notes that in the power structures of most congregations, children are overlooked. Clergy children, though, are very aware that some of the adults around them supervise their clergy parent's work, and are a source of tension. When conflict erupts, adults who had been supportive sometimes become suddenly absent or angry, and the children may feel even more isolated and alone. Some children face conflicting loyalties between parishioners and their clergy parent.[25] My daughter grew very close to a couple who suddenly left the parish, furious at something I had done. She didn't understand why her "friends" no longer wanted to see her, and I was hurt both by the conflict and the hole they left in my child's life.

Teenagers have their own issues. Upon hearing that her mother was going to start seminary and eventually be ordained, one thirteen-year-old lamented that this was the most embarrassing thing her mother could ever do to her. And for several weeks my daughter, at twelve, wanted to be an acolyte; "I just want to be close to you," she said. I never found out what that was really about, but I enjoyed it while it lasted, and tried to make some more private time with her as well. Then there's the public face of the church. Peter's son, at eleven, has had to defend some of the controversial stands of the Episcopal Church from accusations of heresy by his classmates. My five-year-old was quite indignant when, after I had presided at a commitment ceremony for two men she knew well, her teacher told her that gay men could never be married in church.

The sliding between roles of clergy and parent can be both frustrating and life-giving. My plan for one morning was to take my daughter to school, host a community clergy meeting, and then officiate at a funeral. A fine plan until Avery woke up fretful, with a fever of 101. I could manage the clergy meeting with a sick child on my lap or coloring beside me, although I did comment to the Roman Catholic clergy that there might be some wisdom in a celibate clergy. But who would take care of her during the funeral, when my husband was unavailable? The ever-obliging ninety-year-old altar guild member sat with her in the back of the church, while I prayed that Avery wouldn't give her the fever. (She didn't.) Eventually we could go home and Avery could get the sleep she really needed while I did some paperwork. Everyone survived, but I still feel a little guilty as I write this — "good moms" would never make their sick child go to work for five hours, and "good priests" would always have not just Plan A but Plans B, C, and D to ensure that children wouldn't have to be at work. And yet, we juggle. As do working parents all over the planet. One clergy single mom said that that was her definition of "good enough mothering": "If I always have a Plan B, and sometimes a hint of Plan C, I'm good." There are unique tensions in this position, but there are strengths as well, not the least of which is a sense of being faithful to God as a parent and a parish ordained leader. Kate Moorehead sums up the benefits well: "It is possible to balance the life of a parish priest and the life of a parent. In fact, sometimes I wonder if God intended for the two to go together, for there is no other relationship that has taught me more about the love of God."[26]

Nurturing marriage (or not)

Children's demands are usually loud and obvious. When children get too quiet, that too can be a cry for help. Parishioners' needs are also obvious, either in individual requests or in program plans. Yet most of the people with whom I talked, male and female, worried that they weren't spending enough time attending to their marriage or primary relationship. Sometimes those danger signals are hard to see. One woman said that she absolutely loved her inner-city parish work, loved it with a passion that blinded her to the effects her eighty-hour work-weeks were having on her relationship with her partner. Not until it was time for her to think about having children could she hear her partner say, "No, not until you make time for me first." A discussion about time and priorities led to a redefinition of her self over the next two or three years that ultimately provided a much healthier foundation for parish ministry, marriage (in fact, if not law), and parenting. "I moved from rescuing the world, trying to save everyone myself, to evangelizing — sharing the good news of how God has enough love to save, heal, and sustain all and how each person needs to claim that gift."

Vanessa reflected on ten years of parish ministry, now that her children were in college:

Perhaps the best thing to say is what I would do differently in hindsight. I would be more realistic about the impact on the family and my ability to handle it, I would not let myself get frozen by guilt about not meeting all my family's needs (maybe even find a way to have a house-cleaner twice a month), I would work out a more conscious partnership of schedules, house-work, and cooking with my husband, I would also insist on making time in my schedule for my husband to continue his interests/career/activities in a way that would be more life-giving for him.[27]

Parish ministry is also not the type of work that can always easily be left at the door. Charlie, a gay man, complained that often when Sean, his clergy partner, came home, he brought some of the issues of the parish home with him, and was distant when it was time for them to be together. Some conscious acknowledgment of this dynamic allowed them to accommodate it and honor the time they had set aside just to have fun or talk or be together. Charlie works Tuesday through Saturday, and they keep Mondays as sacred. For them, keeping the day free for each other is part of fidelity. "On Mondays," Charlie said, "nothing else takes precedence over us." That attitude filters through the rest of the week. Each week they look ahead to the schedule of meetings. Over time they have found that usually they have Friday through Monday evenings together, but that Tuesday through Thursdays, Sean usually isn't home until 10:00 p.m. or so.

A straight clergy couple faced the same problem. "As we left the parish setting, we purposefully chose to do some marriage counseling. Our second and third parishes were very conflicted, and we realized that we were bringing far too much of that home. We wanted help to unravel our marriage from the tentacles that had crept in."

Pam is a psychotherapist married to Les. She said that her greatest stress throughout the marriage was that she has had "to keep her mouth shut." Her personality is extroverted, while he is more laid back, reserved. Often she wanted to tell people how horrid they were being, and she had to keep quiet. She said that there are disturbed people in any parish — an article she read about "clergy killers" named formally some of the dynamics she knew intuitively. Les would spend so much time trying to reason with them, win them over, and they would hurt him and occupy too much of his energy. He would bring his hurt and disappointment home and instead of Pam offering sympathy, she would get mad. Les believes he belongs to the church and God first; Pam loves her husband more than God, because in learning to love her husband more she learns to love God. She has a love/hate relationship with the church, because the church is Les's mistress, his other woman.

And yet, say both Les and Pam, they made time to talk daily, and never ran out of things to say. Their relationship had lots of friction, but is also a genuine love affair. "There's no one else I could be as happy with," she says. One of the benefits for them of being a clergy family was lots of family trips. Les would do summer supply at the same places year after year so the family would have good vacation spots with friends for their children (such as a New Hampshire lake, a Vermont lake, Boothbay Harbor, Maine — always kids the same ages as their children, and continuity from summer to summer). Twice, Les didn't take a vacation one year so that the next summer he could have two months off for wonderful family adventures. Now they go visit children and grandchildren scattered around the country, and twice a year they have a romantic weekend getaway, just for them.

Pam developed a counseling career out of her work in the parish when her children were in junior high school. She felt lucky to be able to stay home with their four children when they were younger, despite some financial sacrifices. For couples now trying to honor two careers and children and home life, juggling becomes even more complicated. Peter's wife, Maya, is a social worker, working on a dissertation while working part-time and being the primary parent for their three children. She is also active in the life of the parish and responsible for organizing hospitality for long extended-family visits, given that both her family of origin and Peter's live in India. She generally assumes that she has to do more for her family and for her church, and often feels guilty. Her dissertation is going slowly as she struggles to identify and honor her own priorities and develop her own voice. Peter tries to support her, but he notices that at the end of a day when they finally have time to be alone together, each wants the other to take care of them because they both give so much of themselves during the day.

Not all marriages succeed. Zikmund et al. note that the rate of clergy who have been divorced one or more times is about the same for clergy as for nonclergy. In their study, 24 percent of clergy women and 19 percent of clergy men had ever been divorced, compared to the U.S. Census Bureau's 1985 survey that found 23 percent of women and 22 percent of men in the United States have been divorced.[28] Divorce is not the norm among active clergy: 50 percent of the women and 75 percent of the men were in their first marriage. There are differences among denominations. The Zikmund study included fifteen predominantly white Protestant denominations, ranging from Southern Baptist and Church of the Brethren clergy, less than one-sixth of whom have been divorced, to Unitarian-Universalist clergy and Episcopal clergy, nearly 50 percent and 25 percent of whom, respectively, have been divorced. For women, most divorces happened before they started seminary or were ordained, and were not related to the stresses of parish life. Most divorced clergy men get divorced in the middle of their ministry career, and their divorces are more likely to upset denominational officials and upset parish life.[29]

Hoge and Wenger's study of five denominations parallels Zikmund et al.'s findings. Five percent of their sample had left the parish because of divorce, either because their denomination forced them to leave or because they felt they could no longer continue. Forty-two out of the 44 divorced clergy in that 5 percent were male; the reasons cited for their divorce that were related to parish ministry included emotionally demanding work, the need to be constantly on call, and "unspoken expectations from laity about the role of clergy spouses."[30] Comparing people who left because of divorce with all people who left parish ministry reveals some interesting differences. Seventy-nine percent of these clergy felt they had problems creating a private life apart from their ministerial role, versus 63 percent of all others. Fifty-two percent versus 31 percent felt that their work did not give them enough time with their children, and 68 percent of their spouses had expressed strong resentment against the amount of time given to ministry and against their financial situation.[31] There were not enough women in the sample to draw comparisons based on gender.

Work-home boundaries

Parishioners often expect clergy to be available at any time, for reasons varying from a serious crisis to a request for a key to the church or a phone number to a "I just need to talk to someone," which could be serious or not. Zikmund et al. observed that "not only do people have many roles and relationships with a variety of persons, but when expectations call for conflicting behaviors or management of time, private and public roles become entangled and confused."[32] Church consultants recognized in the 1970s that ordained clergy are particularly susceptible to role strain because of ambiguous and conflicting expectations about behavior and time management. Jackson Carroll noted that clergy role strain and burnout due to role confusion have not changed in the past thirty years.[33]

Listening to mothers in ministry more carefully may challenge that finding, however. Many mothers I have known over the years, in secular and ordained positions, say that the arrival of a child, or some developmental changes in their children's lives, make them much clearer about priorities. Brenda, who had been a professional fundraiser before having children, waited until her children were in elementary school to go to seminary, and was excited about a full-time assistant's position that would use her energy and skills. About a year into the position, however, work was spilling into marriage, and, more importantly, one of her children had a crisis. She said that she'd been watching the lines between work and home grow blurry, but she thought she had everything under control until then, and suddenly her priorities became clear and her boundaries firm. She reduced her hours, insisted on only being available two days a week, and set up an office in the church so that no work would come home. Eventually she moved out of parish ministry and into part-time diocesan work.

Lisa found that having one child helped her to say "no" more easily, at home and in the workplace. When her second child arrived, she returned from maternity leave after six weeks (the maximum her position allowed), exhausted but determined to function at work. After a few weeks, first her husband and then her older child became sick. She tried to take care of everyone but finally insisted that the older child stay in his own bed and that her husband not wake her up for his needs or those of the older child. "The combination of work and intense baby-care forced me to take care of myself enough to be a good human." Lisa notes that some of her friends who stay at home full-time with young children seem not to be able to set boundaries with spouse or children, so they are exhausted all the time and unable to let themselves take a break away from household duties. Congregational ministry and parenting can each absorb all available time and energy and still demand more. This isn't healthy for anyone — clergy, parish, or family

Collar stories

Different denominations have different understandings of ordination, sometimes reflected in clerical attire. Many mainline Protestant clergy don't wear collars or other symbols of their role outside of worship robes. Many Roman Catholic, Episcopal, and Lutheran clergy do wear collars with some frequency. A discussion of collars among clergy who do wear them illustrates a variety of attitudes and expectations that occur whenever it's known that someone is a clergy person. Father Joe is never seen without his collar, "but he was Roman first [before leaving the Roman Church and having his orders received in another denomination]," says another priest, in explanation. Mother Susan, ordained less than a year, also always wears her collar in public, even on airplane trips unrelated to church business (which was where I met her, out of my collar). She said that she felt she ought to make herself available to anyone who felt the need of priestly counsel or sacramental confession. Constant availability was part of what it meant for her to be ordained. I was traveling with a six-week-old baby and had a dawning sense of what constant availability to an infant might really mean, and it scared me.

In another conversation, a group of women clergy agreed that they wore their collars to tell others and remind themselves that they were "on duty," either fulfilling church responsibilities or representing the church at public functions, or on their way from one to another. One woman says she never takes her collar off or puts it on in front of people; it feels as if she's changing identities "before their very eyes," which makes her and others uncomfortable. Women have stories about not being recognized as clergy even with collars on, because people expect clergy to be male. Yet women clergy are more accepted than in the early 1980s, when one female priest recounted how she had been asked by a man in the grocery store whether her collar meant that her husband was ordained!

Children know that collars are important. More than one clergy parent has said that toddlers will start crying when Mom or Dad puts on a collar, because they know it means the parent is leaving. When asked, "Do you wear a collar when picking up your child from school, or to school functions?" both men and women have said that it depends on where you're coming from, what else you're doing, and how your children feel. One man talked about watching his daughter's face fall as she said, "You're wearing the God suit to school *again?*" Yet collars at parent-teacher conferences or in the school office can command extra respect and attention, whether they should or not.

Clergy themselves may change the way they choose to make their professional identity known. For years Ron almost always wore collars, because he and others expected it of him. In his late forties, he began to face and significantly change some unhealthy patterns of self-care. As he begins his fifties, he has a radically new sense of himself as priest "from the inside," grounded in prayer and counseling, where the collar itself is increasingly irrelevant. He now rarely wears collars at all, except to worship that he's leading, and feels much more faithful to his vocation.

Sharing of self

Collar or no collar, one unique dimension of ordained ministry is that clergy are both believers, engaged in their own process of spiritual growth, and "meta-believers" who share stories and teach about the process of spiritual growth, their own and others, at home or in the world, in their professional life. Almost any experience can become food for a sermon: Most family members of clergy fear that they will hear about themselves from the pulpit. Yet a willingness to share appropriately from one's own experience, or at least let one's own experience inform preaching and pastoral care, is essential to authenticity for clergy. Pregnancy, pregnancy loss, and parenting are experiences that often seem to bring people from different ethnicities or economic classes together. Pamela Cooper White gives one example: "When I first went [to my parish], there was a *huge* gap — I was an urban professional who hadn't taken her husband's name. They were small town, rural folks who really saw me as 'other.' Then I got pregnant. The women got together for the first time in years to give me a shower."[34] The physical changes in women's bodies and often the greater exposure of children at work demanding food or care mean that mothering is often more visible, and therefore more a part of congregational life, than fathering. Lisa became pregnant when she served on a task force on sexuality, and she found that people's responses to her pregnancy personalized the work they were doing in a helpful way. Experiences of miscarriages often evoke stories from parishioners of similar experiences that may never have been shared with clergy. The sharing can open avenues of healing for clergy and parishioners.

Workaholism

Clinical Pastoral Education (CPE), or some pastoral care classes, can leave students feeling that the only reason they were ordained is because of unresolved issues of needing to save everyone, or prove oneself worthy, or be liked and needed. Parish ministry is a perfect storm of opportunities to give continually of oneself or lose oneself in work trying to do any or all of the above. Barbara Brown Taylor illustrates this eloquently:

> No matter how many day planners I bought, none of them told me when I had done enough. If I spent enough time at the nursing home then I neglected to return phone calls, and if I put enough thought into the vestry meeting then I was less likely to catch mistakes in the Sunday bulletin. As soon as I managed to convince myself that these were not cardinal sins, one of them would result in an oversight that caused a parishioner's meltdown. The demands of parish ministry routinely cut me off from the resources that enabled me to do parish ministry.[35]

Many clergy are aware of their particular psychological dynamics that lead them to overwork or overfunction, and are working hard to counter these tendencies through self-care, therapy, or supervision. Many mothers are also aware of how these dynamics play out in their family life. (The differences in male and female socialization usually make the drive to overfunction as a parent much less compelling for men than women.) Yet usually the external demands of parish work are as compelling for men as for women; it's just that many women feel the conflicts between commitments to family and work more acutely and can sometimes use the demands of parenting to help set limits on work life.

Roger talked about workaholism in passing, as a way to avoid dealing with family struggles and his own weight issues. He couldn't go to Weight Watchers because he already had too many meetings, or he had to eat fast-food on the way to the hospital because others' needs are more important than his. However, he also talked about how he could stretch some parish work out to take much more time than the tasks actually needed. Procrastination and avoidance of less-favorite parts of parish ministry can waste lots of time. Roger found that his wife helped get him moving sometimes and called him on his avoidance. The lack of accountability in parishes and fuzzy boundaries between work and home can allow procrastination to fester, and then family time is sacrificed as deadlines approach.

Richard talks of workaholism as part of his character: A drive to perfection-ism and a drive to overachieve in order to meet eternally higher standards mean seventy-hour workweeks, or accepting a position on town council, adjunct teach-ing, or huge diocesan commitments in addition to parish work. Now in his fifties, he has become more aware of the costs of this kind of overwork, and is finally hearing what his partner has been saying for years about the benefits of one day a week off or taking on less. For Peter, the needs of a growing parish and his own drive for excellence mean that he often feels he should be working all the time. He has had trouble honoring his day off; about the time he began to succeed in doing so, the parish started a capital campaign and he was back to working seven days a week. He says he knows the literature about self-care, and respects it, but he has a drive to do parish work not just well but excellently, and it doesn't feel like there's time to do excellent work and take care of himself.

Women often talked of the same dynamics, but mothering was often the unavoidable counterpressure. Karen found that with each child (she and her hus-band adopted three) she had to become more efficient at church and at home. She and her husband worked out ways to communicate schedules, carpool, and shop more effectively. Another woman found that pressure to be finished so she could pick up children meant that newsletter articles "weren't as perfect in [her] eyes (though no one else noticed a decrease in quality), but they were done." One woman said, "I drove myself at an insane pace — child-care, part-time job, and seminary." It didn't occur to her or to her husband to ask him to take on more household responsibilities, as it seems that more of the younger mothers I interviewed did. Madison felt guilty when she asked for an extension on semi-nary finals because her baby was due in mid-December. She took the exams in January, did very well, and then wondered whether she *really* did well or whether her professors gave her a break? She felt that many women don't want to be characterized as needy, especially when need comes from parenting responsibili-ties, because that reinforces the (incorrect) assumption that mothers can't fulfill parish ministry responsibilities adequately.

Madison also named another powerful dynamic. In our culture the "original sin" seems to be valuing people for what they accomplish, not who they are — holy, sinful creatures of God. She worked for a rector who seemed to be perpetually busy, as if by completing more tasks in his calendar, or filling the church's calendar, he could earn salvation. She hoped he would learn in time to differentiate what he thought he should do from what he actually needed to do. Barbara Brown Taylor observed that her drive to accomplish things got in the way of modeling the faithfulness people also expected from clergy. In her words, "I knew attorneys and emergency room doctors who worked longer hours than I did, but 'wholesome example' was nowhere in their job description."[36]

Annette, an African-American co-pastor, with her husband, of a nondenom-inational congregation, reflected on experiences in a group of women serving churches with their husbands as either pastors themselves, or "designated pas-tor's wives," or teachers. In any of these positions, the women often spent time "just being"; at meetings, with parishioners, on the playground with their children, socializing. They (often with their children) also ran into parishioners (and often their parishioners' children) at school meetings, in the grocery store, or in doctors' offices, or on the street. If women were pastors, this was often not considered by their male colleagues as "real ministry," which involved leading or organizing. Yet male leaders would consistently seek out the perspective of the women, who by "just being" often had their fingers more accurately on the emotional pulse of the congregation.

I also find that I overfunction when I'm afraid or unwilling to let change happen. When Avery was three, we moved to a new parish and new nursery school. She was miserable. After judging at least seven other nursery schools unsatisfactory, I realized that the problem was probably not with the schools but with my guilt at moving her and focusing on a new job. On more than one occasion I have invested lots of time and energy in a parish project that seemed to go nowhere. When, out of exhaustion, anger, or despair, I let go and let others take appropriate responsibility, the project took off. Learning when to be directive and when to let go is a spiritual task intimately connected to how I am trusting or failing to trust God.

Trying to prove self by doing everything

Women in seminary with young children and in parishes also found themselves overly eager to show that being a mom made no difference in their professional lives. They would make every meeting, drag children to hospitals in order to make pastoral visits, and never tell anyone about the rearranging of family life necessary to meet parish or school obligations. Sometimes there are real bosses who make real, sometimes absurd demands. One rector, while professing sympathy for his assistant whose father was within days of death around Holy Week, also insisted that she not miss any Holy Week services to visit him. Sometimes we do what was modeled for us: One woman wrote that three or four days after one of her seminary professors had a baby, she invited people to her home so she could teach class. At the time, the woman thought this was a great model; once she had children, she wondered if the professor ever looked back to say "it was the dumbest thing I ever did."[37]

Sometimes there are internal voices. The last three months of my pregnancy were very snowy. It was often difficult for anyone to get to church, yet I made it every Sunday, sometimes walking a mile or so from the train station. I was amazed to hear from the rector later that most people thought I was crazy to do so. No one else expected me to be there. Of course, it would have been interesting to hear what would have been said if I had used snow and/or pregnancy as an excuse to stay home.

Lone ranger

Les was the sole pastor at his church, where all his predecessors had had an assistant. There was more work than he could handle, but he continued to do it rather than train laity to help make up the difference between a one-clergy and two-clergy staff. Les saw himself as a bit of a loner, making decisions apart from the community; his personality, strengths and faults, had much to do with how he ran the parish, and would sometimes cause friction. He and his wife agreed that he almost always took his day off and spent it with his family, but that didn't make up for the stress and exhaustion of continually unrealistic and unmet expectations.

Sometimes clergy in under-resourced parishes, or in parishes where attendance and revenues are slowly but steadily declining, are afraid to let the congregation know the effects of diminished resources, for fear the parishes will get discouraged, angry at the pastor, or disappointed. It seems easier to just soldier away, not counting costs on self or family. Blair felt that the "lone ranger mentality" seriously impaired the ability of her parish to consider merging with one or two other churches within three miles of each other. She and her congregation recognized that they were no longer financially or emotionally viable. When they turned to the other congregations, however, the ordained clergy in those churches didn't want to hear of joint worship, rejected pleas to have youth groups work together, and seemed intent on keeping their own struggling parishes alive at all costs by overfunctioning and then loudly complaining about how they have no time for their families or themselves because they have too much work to do. Blair was eager to explore new models of doing ministry together.

Chronic sources of stress

"Too much work." Some long hours and overfunctioning seem to be built into the structure of a job. For the women in the stories here, the desire to work less or the sense of genuine sacrifice of mothering in the service of the church meets financial or structural realities. Regina's parish survives financially because it has a day-care center. Regina had been at the parish for a few years, and had hired the current the day-care director full-time. This director was very competent, but she had been out on medical leave/disability periodically, and when she was out, Regina had to fill in for her, often working sixty-hour weeks. Regina is a single

mom, so every hour at the church or center is time her son is away from a parent, and that hurts. The blurring of priest-employer boundaries in times of employee crisis also takes her time and energy. The work at the day-care center (and much of the parish) is administrative, not priestly, so it feels draining. Regina is afraid her short temper or fatigue comes home with her too often lately. She also notes, ironically, that she can negotiate a fair wage, with annual raises and the medical leave the director is now using, for the day-care director but not for herself.

The single most important determinant of clergy women's feelings of satisfaction, self-worth, and motivation to remain in parish ministry is how lay church leaders respond to their work. "Negative feedback, often deriving from negative attitudes to women's ordination in general, can be the clergy woman's most daunting 'downer.'"[38] Men are daunted by negative feedback as well, and some cite their inability to establish and maintain a healthy relationship with lay leaders as a reason to leave a congregation or parish ministry altogether. Yet even the most self-differentiated women can't always determine whether a conflict in the parish is really about money, or resources, or personality, or buried sexism. When the criticism or conflict comes from their male senior pastor to women who are associates, the stress can be even stronger. One Presbyterian woman put it this way: "I was advised to [leave the parish] by the center on ministry psychologist — to get out before the senior pastor destroyed me. . . . I needed to find a senior pastor who was secure enough in his own ministry and identity not to be threatened by mine."[39] While only a few more women than men reported conflict with the senior pastor, difficulties reported by women involved feeling that the men were threatened by their presence on staff, differences in ministry style, overprotectiveness, and excessive criticism.[40] I would add to this differences in home-work boundaries, and often a resistance to the different models of ministry that arise when women are committed to honoring family life as well as parish responsibilities.

Blair spent five years in a third parish as associate, where she felt her gifts and talents were used despite some conflicts with the senior pastor. This was where she felt most comfortable as a pastor, and most proud of her accomplishments. This was also, however, where she had a miscarriage fairly late in her pregnancy. She had been scheduled to preach and lead worship because the senior pastor was on vacation. When she called him to tell him about the miscarriage, he saw no reason why she still couldn't preach two days later, or why she might have to miss any work. A part-time colleague saw her distress and led the service for her. At the time she felt devastated by his insensitivity, but in retrospect she wondered why she should have expected anything different. Eighty-hour weeks happened for all clergy on that staff more often than not — all clergy were expected to put parish needs first, and she kept that schedule even when pregnant.

Sexism, and resistance to women's ordained ministry, is another ongoing source of tension. A study of Presbyterian women clergy began with a case study of Elizabeth, a married forty-year-old woman with two small children. Her first call was as an associate in a medium-sized parish, with a long commute and a relatively low salary, but she liked what she saw of the congregation and felt the advantages would outweigh these problems. After a year and a half, however, Elizabeth was miserable. She was expected to take over the nursery when the children needed care, unlike her male colleagues. Male members of the staff made repeated sexual advances, and when she reported this to the presbytery, she was told to ignore them. Her salary was lower than her male associates. She and her husband decided that she should look for another full-time call that paid enough for him to work part-time for a while, so they could accommodate a demanding parish ministry schedule.

The study went on to find that "more than a third of all clergy women reported leaving a congregation because of difficulties within the position, including church politics, gender discrimination, schedule expectations, and low salary, etc."[41] Many women did not label their decision to leave "gender discrimination," but explanations of their decisions included frequent references to discrimination, "not ready for a woman," the session was not female-friendly, recommending women only for interim and supply positions, perceived competition with female parishioners or lay staff, lower salaries for women than for men in comparable positions, disrespect because of gender, or sexual harassment that was ignored by denominational authorities.[42] J. Elise Brown, a Lutheran pastor who responded to a review of women in ministry by *Pulpit and Pew,* believes that women clergy are experiencing a backlash resulting from "sexism gone underground." Most mainline denominations ordain women, and questioning women's general abilities or right to be ordained is taboo. Even the use of theological or biblical perspectives, still a mainstay of denominations that refuse women's ordination, are rarely used overtly in mainline denominations. Yet behavior, and even attitudes expressed in writing, contradict expressed beliefs, and unresolved, repressed emotions contribute to dysfunctional behavior. "Finding a way for the appropriate expression and working out of these emotions could be lifesaving for clergywomen and their congregations";[43] by extension, allowing them to fester can be death-dealing. Several studies reviewed by Edward Lehman found that often the number of people in a parish actively opposing women's ordination or leadership is fairly small, but those members tend to be very vocal, obscuring acceptance and good pastoral ministry by expressing opposition strenuously.[44]

Vashti McKenzie described several reasons why African-American lay women resist the idea of women in the pulpit that have nothing to do with theological or biblical perspectives. McKenzie listened to reasons given in a "Women Surviving in Ministry" seminar. One set of reasons has to do with the limits placed on African-American men in a racist culture. "The pulpit is historically one of the few places African-American men can exert strong, positive leadership," she wrote, and therefore women should let them have that place. Or the pulpit is one of the few places where women interact with men who are sensitive to their spiritual needs, willing to listen to women attentively and respond to them in a crisis, all of which are male behaviors that are valued and need to be modeled for the larger community. Or — and this is telling — in these denominations the moral rectitude of women's ordination is neither articulated or supported by authorizing bodies. "Perhaps there would be a different attitude if these bodies took the same care in introducing female leadership to congregations as they do in introducing a new denominational thrust, stewardship drive, or liturgy."[45]

Then McKenzie explains some of the pressures felt by African-American clergy women: "The constant pressure to explain and defend the call to gospel ministry; the pressure that your success or failure affects the women who follow you; and the realization that you must be better than, or just as good as, the best male for the position in order to be considered."[46]

The stories of the first women bishops in the United Methodist Church are replete with examples of the toll that sexism, skepticism about women's authority and ability to lead congregations, and even appeals to Scripture prohibiting women's leadership, take on women's career paths and their own sense of themselves. Equally consistent, however, was the conviction that God was inviting, empowering, insisting that they lead. Their experiences are too numerous to include, but a quotation by Charlene Kammerer, a bishop for the Western North Carolina Conference, of the United Methodist Church, sums it up well: "It is still true that women must lead the way in helping congregations or other settings of ministry experience a woman as a pastor. This takes enormous energy and a need to validate yourself with each new setting that our brothers simply do not encounter."[47] I would add that for clergy women with children it still also takes energy to trust that they are "good enough mothers" even when they are violating some cultural, and perhaps internal, expectations about what good mothers really do.

Self-differentiation

Another reason to understand vocation as including ordained ministry and family life, and self-care as parts of an integrated whole, is to care for the semipermeable boundaries between self and other that can both illumine and endanger relations with family and parishioners. The recent appreciation of systems theory, developed by Murray Bowen and made popular for clergy by Rabbi Edward Friedman, reveals the impossibility of separating selves into work, family of origin, and current family sections, and the dangers of not noticing when issues in one part of life influence the others in conscious and unconscious ways.

More than once I have come home angry from a premarital counseling session, where I've talked about the importance of maintaining "date nights" with one's spouse or partner, because my husband and I never seem to be able to keep a date with each other. The hypocrisy of preaching what I don't live, and want to live, rankles. Sharing mutual stories of the struggles and joys of parenting with parishioners can provide laughter and create appropriate bonding (sometimes to my daughter's chagrin, as can happen in any conversation between parents about children that is overheard by the children themselves). But what happens when the pastor visits a child in the hospital who is the same age as his child, and the parents' choices for treatment are radically different than those he would choose? A clergy friend called me, ranting about those parents, because the issues were too close to home for him to discuss with his wife. He wanted to think through what he was going to have to do to be an effective pastor to the family. I remember watching a terminally ill woman about my own age say last good-byes to her twenty-something children, trying not to cry until I reached the car, but only cry in the car because I was going home to my own teenager's slumber party.

Three women in their late seventies recently told me how disappointed they were in the way I handled a situation in the parish. I made a mistake that I rectified quickly, yet I was much more upset with myself than the situation warranted. Is it any coincidence that my own mother is also in her late seventies, and that she hasn't been universally pleased with every decision I've made? Jane was irrationally furious with her husband for a fairly trivial remark that played right into conflict in her parish; it took everything in her power not to start a full-scale battle with him at home.

Those are negative examples of the dangers of sharing oneself authentically, when unresolved issues in one area of life pop up in another area. Yet the power that comes from using the love God has given people to love and heal others is essential to ordained ministry. People from any walk of life — lawyers, accountants, welders, administrators, gardeners — can love their work, and love who they are becoming as a result of the work they do. People in the helping professions also generally use their capacity to love as a tool in their work. It's hard, and yet also a privilege, to officiate at the funeral of a long-time active parishioner, and I find love in preparing the liturgy. I also find love when I meet the family of a stranger in the funeral home as I help them say good-bye. Love is part of listening to people's experiences, showing up at the hospital, seeking desperately to reestablish a sense of order and respect in an unruly vestry meeting, cleaning up the kitchen after a parish event with the "usual crew" of folks who won't leave until the work is done.

Psychotherapists are trained in the uses of transference and countertransference so that they learn to use themselves as an instrument in the treatment of others while never forgetting the differences between self and client. They also rarely see clients in informal settings, while parishioners watch clergy and their families interact at work and expect some level of friendship and shared activities in parish life. Barbara Brown Taylor notes that "the real problem with transference with clergy without the skills to deal with it is that it feeds our sense that we are more powerful than we really are."[48] A small kindness accepted with excessive praise, or a small mistake vehemently protested, can distort appropriate self-evaluation. More often, clergy avail themselves of pastoral supervision, so that they too can learn how to use their own psychological issues and experiences most effectively. One man followed a dearly loved rector who had quietly misappropriated funds, and he knew enough about himself to insist when he negotiated his contract that either the parish or the diocese pay for monthly supervision for him. Clergy and parents who offer themselves appropriately are a gift to congregations and families, but most of us need some sort of structured opportunities for reflection to help the process of self-differentiation along.

Personal crises

There have been many studies of how conflict and crises in the parish affect clergy and their families. Talking with couples about their life together revealed how personal crises also affect life in the parish and clergy ministry. One family had to move across country because their son needed a special school. Roger found an exciting parish soon after they realized they had to move, but his wife, Roberta, was devastated. It was good to be closer to her son, who still needed special attention, but she was angry and miserable. She had just been awarded tenure at "the best teaching job on the planet." Their younger daughter was good at adapting to wherever she was, but Roberta and Roger both said that their forties were hell because of internal contradictions in their own lives and in the family. For five years Roberta was quietly miserable in a job that paid the bills but didn't bring her much joy. Then she began to be more proactive. Roger was struggling with weight issues. They both began therapy and support groups, which helped some over the next few years. Roberta found a teaching job she enjoyed, and began extra education to become a master teacher. Their daughter graduated from high school and began a prestigious college. Their son, also in college, became too dependent on drugs and alcohol, so an intervention with him led to Al-Anon for everyone. Then their daughter was diagnosed with a rare but very dangerous chronic medical condition, and underwent a few years of diagnosis, surgery, and illness before her condition stabilized. As Roger said, he was doing relatively effective pastoral work, in part because of God's grace and in part because attending to parish work was a comfortable diversion from so many crises at home. While not many people were as honest as this couple was about their struggles, it is clear that alcohol, depression, children with special needs, and other struggles of human life are part of clergy life as well, influencing parenting and ministry in conscious and unconscious ways.

And then September 11, 2001, happened, and out of the bowels of a national crisis came some resolution of internal ones. Roger found real meaning and purpose in intense trauma work at Ground Zero. His experiences led to a trip to Hebron to witness struggles of Palestinians, over Roberta's strenuous objections. Roger heard her objections but felt inwardly compelled, and went anyway. When he came back from Hebron, he said that finding courage in the midst of struggles for life helped him find the inner courage to face his own weight issues head-on, with surgery and intense therapy. In his experience: "The image in the mirror didn't match the image in [his] head and heart, and that image needed to change." Roberta was a support, but also a bystander, since Roger had to decide to make and stick with changes. Roberta found herself slowly able to let go of trying to control the lives of everyone close to her and do her own inner work. They both turned fifty, and life started really looking up. All the internal work they both had done bore fruit in much greater health for both, and for the relationship. Both children are now stable, happy, and living independently, which is both bittersweet and happy. Roger is almost through with CPE supervision training, and in two years can retire, perhaps to full-time counseling, perhaps to nonparish church ministry. Roberta is a master teacher and has time to train other teachers; she loves the professional respect she has gained. Roger is much less concerned with the "trappings of institutional church," and much more attuned to God's presence in oppression and suffering, in pastoral needs of parish, and in clinical settings. He finds he has more energy than ever.

Midlife change for spouses out of involvement in the parish

Pam, a clergy wife, was fortunate to be able to stay home with her four children when they were young. At their first parish, she attended parish events, threw parties, and taught confirmation classes; in the next call she felt more like a leader in the suburban parish. When her youngest child started high school, she started a master's program in marriage and family counseling, because she had found that she was doing lots of informal counseling and pastoral care in the parish. Les picked up some more household and chauffeuring responsibilities for their adolescent children. This was a difficult change for Pam, who found herself being moved out of roles that no longer fit, out of circumstance and her own choice. She had to give up entertaining large groups of parishioners, and she had enjoyed that role. Les retired, however, and began to serve as a nonstipendiary associate at an urban parish where he is on the vestry, preaches occasionally, and leads workshops on marriage and family health. The roles are reversing, and again their marriage needs renegotiating. However, retirement gives them time to visit children and grandchildren living in various corners of the country.

My children are so young, and my years in the pension fund so few, that retirement looks like its never going to happen. Yet I admire the energy and wisdom of female colleagues who used retirement from secular jobs to begin parish ministry as deacons or priests. I envy a survey response by a man who went to seminary right out of college, got married, had children, "took a break between positions" because he was imprisoned in Vietnam for over three years, came home and served two more parishes for over twenty-five years, retired, but continues to serve as a nonstipendiary priest. He says in conclusion: "We just celebrated our fiftieth [wedding anniversary] and both my wife and I have been very much involved in child-care and church work. Maybe it has not been a very exciting life, but we think it was, and we would re-run the same path at any time." I see retired colleagues continuing to grow and learn in their profession, visiting grandchildren, worrying about aging parents or adult children's decisions, and facing growing numbers of doctors' appointments with humor and grace. Usually the choices people have made throughout their lives shape their retirement and the way they face aging and death. My goal is not only to live long enough to retire but to make choices along the way that will bring more satisfaction than regret in parenting, ministry, marriage, and life.

When I think about my own experiences, stories people have shared about how to juggle family and parish and personal crises, and the qualities of clergy I respect, it seems that a sense of God's invitation and grace, a sense of humor, and the ability to forgive self and others when sin happens make this crazy life possible. Books about clergy self-care emphasize the need for regular prayer. So do many faith-based parenting books. There are wonderful stories of parents trying to meditate with toddlers crawling into their lap, of a "wave offering" to God as they collapse into bed or wake up late and start the morning routine, of finding new disciplines of prayer and refreshment with each new stage of child development and each new phase of parish life. One woman remembers a clergy conference when the bishop strongly urged all clergy to spend at least forty minutes in prayer and reading the Daily Office; her first thought was that "he doesn't have a four-year-old who always wakes up ten minutes after I do no matter how early I rise or how quiet I am." Yet she found her way into prayer that made sense for her.

Humor is essential. Even serious crises have some humor in them, usually discovered in retrospect. Most of my conversations for this book were punctuated with laughter at children's antics, at parishioners' expectations, or at our own belief that "all things were possible" until we discovered that they were not. (Yes, you can nurse a baby and type at the same time, but is this good?)

And then there's forgiveness. I have worked with battered women and sexual abuse survivors enough to know that forgiveness is often bandied about too easily. Forgiveness for sustained damage requires accountability and repentance, does not mean returning to or remaining in a toxic situation, and is a gift from God often found by grace rather than will. But there is a level of forgiveness for the ordinary faults and failings of daily life that can help ease the juggling. No pastor and no parent is perfect, and freedom to admit mistakes, to name unhealthy patterns to appropriate people and take overt steps to change them slowly, to say sorry and to keep trying, to accept apologies and support life-giving change can ease life at home and in the parish. Usually that freedom comes from God, through others, and into the healing of relationships. Maybe the church should distribute "grace cards" that can be played to help people in the midst of conflict step outside the box and look with God for a new way out. Then there's letting go of false guilt. Sorting through the many expectations from self, family, parishioners, the culture at large, and God is a lifetime task. Some days I can actually trust that not all evil in the world is my fault (though I did break a mirror one presidential election day and my candidate lost narrowly). But too often clergy and parents both feel guilty for things that are not their responsibility and spend time lamenting things they cannot change.

Chapter Five

Unchosen Dimensions of Vocation

It was Maundy Thursday. "Before children," Maundy Thursday had been the time when I threw myself into the drama of Holy Week. I came into the Episcopal Church in a community that took Holy Week very seriously, with fasting, all-night vigils, and all possible liturgies. I would often stay at church all night, meditating in silence and, usually, in solitude on the meaning of Jesus' passion for me. It was one way I lived out my vocation as a Christian in the world.

I found that my first child was due during Holy Week while I was serving in a very "high church" parish — laity and clergy seemed to compete to see how many Holy Week services we could offer. The inability to count on my participation in Holy Week services should have been a clue that with children, things would be different. I waddled through liturgies, refused the youth group's invitation to give birth during the Good Friday liturgy and baptize the baby at the Vigil, and delivered Avery on Easter Monday. During the next few years, I needed extra child-care during the Holy Week rush if I were to catch a few hours of prayer for myself. Fast-forward ten years, when we were living in a rectory next to a church. The Maundy Thursday service was over, I was uncentered and wanted nothing more than to stay by myself and enter into the drama of the Passion. That's what "serious priests" do.

But I went home, to catch up with my husband and sleep — I'd have the next morning to finish the Good Friday sermon. I found my older daughter patiently throwing up into a bowl by herself while Mike was changing the younger one, who'd also been sick. We spent the night sitting with first one child and then the other and washing sheets and pajamas again and again and again. Around three in the morning, I realized that this was our vigil at the garden of Gethsemane. Mike and I learned something about trying to remain loving when it's smelly and inconvenient and exhausting to do so, a working definition of "God's will, not mine." The beautifully decorated sanctuary, with no distractions, would have been an unholy (but not entirely unwelcome!) escape from my vocation as parent and priest.

Much literature on parenting talks about the way having a child "de-centers" parents, shifts their focus from their own needs to the needs of a dependent other. Marriage can be described in terms of learning to set aside some of each partner's own needs and desires to make room for the needs and desires of the other and the couple. Shifting attention from the self to God is a powerful theme in Christian spirituality. After all, Jesus said, "If anyone is to be my disciple, they must deny themselves, pick up their cross, and follow me. Those who save their life will lose it, but those who lose their life for my sake will find it."[1] This injunction is repeated in all four gospels, and is central to understandings of vocation. The idea of self-denial, of losing life either literally or the life one has planned, or expected, for the sake of greater growth is a Christian ideal.

It has also been misinterpreted. Barbara Brown Taylor eloquently describes a view of Jesus' life that is implicit in many theologies of priestly vocation. She was looking to Christ for a model of how to be a faithful parish priest when she was discouraged and fantasizing about beach cottages and all night cafés where she would not be recognized.

> When I looked at his life I did not see any beach cottages or all-night cafés. Instead I saw someone who was always feeding people, healing people, teaching people, helping people. When he tried to withdraw from these people, they followed him. When they tried to eat him up, he did not resist. "Take, eat, this is my body, given for you," he said, holding out a loaf of challah to them. . . . He fed his spiritual offspring from his own flesh and blood until all of his reserves were gone. Then he died, and though he rose from the dead three days later, this was quite an act to follow.[2]

When Jesus gave up his life, he did so for the sake of resurrection, to show people that God could bring good out of the worst of what humans can do, and that God's love is stronger even than death. When the desert fathers and mothers fled society and withdrew into the desert, they gave up property, sex, some food, and other things of value in order to experience God in a life-giving way. They *chose* to renounce "the world" for the sake of a deeper joy in Christ. When people choose careers in ministry or helping professions, they often sacrifice the possibility of financial success for the meaning and value they find in certain jobs. Spouses may choose to leave a home they love to be near the job of the spouse's dreams, trusting that they too will find joy and meaning in new opportunities and in the deepening of their intimate relationship as their partner blossoms. Parents find themselves changing priorities when children arrive, giving up anything from a motorcycle to unrestricted schedules to sleep. Adult children find a similar shift if their parents become chronically ill and in need of ever greater care. Self-denial is part of Christian tradition and of everyday life, and can bring great good even in the midst of suffering and deprivation.

Self-denial has also been misused and misunderstood. Liberation theologians have noticed that self-denial is often preached by the dominant group (e.g., men, white people, rich people) to groups over whom they have power, as a way of reinforcing social control.[3] "Good" wives, or slaves, or workers, are those who put the interests of their superiors first and set their own interests aside "for the greater good," while their superiors do not expect to make similar sacrifices. Ascetic disciplines are also taken out of context in ways that encourage unhealthy self-denial: Mainline Protestant clergy, especially Episcopalians and Lutherans with a "higher" view of ordination, are often haunted by implicit expectations of "poverty, chastity, obedience," though in fact these are monastic vows chosen by some clergy and lay people as part of a commitment to community life. Feminist psychologists bemoan the tendency of many women to deny themselves so completely that they forget they even have a self, and to define their lives in response to others' needs and desires.[4] It's not uncommon for male and female clergy to pour time, energy, and resources into a struggling congregation at their own expense or that of their family, telling themselves (or being told by others) that this sacrifice is necessary to do God's work well. These kinds of self-denial, especially when imposed on some for the well-being of others, are dangerous and unholy for clergy and their families.

The sacrifices that come from institutional racism or other forms of prejudice are also dangerous and unholy. Racism, sexism, homophobia, and other forms of discrimination all try to deny the intrinsic humanity of certain groups of people. When such biases are built into law, education, housing, medical care, churches, and other social institutions, some people's lives and opportunities are sacrificed; but more insidiously, people internalize the oppression and spend energy questioning their own value and potential. In *Not Without a Struggle*, Vashti McKenzie summarized interviews and surveys of one hundred African-American women pastors, primarily Methodist and Baptist pastors in the northeast United States. "One full-time pastor of a rural church stated, 'I'm tired of all the people who keep saying no to my femaleness, my Blackness, and my ministry. Sometimes I feel as if the whole world is against me!' "[5] Women with similar experiences found support in prayer, in colleague groups, and in groups of "girlfriends," so they could "keep on keeping on" despite the costs of rejection, insults, and extraordinary difficulties.[6] Denominations that make gay and lesbian clergy choose between ordination and either intimate relationships or honesty about their sexuality and relationships exact a toll on the institution, which often loses gifted clergy, and on the pastors who give up part of themselves to remain in ministry they love.[7]

And then there are what Karl Jaspers calls the "boundary situations" of life that no one chooses, although humans have some measure of control over how to respond. "Situations like the following: that I am always in situations; that I cannot live without struggling and suffering; that I cannot avoid guilt; that I must die — these are what I call boundary situations."[8] Jaspers argues that the way people respond to these situations shapes their character and defines their humanity. Carol Ochs argues that often Christian tradition proposes a solitary journey of rejecting this world, with its limits and unpredictability, in order to achieve an otherworldly salvation. Instead she offers the image of a walk with others, delighting in the God known in daily struggles and joys of this world.[9] Her notion of vocation rooted in women's experiences of mothering sets self-denial in a larger context of love.

How does understanding self-denial as something affecting a family or congregation, as well as an individual, help protect against abuse of self or others? How can awareness of the multiple dimensions of human life, commitments to work and self and God and others, help discern which sacrifices are truly life-giving? How can analyses of the power dynamics shaping occasions for self-denial help flag potential abuses of self and others? How can God transform experiences of suffering and struggle into a source of love and life? These questions will reveal the broader context within which vocation and self-denial should be understood.

Corporate rather than individual understanding of vocation and self-denial

The local clergy group wanted to get together to say good-bye to a rabbi who was moving. When talking about schedules, one of the pastors asked that we meet at 6:30 because, he laughed, "That way the dinner takes away time from family, not church." Ouch — I imagine his family misses him. Yet the family's sacrifice would be expected in a schema of meaning where the husband's career is seen as the holier vocation, for him and for the family. Forty years ago, most clergy spouses were women who took care of their home and children, while the clergy man earned the money and determined the family's social standing. The family's job was to support his vocation as would any family of a working man, whether that meant frequent moves or an absent father on evenings and weekends or other contingencies. When the husband is doing God's work, and the congregation's needs are urgent if not always important, expectations of the family to support his work unquestioningly were even greater than with secular jobs. No one asked men to take their vocations as husbands and fathers as seriously as their professional vocation except in the role of economic provider. Often the sacrifices they expected their wives and families to make were unnoticed or unappreciated, except in occasional speeches where their spouses' sacrifices were applauded and seen as an intrinsic part of women's roles.

Joanna Trollope illustrates the many levels of sacrifice expected of clergy wives in England in the 1980s in her novel *The Rector's Wife*.[10] Anna Bouverie never liked the role of rector's wife into which she was thrust, but she did what her husband and the parish expected, until the pain of deferring her own dreams, watching the consequences of limited income on her children, and seeing her husband become more and more absorbed in the life of the church became too much. When she takes a job, she faces ridicule and scorn at home and in the parish. When she dares to take her own professional and personal aspirations as seriously as those of her husband and family, the dysfunctional system implodes to reveal life and death. Her goal was to create a family where the vocations of all the members were named and supported. When vocation and self-denial are understood individualistically, it is easier for people to abuse themselves or sacrifice people around them and for those around them to come to expect such sacrifice.

Too many clergy boast of their busyness, their long hours, the vacations or days off that they have never taken, in service of the church. A middle-aged African-American pastor went into the hospital to be treated for heart disease, only to die of a heart attack while awaiting surgery. He was well-loved by his parishioners in part because of his devotion to the parish and his willingness to give himself wholly to the work. Some people would urge him to slow down, or take it easy, but there was always something important to do. At his funeral, however, his wife lamented the ways she felt the parish had robbed her of her husband's attention, energy, and ultimately his life.

Fuller Theological Seminary conducted a survey of clergy men in the late 1980s that found that 90 percent of pastors work more than 46 hours per week, and 80 percent believe that pastoral ministry negatively affects their families.[11] In Matthew Price's analysis a decade later, including male and female Episcopal clergy, 20 percent of clergy reported "that their spouses regularly complain about the amount of time they spend working." Thirty percent of clergy women with children felt that ministry did not allow them to spend enough time with their children, and 20 percent of rectors with children in the home regularly consider leaving parish ministry for ministry in another setting.[12]

Now, when clergy can be male or female, when many clergy spouses have their own careers, and when time with children becomes increasingly scarce and increasingly scheduled, it may be useful to uphold care for the family as a central Christian value for clergy. Most denominations are trying to change the culture of clergy self-sacrifice by preaching wellness and self-care. A "corporate" understanding of vocation includes attention to the quality of intimate relationships as well as the opportunities for professional meaning and advancement for each member of the family. It could also challenge unhealthy self-sacrifice either by clergy or by clergy family members. Family members still will need to deny themselves for the sake of others in the family, but with some intentionality, accountability, fair distribution of sacrifice, and recognition of the gains and losses involved in vocational decisions, these decisions may be more life-giving for all involved.

Clergy women I interviewed often model a more corporate understanding of vocation. Many women talked of needing a new job, but needing to wait until their spouse or partner could also find a life-giving job. Madison's husband is in a very specialized field, with very few opportunities. When her job ended (shortly after the birth of her fourth child), she and her husband talked incessantly about which of them would need to set professional dreams aside, since the possibility of finding positions for both of them geographically close enough to each other to allow them time to care for children too seemed remote. Yet, she said, "after four children and fifteen years of marriage, I have discovered that God is a better organizer than we are." Within six months (a scary, "can we really trust God for another day?" six months) they found two positions that fed both of them professionally and met their family needs. She felt that it was their unwillingness to settle for options that were good for one but not the other, even when the money looked more and more essential, that gave the Holy Spirit space to move.

Understanding self-denial in multiple dimensions

When vocation includes multiple dimensions, the decision-making context widens to reveal how a sacrifice in one aspect in fact brings greater life overall. The insight I gained as a parent, caring for sick children on Maundy Thursday, was life-giving for my life as a parent, a wife, and a priest. As a parent, a sense of connection with Jesus in Gethsemane, however different in degree, helped me find meaning in exhaustion. As a spouse, I found and gave support that Jesus didn't have, and that support enabled both of us to keep caring for our children through the wee hours of the night. As a priest, my experience helped me interpret Scripture and theology in a concrete and practical way that may help parishioners find God in everyday life. In this instance, two aspects of vocation complement each other. When vocation is identified primarily with one aspect of life — a career or parenting or volunteer service — the understanding obscures the richness of life.

Jack had been a parish priest for many years when he was elected bishop of Newark. He could articulate clearly why he felt called to be bishop and the vision he had for ministry and congregational health. After three or four years, when it seemed he was becoming increasingly comfortable dealing with a role full of conflict, challenge, and grace, his wife was diagnosed with a serious medical condition. As he said publicly when announcing his decision to retire earlier than he had planned, "When my wife asked me to spend some quality time together before she became too ill, it was time to retire." Whatever misgivings he had about letting go of a fruitful professional role, he was clear that marriage vows were as important to him as ordination vows, and that honoring one meant living into the other differently than he had expected or probably desired. God, and a fulfillment of Jack's vocation, can surely be found in either path.

A study of pastors from five denominations (Assemblies of God, Evangelical Lutheran Church in America, Lutheran Church–Missouri Synod, Presbyterian Church USA, and the United Methodist Church) who left local church ministry found an interesting phenomenon. Four percent of the pastors they studied left parish ministry to care for children or family. Twenty-eight of these forty-one pastors were female, and 49 percent of the pastors were associate pastors. There were a disproportionate number of Presbyterians in this group. In general, these pastors were much happier in their ministry than pastors who left for other reasons, according to several measures. These pastors reported more dissatisfaction with their family life, however, and said more frequently than other pastors that ministry interfered with the time they were able to devote to their children. Several male Assemblies of God pastors complained that "ministry was a day-and-night obligation that paid too little and took too much of a toll on spouses and children." One Presbyterian woman said, "My call is to be a good wife and mother and person in my community giving back, as opposed to serving a particular parish and a particular group of people. The feeling that I have to be a minister or there's nothing else for me, that this is what God wants me to do, is definitely not the same as it was when I started seminary [as a single woman]."[13] In and of itself, work in the parish was satisfying. But when considered in context of their whole lives, they chose other work that allowed them to care for children or ailing parents more faithfully.

Power, self-denial, and vocation

Self-denial implies that someone chooses to let go of something of value, often in response to circumstances beyond their control. Sacrifice may be a more appropriate word for situations where other people or institutional rules force someone to give up something truly essential to their well-being. Sexism, racism, ageism, and declining churches limit opportunities and make it difficult, if not impossible, for all people to use their gifts. One Indian pastor serving a largely white suburban congregation talked of a different kind of sacrifice imposed on his family. While this was an immensely satisfying and financially adequate parish for him, his children were often the only children of color in their schools, they were teased for eating ethnic food, and there was no support network of other peers or families to help mitigate the effects of both overt and subtle prejudice.

The raging conflicts in all mainline denominations over whether gay men and lesbians can be ordained, can live in committed relationships, or can be open about their sexual orientation is another festering wound. The refusal of many denominations to allow gay and lesbian clergy to live in committed same-sex relationships hurts both the people involved and the church as an institution. In the Hoge and Wenger study, twenty-seven gay men and lesbians had left their pastorates unwillingly, either because they had been forced out by their denominations or because they no longer felt safe to be honest about their sexual orientation.[14] Several pastors commented that their parishes generally respected them as effective, more or less open, gay and lesbian pastors; that trouble arose when a parishioner angry about something else made an issue of their sexuality with denominational superiors. These pastors felt angry, betrayed, unappreciated, and that the institution was confusing authentic Christianity with the institutionalized church. Those who stay in the institution quietly pay a different cost because they cannot share all of who they are with the people they love, and either give up intimate relationships or live in dangerous secrecy. Even in the Episcopal Church, where some dioceses support openly gay and lesbian clergy and their families, the controversy swirling around them takes its toll.

Denominations may be just beginning to recognize another important cause of sacrifice. Loren Mead, writing in 1998, observed that most denominations (and past experience) lead church members to expect a professionally trained clergy person to lead each parish. "We continue to foster an image of church that the overwhelming number of congregations do not and cannot pay for. We are unwilling to name the truth that more than 50 percent of our congregations are below subsistence level."[15] Lois, an Episcopal priest, lamented, "I moved to a parish where, after struggling valiantly for two years, the parish, diocese and I decided the parish had to close. I had poured my heart into the parish and found my priestly vocation confirmed at every turn. But the reality is, there are two other stronger Episcopal congregations in the same town, and it became a question of how to use limited resources most faithfully." Walking with a parish through that decision involves listening to their often-wrenching emotions and practical decisions, while simultaneously wondering where the clergy will move next and whether timing will be right for a new call.

Lois said, "My husband, retired on medical disability, wasn't moving again after only three years. There were several full-time parishes open in the same diocese, but as a sixty-something woman, with only seven years of parish experience, I didn't even get any interviews. I'm working in social services to pay the bills, but I'm miserable — why did God make me such a good parish priest if I can't find a place to use my gifts?" A Methodist pastor in a similar circumstance resented the fact that her parish had consistently offered creative ways to combine ministry with two other nearby Methodist churches, only to be rebuffed out of fear of diminishing resources and too much change. My impression, and that of the Methodist clergy woman, is that white women and male and female clergy of color are more likely to be in charge of parishes most at risk of closing, but we haven't yet found official statistics to verify or refute it.

The institutional context creates some unhealthy options. A clergy wife lamented the fact that "the bishop required my husband to live on campus in seminary, so we sold our first home. We've been in rectories ever since; we've never been able to buy our own house [again]." A male pastor said that "we wanted my wife to work part-time, so she could be home with the children, but now we can't afford my child's first choice college." A Methodist woman with a special-needs child would prefer to work part-time to care for her child, but her family is dependent on health benefits only available to full-time clergy. Main-line denominations have been trying to raise clergy salaries to rectify some of the financial burdens caused by these sacrifices. A 2003 *Pulpit and Pew* study found that median total compensation, regardless of denomination, has risen more than inflation over the past twenty-five years.[16] Their analysis of clergy salaries summarizes some of their findings: "Regardless of polity, only a small percentage of pastors earn what most Americans would consider a professional level salary."[17]

Sometimes the most serious sacrifices come when either a pastor or a parish becomes so dysfunctional that a climate of denial, secrecy, and distorting the truth for the sake of maintaining an unhealthy status quo reigns. The literature on clergy sexual or financial abuse is growing, and all denominations are moving toward recognition and prevention. A new priest was serving as an associate in a medium-sized parish. In her second year, she became pregnant and the senior pastor took an unplanned leave of absence, during which time she was effectively the priest-in-charge of the parish. Her baby was born, she took some maternity leave, and returned to find the pastor had resigned because of some sort of misconduct. Her plans to set and maintain clear boundaries about work and family responsibilities went up in smoke. Eventually an interim came and she could resign and go on about her life. Part of faith is putting trust in fallible humans, and allowing for the real possibility of sin and betrayal, as Jesus knew. Self-denial of one's own legitimate needs has often led to clergy burn-out or to boundary violations that hurt everyone. Yet congregations and denominations are just beginning to recognize how devastating the loss of trust can be in practical, emotional, and spiritual ways. Clergy and lay leaders alike are thrust into maelstroms of grief, anger, and craziness that require their best selves no matter what else is going on in their lives, in self-denial no one would choose.

And yet, a willingness to move through conflict with a congregation, with the risk and pain involved, can be a God-given gift. Many clergy now are trained as "after-pastors," coming into a congregation after the previous leader has been removed for boundary violations of one sort or another. This kind of position requires a certain kind of sacrifice, because good after-pastors will help name unpleasant truths, perhaps change some long-standing procedures, and rebuild trust among people who have been violated and are often wary of authority. Conflict and anger at the new leader are inherent in the situation.

Anne was called by a parish and diocesan staff to help a parish heal after several waves of conflict and abuse of various kinds. She felt that her role was to be the lightning rod, and surface some of the destructive dynamics that had plagued the parish for two or three past pastors. I was speaking with her toward the end of a particularly difficult discovery of yet one more incident of abuse, when most of the lay leaders begged her to "let this one go." Yet because she found grace to endure the insults and actions intended to keep her quiet, the parish had slowly been able to move to a much healthier place that parish and pastor could celebrate. Anne felt in retrospect that she had gained strength and new confidence, but the pain was real and unforgettable. "The truth may set you free, but it makes you miserable first" was the parish's motto in those months. What enabled her to remain firm in the face of resistance was the sense, from prayer and her own therapy, that she was walking with Jesus toward Jerusalem, willingly enduring pain because it would bring new life to almost everyone involved. She talked about it in terms of the vocation of ordained ministry. "Clergy offer themselves in that they model for and with the congregation Jesus' offering of self for the life of the world," she said. "But Jesus was strategic in his self-offering; simply pouring yourself out without knowing how it will bring life is suicide." It is chosen, intentional sacrifice for the sake of ministry that is intrinsic to Christian life.

Facing human limits

"I have to say, you really do do funerals well. I don't understand how you can deal with all that grief." This was a comment from a parishioner after the third funeral of key parishioners in as many months. Clergy are asked to walk with people through the most painful parts of human life — death, crisis, divorce, recovering memories of abuse or exposing current violence, addictions, and chronic illnesses. Sometimes this is not as much a sacrifice as it seems; personality, training, and institutional support all make it easier for me to walk with people through hard times than to create a chart of accounts or solve an engineering problem. Part of parish ministry is opening your heart to people who can suffer, insult, or betray you, yet the willingness to love authentically even when that love will not always be appreciated or returned is central to effective pastoral work. Every vocation, whether in a professional arena, a family, or community service, has its "hard places," where risky self-giving is required and there's no guarantee of a good outcome. Psychological development often requires choosing the hard path for the sake of growth in love. Clergy, families, couples, and congregations some-times choose to do the painful and yet ultimately liberating therapeutic work of changing destructive habits. When I served on committees whose purpose was to discern a vocation to ordained ministry, I would often ask aspiring clergy how they thought ordination would help heal something in them that God couldn't heal any other way. One of my children made me face aspects of claiming author-ity that I had successfully avoided in every other aspect of my life. The idea that God puts us in certain situations, or gives us children with certain personalities, so that we can learn things about ourselves that we couldn't learn any other way and that ultimately benefit self and others helps me keep doing work that is otherwise terrifying.

The basics of self-care for clergy — prayer, supervision, spiritual direction, friends outside of the parish, exercise and attention to physical well-being — are essential for the clergy in their work with the congregation and their family life. There will probably always be some spill-over between emotions at work and home — clergy coming home grumpy after a vestry meeting, clergy children acting out before the vestry meeting because they want you to put them to bed or help with homework, tears at a funeral about clergy's own losses as well as the loss of the deceased, and so on. Clergy will also deal with their children's bad day at school, their spouse's hurt from their work day, the fight at dinner just before the vestry meeting — our ability to give and receive support, to yell and then ask for forgiveness, is part of family life. But in a profession where emotions and love are as central as skills to being an effective pastor, clergy have to be intentional about how they express and process emotions if they are to remain true to God and respectful of those with whom they live.

The situation faced by Blair, a young United Methodist pastor with a special-needs child, has been described elsewhere in this book. She was matched with a rural parish whose beloved pastor had left. Just as she and the parish seemed to be adjusting to each other, she became pregnant again, and again the pregnancy was considered high-risk. One man on the leadership committee called the district superintendent and repeatedly told people in the parish that "there's no way Blair could be a full-time pastor when she needs to be a full-time mom." Blair, her previous congregation, and her bishop know that she has been an effective full-time pastor. She pointed out that if the parishioner had said these things about her in a corporate setting about an employee he would have been fired, but that in a church setting no one challenges his assertion. Her fear is that the congregation has already decided they don't want her — they're afraid of the changes they will have to make to accept her ministry gifts, limits, and family situation. There are unchosen sacrifices all around — her health, her son's special needs, the congregation's loss of a well-loved pastor who preceded her, enforced bed rest when her family and her parish need her, the congregation's desire to have a clergy person without child-care responsibilities. There are gifts, some already known and some yet to be discovered, all around as well. God will provide grace to bring life and joy to Blair and the congregation if they can be open enough to accept it. That remains to be seen.

"Love God and neighbor" as a complement to "deny yourself"

So how do we discern when self-denial and sacrifice are in the service of resurrection life and when they are death-dealing, to self and others? Look at Jesus. Look first at the context of the passage about self-denial. In Matthew, Jesus is sending the twelve disciples out in pairs to heal and preach the nearness of the kingdom of God. First, he urges them to travel light, bringing no food, money, or supplies. He warns the disciples of the conflict and rejection they will encounter: "Do not think that I have come to bring peace to the earth; I have not come to bring peace, but a sword."[18] Family members will be set against each other, and "whoever loves father or mother more than me is not worthy of me; and whoever loves son or daughter more than me is not worthy of me; and whoever does not take up the cross and follow me is not worthy of me."[19] Disciples are asked to give up everything and follow. The key is, why? By letting go of some things we *think* are essential, we will find the presence of God, or God's kingdom, and discover what is *truly* essential.

Luke sets the injunction about self-denial in another context that is also illuminating. Jesus tells the story of a king who invited people to a sumptuous banquet, but the invited guests all had excuses or important reasons why they would have to miss the feast — investments, work, marriage. When these commitments come first, we miss the banquet. When God comes first, we find the reign of God in our work, and family life, and investments. We feast at the banquet. Self-denial is for the sake of finding life, God's life. Jesus is not inventing some esoteric ascetic practice. Jesus is saying, "Watch out! There will be many distractions that will pull you from the love of God right in the midst of everyday life, and if you're not clear about your commitment to God, you will get lost." Let go of that which keeps you from loving God, self, or neighbor in the ongoing dance of discernment. The gospel of John expresses this even more clearly when, in the farewell discourse, Jesus tells the disciples that they are no longer servants but friends, friends who can choose to lay down their life for the sake of another out of love.[20]

We don't need to seek out opportunities for self-denial — they are everywhere. I need to make a hospital visit, my daughter wants to go shopping, my other daughter must be picked up at 4:45 sharp, and I have a book to finish. If I did what I most wanted to do, my day would look one way; when I take a few minutes to pray and remember priorities, the day looks different. I can find the courage to say no when I need to, be present when I need to, and accept that my parenting and pastoring are "good enough," if not up to the expectations of perfection I impose on myself. A Lutheran pastor with three children, married to a pastor, said that she and her husband live by the motto, "You can't do it all ... and you don't have to" because there is no way they can do all that is asked or expected of them every day.

What is true on a daily basis is also true for a lifetime, a life shaped by commitments to find God in church work and family life and even an occasional walk on the beach alone. Jesus was clear that self-denial will be part of faithfulness, but he identified the "greatest commandment" in terms of love: Love one another. Love the Lord your God with all your heart, and strength, and mind, and your neighbor as yourself. Carol Ochs observes that mother love is a useful source to understand love of God, God's love for us, and our love for each other. Given the way mothers have assumed primary responsibility for raising children, and the way human experiences of child-rearing have been largely ignored in Christian tradition, watching how mothers love offers us an understanding of love free from expectations of romance and courtship, and replete with examples of self-giving in the service of life.[21] Given women's fairly recent experiences in ordained ministry, insights from how they love parish work and family may help expand understandings of self-denial and love.

Chapter Six

A Wider Vision of Vocation

Clergy mothers have valuable gifts to offer their parishes, the wider church, and their families. They have been creative and resourceful at making a way through an institution designed for male clergy without daily child-care responsibilities, worshipping a God depicted primarily as male, in a world that finds church increasingly irrelevant and still isn't sure where women really belong. Attending to their lives reveals changes in church practices and social structures that could make it more possible for clergy, family members of clergy, and the church as a whole to live more sanely.

Every year, clergy in the Episcopal Diocese of Newark are strongly urged to attend clergy conference at a Poconos resort from Sunday or Monday afternoon through Tuesday or Wednesday lunch. There is usually a speaker and a theme, chances to eat and worship together, a full afternoon to socialize, shop, hike, play softball, and time generally to relax in the company of other clergy. Spouses and partners are not invited, and on-site child-care must be arranged *ad hoc* at outrageous expense. In a plenary session there are more men than women, many more white folks than people of color, many many more people over fifty than under thirty-five, and three or four children under age four in infant seats or playing quietly. I take notes or journal about the topic of the day. Later I seek out other women with children, catching up on the year; I play a little bit of "mine's bigger" with some colleagues who insist that their ministries are always flourishing and who never have any doubts about anything; I connect more with women and men whom I know are struggling with issues in the parish or home, my lectionary study group (that during the year is often slighted for other activities) goes shopping together, I play softball and laugh and have a glass of wine.

But I haven't been able to stay both nights since my oldest child was two, because my husband cannot cover child-care for three days. His annual professional meeting always happens around the same time, so usually he is out of town during clergy conference. Neither have some of the other clergy women, and one male colleague — their spouses must leave the house by 6:00 a.m. and work in the city until 7:00 p.m. Regina, a single mom, can take her older son to her sister's, but she finds a free afternoon, hours away from her son when afternoons are usually their time together, to be a huge sacrifice. Many of the clergy women have worked overtime to arrange carpools, make sure spouses know children's schedules, and put food in the refrigerator before they leave. I've never asked the men what kind of arrangements they had to make for children or home. Last year I sat at the registration table trying to gather information about which clergy have children at home, because there are no diocesan records of this, while knowing that without any maintenance the list will be out of date soon. Family is still seen as an intrusion into clergy renewal time, and clergy conference is still experienced as in intrusion into family life.

Maybe that is the way life is when two commitments, or three, or more, shape choices of how to nurture relationships and spend resources. God invites people into family and church life. The church ostensibly values parish ministry, marriage, and family life. (I yearn for a day when the institutional church can recognize and value same-sex committed relationships, as well.) Some conflicts, pushes, and pulls are inevitable; so are some joys, as commitments enhance each other. This chapter looks at what clergy, parents, denominational officials, Christians, and the wider culture can do to enable all people to live into God's invitations more fully.

Why should the church care about the well-being of clergy families?

There are practical reasons why the church should care, seen throughout this book: preventing burn-out, enabling gifts to be used fully in the church and the family, remembering that family life is as important to God as the life of the parish. The theological reasons may be more important, however. First, the church is of God. Scripture and tradition show how God values family relationships and the well-being of all people, not just those in the workplace. The idea that people are only valuable insofar as they are productive workers comes from the market, not from God.

Second, the church as an institution explicitly claims responsibility for baptism, marriage, parenting, ordination, illness, and death — for the work of helping people live faithful lives in all dimensions of their experience. It addresses the needs of families; in fact, one measure of church size is the number of families, not individuals, who participate and pledge. Clergy are expected to be models of holistic, faithful life. (The Episcopal Church's ordination service explicitly asks this of priests and bishops.) As one clergy mother said, "Pastor moms have an opportunity to model ways of parenting that are healthier...we have a duty not to try to be superwoman, but to be honest and open about what a struggle it is to combine these roles well....Corporate America...has had no mandate to put families first, whereas the church should have a harder time justifying a failure to do so."[1] One measure of integrity is the congruence between word and action, so when clergy preach care for the family and then work too many hours to care for their own families, everyone suffers.

Third, the church is called to model life in the kingdom, or commonwealth, of God, not accept unquestioningly whatever prevailing social order exists in a culture. The civil rights movement came out of African-American congregations and values, and was later supported by predominantly white religious institutions. It was the faith dimension of civil rights work that kept people going when the going got tough, and that gave people a vision of how we are to live together. It has also been difficult to cut through the patriarchy of religious institutions and recognize that God expects women to be treated as the beloved daughters of God that they are, or through the homophobia that condemns love that God created. Starting a movement for family well-being stumbles on the racial, ethnic, and economic divisions that still plague the United States, and on a work ethic grounded not in God but in employers' and shareholders' needs. These barriers make it even more urgent for people of faith to pray and work for conditions that foster the well-being of all of God's children.

Theological and conceptual insights from clergy mothers' lives

Here is a brief summary of some of the theological implications of the multidimensional understanding of vocation that has been developed throughout the book.

- Commitments to work, spouse, family, and world are the locus of holiness and the context within which a relationship with God develops. They give meaning and value to daily life and have practical consequences for where people live, with what resources, strengths, and faults, and with what supports and challenges.

- Vocation is not a part of life, but rather an ongoing response to God in and through commitments that becomes a way of life, an almost constant discernment process, grounded in prayer, in which people choose priorities, walk in faith trying to honor them, and live with sacrifices and unintended consequences.

♦ The idea that priorities are established in conversation with God rather than in response to social norms or structural limits is profoundly countercultural. Part of faithfulness to God's commitments, when they contradict social expectations, is living through resistance. The church, as Christ's body in the world, should help both with discussing alternate values and with changing institutional structures and public policy to help clergy and family of clergy stay centered and faithful.

♦ A multidimensional understanding of vocation challenges the assumptions that ordination is most holy way to be faithful to God and that church service is the only way to serve God. Privileging ordination and church service over other ways to serve God leads clergy and church to sacrifice marriage, family, and self-care on the altar of Molech.[2] Chronically busy clergy women who are stopped in their tracks by the wonder of a new child, or the struggles of an older one, or the barrenness of a relationship they had always meant to nurture, or sheer exhaustion, could interpret the interruptions as clues to restoring greater health and faithfulness in ministry and life.

♦ When clergy and churches attend to the way God is found in everyday life, including parenting, creation, the lives of the most vulnerable people in the "neighborhood" where ministry is needed, or the lives of the increasingly wealthy and frantically busy people searching for meaning in status and possessions, all believers may be called back to a focus on mission and ministry rather than institutional survival and maintenance.

♦ Too often sermons about feminist biblical family values, or inclusive language liturgies, are seen as self-serving luxuries for women for which the parish is not ready and which it does not need. We need "a few good privileged men" to take risks in denominational hierarchies and parishes, to help bring feminist biblical and theological interpretation into the mainstream of Christian thinking. Women need to value themselves and their experiences enough to keep trusting that the voices of women are essential for the well-being of all. Yet another generation of Christian girls is growing up without knowing the "herstory" of the Christian faith because patriarchy and sexism aren't sufficiently challenged.

♦ The church is foundering on conflicts over sexuality that still seem focused on who's doing what with whom rather than the quality and integrity of intimate committed relationships. Clergy women, gay and lesbian families with clergy members in them, and increasing numbers of straight men can offer new models of egalitarian relationships, fidelity, and sexual responsibility. They have important insights from their experiences to enflesh already existing academic theories of sexuality that are life-affirming, theologically grounded, inclusive, with appropriate guidelines for faithful behavior. Again, systemic and individual resistance to challenging implicit norms keeps people from living fully into their vocation.

- Understanding vocation to include faithfulness to God in and through family life, parish ministry, and community participation implies that family members of clergy also need space and support to name and fulfill their vocation and commitments, respected by clergy and church.

- Baptismal tools of discernment can be a model for how all of us continually name and evaluate priorities, notice how our actions contradict the values we profess, and develop new habits of faithfulness in continually changing contexts. No balance will work perfectly; all of life is a school for love, with wisdom and grace, sin and repentance and forgiveness, discovered in and through prayerful attempts to keep being faithful.

The ethics of vocation, broadly conceived

All denominations expect clergy and their families, when they have families, to live in accordance with Scripture and Christian tradition. Yet significant controversies exist over what Scripture and tradition say about the definition of family, the proper role of women in the home and the public sphere, the holiness of egalitarian heterosexual relationships rather than families where ultimate decision-making power rests with the male head of house, and whether same-sex relationships can be holy and blessed by God. This book includes the broadest vision of Christian families — heterosexual couples and same-sex couples, single mothers raising children, biological and adopted children, and so on, all of whom are clear that God has blessed their families. My interpretation of Scripture is filtered through the experiences of these family members as they struggle to be faithful to Scripture, tradition, and their own sense of God's invitations not just to relationships and family life but also to work and community involvement.

Traditional Christian ethics has also accepted the false separation of public and private life, and has tended to ignore what happens in private life with the exception of norms about sexual ethics. Those norms, like the structural definition of family, focus more on the form rather than the substance of sexual relationships: "who was doing what with whom and when"[3] and how were they related rather than the quality of the relationship, the context of power dynamics within the relationship, or the presence or absence of consent.[4] Larger ethical issues present in family life, including parenting, nurture of relationships, stewardship of family resources, the use and abuse of power, or the foundations of trust and respect were generally ignored in Christian ethical theory until feminist ethicists paid attention to the realities of family violence.[5] Ironically, there are resources in both Jewish and Christian Scripture when interpreted with historical-critical methods that locate family values squarely in the public realm and in the realm of holiness and faithfulness to God. Developing a biblically based ethics of vocation that attends to the public and private dimensions of family and work can help overcome the traditional separation in ethical theory between family and public life.

"Household of God" as a foundation for an ethics of vocation

In *Family Ministry*, Diana Garland proposes that Christians use a functional rather than structural definition of family. A structural definition focuses on "how persons are related to one another by blood lineage or legal bonds of adoption and marriage," regardless of the quality of the relationship.[6] A functional definition looks instead on the roles people take with one another and the quality of their relationships.[7] Garland identifies six functions of family: "Family is the organization of relationships that endure over time and contexts through which persons attempt to meet their needs for belonging and attachment and to share life purposes, help and resources."[8] This is much more consistent with the extended families of Hebrew Scriptures and the concern throughout the New Testament about creating a new "family of God," known by the love members show to one another and to "strangers" they meet — "whoever does the will of God is my brother and sister and mother."[9] In the household of God and among the people of Israel, people love each other, are faithful to the same Lord, take care of one another, encourage and suffer with each other, extend hospitality to widows, orphans, and strangers, and adopt each other as siblings regardless of biological or legal ties.

Basing an ethics of vocation on the biblical understanding of the household of God has an important advantage. In traditional Christian ethics, family values were equated with adherence to household codes and generally left to the discretion of the head of house, without any public accountability. Distinct public and private moral realms emerged, without attention to how decisions and patterns of relations in one realm affected the other. Reinhold Niebuhr crystallized this distinction when he argued that love was the appropriate ethical category for the private realm of family and interpersonal relations, while justice was appropriate for the public realm of economics and politics.[10]

Greek, Roman, Palestinian, and Hebrew households were considered economic as well as social units. Particular work was assigned by gender, but both men and women contributed to the economic and social standing and to the reproductive work of the family. Patriarchal inequalities assumed in these families at the time can now be challenged by the radical equality of all people under God. The underlying understanding of the family as an arena of moral action, "the place where both women and men are called to labor and to struggle with the fundamental challenges of human love and the making of human history,"[11] is key to a broader understanding of vocation. Jewish laws regulated most aspects of family life. The daily working out of relations in the family was holy work, which deepened members' relationship to God.[12] The understanding of family as a central moral arena of public and private life remains strong to this day in Judaism. Perhaps the adaptation of Christian tradition to Greek philosophical categories, or the skepticism about sexuality and Jesus' challenge to narrow family loyalties, or the influx of Gentiles with different understandings about the search for meaning, truth, and relationship with God, or the evangelical emphasis on personal piety, obscured the moral dimensions of family life for Christian ethicists. The "household of God" metaphor sets family life, social, economic and political life in the largest schema of participation in God's work of creation and restoration. Vocation then has a broader context within which responsibilities to the needs and well-being of the family, the individuals in the family, the larger society, and ultimately to God can and must be integrated.

From that foundation, other biblical categories emerge to help Christians evaluate the quality of their relationships and how well they live into their vocation by fulfilling the responsibilities entrusted to them. Values of the reign of God, love, mutuality, accountability, and abundant life are central to Christian Scriptures and to a broader understanding of vocation. They may also help progressive Christians reclaim "family values" authentically grounded in the Bible, in contrast to the rhetoric of the Christian Right, but that is another story.

The "Commonwealth" of God: sharing resources meant for the well-being of all

Jesus' most consistent message was that the kingdom, or commonwealth,[13] of God was in our midst. His teaching, healing, miracles, life and death and resurrection opened believers' eyes and hearts to the presence of God in all places, to the righteousness God desired, and to the love continually available for all of creation. The "common-wealth" can never be imposed, as many expected and many through history have tried. God's wealth includes love and justice, healing and service, dignity and respect, repentance in the face of sin and hope in God's future, meant to be held in common for the well-being of all. We have glimpses of this commonwealth in this life, and trust that in time it will be finally fulfilled, "on earth as it is in heaven." The more we live and pray into God's vision, the more we are able to align our choices about parenting and work with God's desires and intentions for humanity and creation.

Hospitality is one way to broaden our vision of the commonwealth of God. In *Jesus' Family Values,* Deirdre Good shows how Luke situates much of Jesus' ministry in respectable households, "enlarging the function and role of family and household with a program of expanding hospitality. Disciples may need to leave their families of origin, and those families will need to extend themselves further in hospitality than might be considered usual."[14] Luke shows the household of Mary and Joseph as a source of the stability, quiet, and order within which Jesus could "grow in wisdom and in stature," while the incident of the adolescent Jesus remaining in the temple shows his primary commitment to God as his father. Good argues that the example of healthy differentiation of Jesus from his family of origin in the temple also provides a context within which to understand Jesus' rejection of his biological family (Luke 8:20–21 and 12:52–53) in favor of those who "hear the word of God and do it." In Acts, Luke portrays house churches as similar sources of stability, order, and resources for the early Christian community.[15]

Our vision of the commonwealth of God is constantly expanding. The story of the Ethiopian eunuch offers particular insight into the inclusion of folks labeled "damaged" or irreparably broken. Through baptism those who have been excluded from ritual participation become acceptable, wanted, and necessary to the new family of God.[16] Garland goes a step further when she argues that hospitality is not constrained by biology. God fulfills the prophets' promise that the Messiah will come from the line of David through adoption, not direct biological descent. In so doing, Jesus, as an infant, models what he will preach as an adult. "From this point forward, no one must be without family because wombs are barren, marriages are broken or never formed, or loved ones die. The human experiences of conception, birth, and marriage are transformed by the in-breaking Spirit of God, reforming family."[17] This is often dramatically illustrated in families headed by same-sex couples, especially those who have chosen to adopt special-needs children or assume their care when other family members renege on their responsibilities.

Many of the epistles invite believers to trust God's commonwealth in their general prayer of thanksgiving. The prayers follow a typical formula of thanks to God, thanks to the recipients of the letter for faithfulness, and a plea for continued faithfulness because of one or more attributes of God or Jesus. They reminded congregants then and remind readers now of our ultimate purpose: to grow into the people and the society God intends us to be. 1 and 2 Corinthians[18] promise the development of spiritual gifts for the well-being of congregations and the world. Philippians 1:2–11 promises that "God who has started a good work will bring it to completion." The hope and truth of the gospel is growing and bearing fruit in your life and the life of the world so that you may sustain a worthy manner of life and be about the work of reconciliation entrusted to us by God, promises Colossians 1.[19] Promises, promises — but "in Christ every one of God's promises is a yes."[20] They are a powerful reminder that all of our lives are a process of growing in faith, not necessarily linearly but in and through the joys and struggles of daily life. The ways we treat family members, congregants, and "local others" now helps us live into God's global vision, and sets our daily life into a larger context.

Colossians' compelling image of faith bearing fruit and growing in the world, the congregation, and individual Christians reminds me that I participate in the unfolding mystery of God's life in the world even as I'm nagging my seven-year-old to "brush your teeth *now* or we'll be late for school."[21] As I watch children sleeping, or as I prepare for a vestry meeting, the prayer in Ephesians to let God enlighten the eyes of their hearts and mine to discover the hope intended for each of us and for the world[22] restores perspective. Recalling the "breadth and length and height and depth" of the love of Christ, and the promise of God who, working "within us, is able to accomplish abundantly far more than all we can ask or imagine"[23] helps me find strength, grace, and forgiveness of self and others. Just to set the events of the day, and sometimes tomorrow's plans, in the context of thanksgiving to God helps me remember my ultimate goal of strengthening my love for God, neighbor, self, and creation in all that I do.

Love: expanding my capacity to give and receive love

Theologians and ethicists have waxed eloquent about the centrality of biblical love for centuries. Two particular aspects of love, however, are especially useful as an ethical category for vocation: the examples of love as nurturing, service, caring for the vulnerable, often illustrated in images from family life, and the understanding of love as covenantal relationship with God, self, others, and creation, found most clearly in Deuteronomy and the prophets.

Gail R. O'Day understands the gospel of John as an introduction to the language of intimacy, relationship, and family not found often in the synoptic gospels. Members of the beloved community were to experience God's love and demonstrate it in the ways they treated each other. O'Day notes that many of the signs by which believers are to recognize Jesus as the Christ are revealed in family settings — the wedding in Cana, the raising of Lazarus, the anointing of Jesus — and when the setting is public, parents are often included, as in the healing of the blind man or Jesus' giving of John to his mother, Mary, while on the cross.[24] John includes the foot-washing as an example of discipleship as intimate love and service that most parents know when giving their children baths, and many adult children know when they bathe their ailing parents.

In John's gospel, love is dynamic, flowing from God through Jesus to the dis-ciples and the world and back to God. Often when I was nursing, I had the distinct sense that I was abiding in God's love as surely as my infant was abiding in mine, and that the love God offered me, that I offered my daughters, that they offered me, that I offered God, was both safe haven in which to rest and energy to release into the world. Many of the clergy I interviewed said that part of what makes parish ministry so satisfying is that in worship, or counseling, or designing programs, or even structuring safe and effective meetings, they were a conduit for God's love. O'Day observes that in John, disciples give out of the abundance of their love, love continually replenished by God, rather than out of self-denial. An ethics of vocation needs to value the sharing of love out of fullness that often is known in acts of caring, nurture, attachment, and belonging.[25]

Kathleen Chesto offers an interpretation of Matthew 25 that is useful for par-ents. Parents get to heaven and find themselves on God's right hand, astonished because they felt that caring for children kept them from the acts of mercy Jesus commended: tending the sick, clothing the naked, visiting prisoners, and so on. "When did I see you hungry and feed you?" Jesus replies, "How could you ask, you of the three-and-a-half-million peanut butter and jelly sandwiches! When you stayed up all night with a sick child, when your days were filled with cleaning babies and changing diapers and washing clothes and dressing children, when your conversations, or sometimes silences, freed adolescents from the prison of their own bodies and emotions, you were taking care of me."[26] Of course, car-ing for those who are literally sick, naked, in prison, or hungry is also essential. Domestic duties, real and created, can blind parents to the needs of the wider world. It is a reflection of some understandings of piety, however, that parents would discount their daily work of nurturing children because the tradition has emphasized only care for those outside the family.

Yet love is not just an emotion between individuals or exclusively within the private realm.[27] Love in Hebrew and Christian Scriptures is a divinely initiated covenant, intended to make the Israelites a holy people, aware of God's power and presence in their lives and righteous in their dealings with others. It is expressed in commandments about behavior regardless of the emotion of the doer. Sometimes when a child or a member of the congregation calls in the middle of the night, or when a discerned call to ordained ministry is rejected because of gender or sexual orientation, or when a marriage or a pastoral relationship falls apart, any felt sense of God's love or our own ability to respond to others' needs is absent. "Going through the motions" of care prescribed in the Bible can sustain us until healing happens. The covenant defines the vocation of the people of God: for Jews, to be a light to the nations, for Christians, to be a people admired for they way they loved one another. "By this everyone will know that you are my disciples, if you have love for one another."[28] Vows of marriage, committed relationships, baptism, and ordination (I wish there were explicit liturgical vows for parenting), however imperfectly kept, are rooted in the radical faithfulness of God's covenant of love with us and, when kept, lead us to greater holiness.

Mutuality: living together justly

Mutuality is a category developed by feminist and womanist ethicists out of experiences of friendship, intimacy, connection, and respect. It includes equality and interdependence, and is a norm of healthy relationships. For John, anyone who recognizes Jesus as the Son of God, sent from the Father, becomes a child of God and part of the beloved community. O'Day argues that the extensive Father language in God, though grating to feminist ears, is intended to express first the centrality of the relationship between Jesus and God, and later between God, Jesus, and believers, and second the equality of all believers under God.[29] Mutuality can counter the temptation of congregations and clergy to see only ordained people as "real ministers," and can help determine whether responsibilities are shared widely and fairly enough among all involved. Jesus' farewell speeches in the gospel of John are full of the language of interdependence. "As you, Father, are in me and I am in you, may they also be in us."[30] Believers, God, Jesus, and the Holy Spirit are intimately knit together, working together to make love known. John describes the immanence of love as well as its transcendent power; vocation too both draws on an internal source of love and reaches toward a God who is ever unfolding.

Matthew models the idea of mutuality in a different way. Amy-Jill Levine notes that whenever Matthew defines a family unit, he usually describes only mothers and children (cf. 12:50). The one exception is Jesus' birth, where Mary is entirely passive and Joseph, the one whose action is neither legally necessary nor socially expected, adopts Jesus and thus brings Mary and Jesus into the line of David.[31] A biological father, however, is still missing, and Joseph's role seems primarily to serve and protect Mary and Jesus, not rule over them. She argues that Matthew does this deliberately, because fathers in his day automatically had power over women and children. The gospel author is intentionally eliminating all relationships in which one group exploits or dominates another.[32] Levine reinforces this by pointing out that the women in Matthew's genealogy "were initially removed from traditional domestic arrangements: unmarried [Mary], separated from their spouse [Bathsheba], widowed [Ruth, Tamar], or prostitutes [Rahab]."[33] His illustrations of people in mutual relationships fulfilling unexpected roles can encourage churches and families to think "outside the box" about how to organize congregational or family ministry. They free vocation from narrow identification with any one particular role.

The first few chapters of Genesis also provide an image of mutuality. In the first chapter God creates humans, male and female, in God's image, blesses them, commands them to be fruitful and multiply, to rule over and care for all of creation, and to eat only plants.[34] These verses focus on humanity's God-given responsibilities for the rest of creation, as participants in God's creating work. Chapter 2 has a different emphasis. God created Adam, an "earthling" of undifferentiated sex, and put the earthling in the Garden of Eden to till and care for it. Again, the first purpose for humans is caring for God's creation. God notices that "it is not good for [Adamah] to be alone. I will provide a partner fit for him."[35] Garland observes that again men and women are created as equals, who mutually participate in productive and reproductive work, a challenge to the gendered division of labor common then and now. The animals were fit for service, or because of their particular role in creation, but humans need other humans to be fully human themselves. The companionship partners or spouses can provide to each other, in their work in the family and in the professional arena, has been part of God's intention for humanity from the beginning. In Mark, Jesus later grounds his defense of marriage in God's establishment of relationship in creation.[36] Mutuality creates a safe place where vulnerabilities can be shared and intimacy deepened. Nurturing intimate mutual relationships helps both people tap into the divine "love that moves the sun and the other stars."[37]

The third chapter of Genesis explains how this original equality in relationship was distorted by sin. The abuse of power in families, the systemic development of patriarchy, the gendered division of tasks, and the lack of support or recognition of caretaking, are formidable examples of sin that still plague human families today. When people use Genesis 3 to justify male headship in families, they distort the account of creation.

Accountability: promoting the safe use of power

A biblically grounded ethic of vocation needs to include guidelines about holding people accountable, to each other and to their ministry, for the way they use all their gifts. Because the epistles are addressed to specific congregations with specific issues of how to live together faithfully, they flesh out a principle of mutual accountability for members of this new family that is useful in living both congregational and family life. Each of the letters uses its own languages to encourage the community to attend to the way members treat each other "to build up the body of Christ."[38] Authors employ different theological metaphors — reconciliation, participation in the body of Christ, the household of God — to express an ideal for community life. Then the authors address particular issues, which threaten to weaken the congregation, whether eating meat sacrificed to idols, quarreling, insisting on circumcision, women covering their heads in church, or people not doing their fair share of the work involved in ministry. First Corinthians concerns the right use of spiritual gifts.[39] Second Corinthians offers standards of stewardship and proportional responsibilities (although not at the expense of one's own needs[40] — a useful caveat). First Timothy 4 offers rather harsh criteria for the congregation to determine which widows are worthy of support, balancing their needs with their willingness to assume some responsibilities. I hear echoes of this in vestry meetings about "whose job is it," in home discussions of why chores differ for seven- and fourteen-year-olds, and in welfare policies seeking a balance between an essential safety net and a "free ride." Many of the epistles give specific guidance for banning people from the community when their behavior threatens the well-being of the whole,[41] though 2 Corinthians also describes a process for readmitting offenders and forgiving them, as does Matthew 16. Ultimately, evaluating actions by "the fruit of the Spirit," or by what "builds up the body of Christ," whether actions lead to quarreling, licentiousness, gossip, adultery, incest, fornication (interpreted as sex without mutual respect), and other behaviors destructive to community or to patience, gentleness, kindness, joy, and generosity[42] is an essential criterion for families and congregations alike.

Not all relationships can be mutual, and not all power over others is exploitative. Parents appropriately care for vulnerable children, providing safety, resources, nurture, and care. Clergy have been given authority to lead their congregations, making decisions, controlling resources, and representing the sacred in holy space. Often lay leaders have authority over church finances or other resources. The parable of the faithful steward, who cares responsibly for those in his charge, speaks well to the right use of authority: "From everyone to whom much has been given, much will be required; and from one to whom much has been entrusted, even more will be demanded."[43]

A lawyer and Catholic lay woman has been dealing with sexual misconduct cases in Christian and Jewish denominations for over fifteen years now. After the initial outrage when abuse is discovered, she finds a consistent pattern of institutional unwillingness to insist that abusers accept consequences for his or her actions. The clergy appointed to judge their peers are often so concerned with bringing the abuser back into the family that they accept immediate promises of repentance rather than wait for demonstrated changes in behavior and a willingness on the abuser's part to accept responsibility for their actions. They focus on the abuser's needs rather than the damage done to the victim(s), their families and their congregations.[44]

Most parenting manuals also stress the need for parents to help children face the consequences of their actions and take responsibility for making amends and changing their behavior when it threatens the well-being of others. Wendy Mogel is a Jewish clinical psychologist who sets the responsibilities of parents to their children in the context of Torah and religious practice. She describes the difficulties many parents have in claiming and using authority appropriately.[45] Many of the complaints I have heard from clergy spouses are about the emotional strain their partners experience when members of a congregation (lay and ordained) are too afraid to hold each other accountable for truly destructive actions. Accountability can challenge the culture of niceness that was never part of Jesus' mission but is ingrained in the church. Asking clergy to account for the ways they spend time and energy in church and home might help clergy make their priorities explicit, claim their authority for the choices they make, and notice when their actions are in fact no longer consistent with their intentions. Asking congregations to account for the demands they put on clergy might also help distinguish reasonable from unreasonable expectations.

Self-differentiation is another aspect of accountability, for only people with enough ego strength to remain true to themselves will be able to discern how to handle conflicts and choices that arise in a community of grace-filled and sinful people. There is a growing literature about systems theory and self-differentiation, developed by Murray Bowen and Edwin Friedman. Those of us who are working on self-differentiation may find it useful to pray with Ephesians 6:10–17, where the author describes "the armor of God" necessary to fight the cosmic forces of evil. Truth, righteousness, readiness to proclaim the gospel of peace, faith, salvation, the word of God, and constant prayer are all tools to help fight off temptations to please people, or avoid conflict, or accept unquestioningly the way roles have been structured by economic or social systems.

There is another, more subtle dimension of family life present, though rarely mentioned, from biblical times to today. The family is perceived to be a haven of security and comfort for adults returning from an impersonal or harsh workplace and for children as they grow, or for adults, aging or with special needs, who need continued care. Yet families can also be dangerous places, especially for women, children, and dependent adults. We have no statistics about family violence in biblical times, though there are records of life and death authority over women, children, and slaves. In the United States in 2001, 20 percent of violent crime against women was intimate partner violence, compared to 3 percent of violent crime against men.[46] Approximately 906,000 children are victims of abuse and neglect every year in the United States, or 12.3 out of 1,000 children. Children under four are most at risk.[47] Ched Myers argues that Jesus' criticism of family life in Mark comes from Jesus' awareness of how vulnerable women and children were to threats from within the family as well as external threats of poverty, disease, and violence. Jesus' use of children as a model of faithful living, and his repeated healings of children, show that children were persons in their own right entitled to safety and respect.[48] Jesus' prohibition of divorce can also be understood as protecting women who would otherwise be summarily cut off from their home and resources. Those with power and authority over others need to be held accountable for the ways they exercise their power.

Finally, accountability has a political and economic dimension. God, through the prophets, held the Israelites responsible for the way they cared for each other. It mattered how the Israelites organized their society, whether they couldn't wait until Sabbath is over to cheat the poor, or whether they were so much at ease in Zion that they ignored the needs of widows and orphans, or whether they forgot that they were strangers in Egypt and failed to care for the foreigner in their midst. Jesus continued this attention to the responsibility to care for "the least of these," using the amount of care or neglect as a measure of justice. Discerning appropriate responsibility for family, work, and the most vulnerable members of society, and then designing structures of accountability that will protect those in need when personal responsibility fails, is intrinsic to vocation.

Abundant life: delighting in participation in creation

"I have come that they may have life. . . . " "I have said these things [about abiding in God's love] to you so that my joy may be in you, and that your joy may be complete."[49] Abundant life and joy are themes throughout the gospel of John and the Johannine epistles. They do not occur per se in the synoptic gospels, but Jesus' delight in the children who sought him out, his frequent descriptions of banquets, and his refusal to fast in the way prescribed by religious leaders of the day suggest that Jesus experienced and valued both. Sheer delight in God's creation can be found throughout Hebrew Scriptures. People of faith are continually being invited to a banquet whose joys are revealed in everyday choices of work, family, and community life. Often we refuse. Sometimes we're blind to them — an absence of joy over time is a sign that something needs to change. Sometimes the invitation seems too hard, or amorphous, or crazy. Yet vocation is about discerning and honoring God's invitations to abundant life.

John offers the metaphor of a vine, a "radically nonhierarchical image for the composition and constitution of the church"[50] that includes accountability and interdependence. Jesus is the vine, God is the vine dresser, and believers are branches that grow and bear fruit only in connection with the divine source of life. The vine dresser prunes whatever is dead or no longer useful. This is the most concrete image of the love of God, Jesus, and people for each other, offered by Jesus "so that my joy may be in you, and that your joy may be complete."[51] Congregations and families both could benefit from living into this metaphor. An article in a parish newsletter compared my behavior in the church building during the week to a juggler on roller skates spinning plates. That image brings a smile, but the drivenness it suggests feels more like I've taken a page from Mark's Jesus, who is always immediately responding to one thing or another.

Pruning is that nasty-seeming task of "saying no" to some demands, some desires, some possibilities in order to stay true to God and self. Almost everyone I interviewed — male and female, lay and ordained — expect that parish clergy be available twenty-four hours a day, seven days a week, always. Most of the women I interviewed also felt that as mothers they were expected to be available to their family twenty-four hours a day, seven days a week, always. There's some truth in this, in that parish clergy, like many members of the helping professions, are needed in crises, which can happen at any time. More than one clergy mother has brought her young children to the emergency room in the middle of the night to visit a parishioner because arranging child-care at midnight is impossible. The children may grumble but they know this is part of their family life. But not all needs are equally important or urgent. Jesus focused on God, and what God expected him and his disciples to do. We should do no less, continually evaluating whether our "yeses" to the many opportunities we have to love are of God, or out of a sense of being needed or important or in control, or out of guilt or manipulation by other people's agendas. The vine metaphor reminds us to let ourselves abide in Jesus, and to grow and stretch at God's instigation. In the synoptic gospels Jesus left needy crowds often, to pray, or to spread the gospel elsewhere, or because of the crowd's hardheartedness, or because he was on his way to Jerusalem. When we become ever more focused on God's particular invitations to us, we will be more able to do what God needs us to do, and to let go of that which looks tempting but is not ours.

The vine metaphor reminds us also that we are part of a larger entity, connected to other people, to Jesus, and to God. Humans need each other, so communication and nurturing connection is essential in the parish, community, and family. One clergy couple with three children found that Palm Pilots, where each adult could send daily revisions to their calendar, helped incarnate both accountability and interdependence (the modern day wireless vine!). "Communication and organization are essential for us both personally and professionally," they said. Their rule was that once one spouse had scheduled a meeting, if the other also needed to meet at the same time, the second spouse had to make child-care arrangements. Emergencies were negotiated as they arose. They had another practice that helped keep some fluidity in their lives and schedules: one evening a week of family time, and one morning or afternoon of couples time just to enjoy a walk, or a museum, or a movie, or each other. The fruit of communication and organization was time for joy.

There is a temptation in John's writing and in contemporary life to restrict the circle of people we are expected to love; John's gospel condemns harshly those who fail to recognize Jesus and can perpetuate damaging anti-Semitism. Explanations of the intercongregational battles and persecutions that led to harsh judgments against "the Jews" aren't a sufficient antidote in a world still ready to look for enemies to blame. So we need to counter the tendency to restrict love with clear injunctions in the synoptic gospels to love our enemies, and pray for those who persecute us, and meet violence with loving but persistent resistance to violence in all its forms. Abundant life comes in faithful response to adversity as well as occasions for joy.

We come full circle: vocation understood as living in the household of God, distributing the resources of the commonwealth of God with love, nurturing relationships of mutuality and being willing to hold others accountable and be held accountable to the well-being of the body of Christ, leads to joy and abundant life. Throughout the Bible God is continually inviting individuals, the people of Israel, and congregations into relationship with God individually and corporately. The prophets and Jesus continually keep the picture of the commonwealth of God before us, so we will be moved to share resources justly with all. The synoptic gospels illustrate in Jesus' healing, teaching, castigation of religious authorities, and inclusion of the marginalized how to hold people accountable for their choices and work toward relations of mutual respect. John complements all of these by modeling abundant life lived out of the fullness of God's love. These biblically based ethical categories can help people live into their vocations most faithfully.

Practical steps for clergy mothers

Let's return to the factors that Barbara Brown Zikmund and her researchers found that make it *unlikely* for women or men to leave parish ministry: strong professional self-concept; good mental, physical, and spiritual health; the ability to set boundaries between church work and private life; fair compensation; respect from denominational officials; belief that a better church position will be somewhat easy to find; and participation in a clergy support group.[52] There is a plethora of information about what constitutes strong families, from many different ideological perspectives. Here are some parallel factors that support all kinds of families: strong concept of self as a good enough parent; good mental, physical, and spiritual health; the ability to set boundaries between family life and work in the public domain; adequate resources; respect from culture for parenting responsibilities and a freedom from stereotypes about parenting; the conviction that family life can be fulfilling throughout its many stages; and support from a "village," including family and friends. Each of these factors is considered in terms of what individuals, parishes, denominations, Christian theology and practice, and the larger culture can do to support an expanded understanding of vocation.

Strong professional self-concept and concept of self as a "good-enough" parent

When has a pastor done enough for the church? When has she performed well enough? Professional self-concept is a clergy person's sense of being effective, skilled, and graced by God in her profession, able to handle the routine tasks that come along and the crises that interrupt personal and institutional life. Fred Lehr names several objective components of professional self-concept: Clergy are able to feel confident about their professional performance when they feel they have had adequate training to meet demands of the job and when more training is available and accessible; when they can name one or two core parts of their job that they enjoy and perform competently; when they have an appropriate sense of what their job is and is not, when they are able to take positive and negative feedback from parishioners with appropriate perspective; and when they have a sense that the work they are doing is in fact congruent with what God wants of them.[53] Regular evaluation of a pastor's work is very difficult to institute, however. It requires a relatively healthy denominational and congregational system, and a pastor healthy enough to be able to claim both strengths and "growing edges." In a position where there are usually more demands than time to fill them, frequently a vague sense of the role of pastors or churches in society, no connection between work accomplished and a growing "bottom line" of product or profit, and often an overlay of parish dissatisfaction with demographic factors beyond their control, holding on to a sense of being a "good-enough" pastor is often very difficult.

If objective measures of clergy effectiveness are hard to find, objective measures of good-enough mothering are nonexistent outside of the child welfare agencies' criteria for dangerous parents. One woman measured her effectiveness by the number of back-up plans she had for child-care. Sometimes I obsess about whether I've really spent enough time listening to my teenager, or whether my seven-year-old is eating enough healthy food, or how much therapy will be required when I directed anger about work or spouse at a child instead. Other days I count as a success if they're alive at bedtime! Another woman said that when she could no longer keep her children's names straight, it was time for a break. Yet another woman watched her children sleeping, and thanked God for who they were and for the spark of personality that made each one unique; as long as the spark was still there, she and they were fine. Overall, I heard guilt from almost everyone, rueful gratitude for lessons learned through mistakes, and underlying trust in resiliency — theirs, their children's, and God's.

One barrier to strong professional self-concept, and perhaps to a sense of being a good-enough parent or spouse, can come from husbands. Jackson Carroll found that most of the married clergy women in his study were under age of thirty-five, many of them had children under the age of ten at home, and had spouses who were employed full-time, often as clergy serving churches. Two-thirds of the married women reported serious role strain because of home issues about whose priorities and demands were to prevail, theirs or their husbands.[54] Lehman didn't provide details of Carroll's study. Yet my own life and conversations with women clergy suggest that the stress lines include constant negotiation over care of children and home, when one or both partners assume that that's the woman's job. Finances, and relative contributions to household income as a measure of whose job is more important, are a piece of these negotiations. Less frequent but more anxiety-producing are the conversations about geographical relocation, or one or the other spouse pursuing a new call or job opportunity. A litany of subtle but persistent questions by husbands of wives of whether they really should be working as hard as they are, or in the job they have, or in ways that reduce availability of the wife to the husband, or the wife to the children, can lead a woman to question her own worth and her right to be doing the work she's called to do. In conversations with clergy women in their forties, fifties, and sixties, we talked about fighting conscious and unconscious assumptions, on our part and from our husbands, that the husband's work and activities are more important. I hope that would be less true with a younger generation of married clergy women.

Belief that a better church position and increasingly satisfying family life are achievable

The belief that a better church position is available is connected to professional self-concept. A new call is exciting, because it affirms some qualities one has already and offers opportunities to learn new things and grow in new ways. There are good periods and times of crisis and change, but for a while the position offers more satisfaction than despair. But at some point, clergy get into a position where their ministry is stale, or exhausting, or no longer where their heart is. The hope of a better church position is an affirmation of the need to grow and change. Sometimes a retreat or sabbatical can renew commitment to be in the same position in a different way; other times it's time to move on, and it's helpful to think that other positions might be available. When sexism, or low salaries, or geographical or family constraints dim the hope of a new position, some women turn to opportunities beyond parish ministry. The sense that real gifts and skills will not be used for whatever reason diminishes the sense of being a competent professional.

Increasingly satisfying family life is another entirely subjective goal, yet it's essential for healthy marriages or partnerships and for parenting. Are we still growing together? Many of the women I spoke with and some men, both gay and straight, said that it was too easy to neglect their marriage or ignore the calls of their partner for more connection and quality of relationship. One woman was frank to say that she sometimes used parish work to avoid intimacy with her partner, and it took her partner's repeated pleas for her to notice and, eventually, work to change that pattern. She named an issue that is probably part of many clergy lives. All the marriage manuals remind couples that marriage or relationship is valuable work, work that reveals more love and joy. But it is not easy, and couples' counseling can be expensive on a clergy salary. For those of us in the church who preach nurturance of intimate relationships, giving ourselves the time and space to nurture our own relationships is essential.

Good mental, physical, and spiritual health

Obviously. Wellness programs are sprouting up all over, reminding clergy and others of the need for rest, exercise, healthy food, and relaxing time. Equally obviously, to look at some recent studies of clergy wellness, many clergy are unable or unwilling to honor those needs. One man said it well: "I know the literature about self-care, I agree that it's important, but when? I want to do too many other things too well to make time to take care of myself." Women in Vashti McKenzie's study reported that they saw to the needs of their congregation, church, and family first. On average these women spent only one to two hours a week on personal needs (exercising, socializing with friends, bubble baths, etc.) and about fifteen minutes a day for personal devotion outside of sermon or Bible study preparation. Vacations were usually tied to church conferences, denominational events, and revivals. When demands of ministry and family increased, hobbies and vacations were abandoned, to be picked up later.[55] Barbara Brown Taylor describes her worries about what it might mean to observe the Sabbath:

> Taking a full day off was so inconceivable that I made up reasons why it was not possible...no more weekend weddings...sick people would languish in the hospital and begin to question their faith.... If I stopped for a whole day, my animals would starve, my house would grow mold, weeds would take over my garden, and my credit rating would collapse. If I stopped for a whole day, God would be sorely disappointed in me.[56]

She goes on to point out the folly of these reasons, but her sense of compulsion about so many daily tasks rings true. Clergy mothers, after a "crash" when they realized they couldn't sustain their current schedule, often found they were more motivated to take care of themselves better. They had to establish routines of rest and exercise "for the sake of the children" or "so I could function at work" because they had seen the consequences of self-neglect.

Nourishing a life of prayer and worship

This also seems obvious, and is easier said than done. There are all the excuses of prayer not feeling as productive as accomplishing the "to do" list, or trying to pray but falling asleep from exhaustion. Yet there's a unique dimension for clergy. For most Christians, church is a place to find respite from struggles in work and home. For family members of clergy and for clergy, church is work and engenders its own conflicts. Finding ways to worship or find spiritual counsel that are genuinely nourishing can be difficult. Clergy family members talk about the joy of sharing in leading worship or a parish, but they also talk about the difficulties of not having a priest or of worshipping and passing the peace with people in the midst of conflict between minister and people. Clergy are often so busy preparing or leading worship that they don't make time to let others lead and feed them. Barbara Brown Taylor found that "the demands of parish ministry routinely cut me off from the resources that enabled me to do parish ministry,"[57] including prayer and worship.

Vashti McKenzie also found that in a crisis, most of the African-American women she surveyed turned to prayer and fasting and sought comfort first from God. The ability to connect to a higher source beyond themselves is life-saving. McKenzie made an interesting observation, however. Running alone to God in prayer can promote a sense of isolation and willingness to suffer in silence. She recommended that after prayer, women share their struggles and the insights from prayer with others who can be rich resources and sources of advice.[58]

Michael Jinkins echoes the recommendation that clergy hold each other accountable for maintaining consistent disciplines of prayer and study. His study of Austin Seminary alumni revealed that while most respondents said prayer and Bible study were essential resources for personal refreshment, 62 percent of them had no regular time set aside for either prayer or study, and less than half of them used any sort of mentor, spiritual director, or therapist to help monitor their spiritual growth.[59] Prayer and study often seem like "important but not urgent" activities that too easily get swept aside by everybody else's needs.

Patricia Hayes offers several specific techniques to help clergy maintain a prayer life in times of personal stress, many of which have merit all the time: work with a spiritual director, to reflect monthly on where God is moving. To that I would add: Find someone clear about their understanding of vocation as encompassing commitments to God first, then church and family and self, in no particular order. Hayes goes on to remind clergy to keep in honest and regular touch with five friends outside the congregation. ("Why five? Because at any given emergency time, two will be on vacation, one will be in love, and one will be on his or her own emergency."[60]) Check in at least a few times a year with a personal therapist and a "systems" therapist, to discuss parish dynamics. Do things that nourish your soul, every day, whether you feel like or not. And finally, practice the Ignatian discipline of "looking at God, looking at you." She notes that clergy are usually so hard on themselves that they need to be reminded to ask God what God actually sees and loves in them.[61]

The ability to set boundaries between church work and private life

Almost every story I heard, and every article about home and parish, talks about boundaries. The ability to set and maintain boundaries, to establish priorities based on all the things God *is* asking clergy moms to do and say "no" to all the things asked by anyone but God is a constant process. With constantly changing needs and schedules there can be very few absolutes. (A personal, and illustrative, sidebar: As I write this, I had carved out two full days to finally finish the manuscript, promising myself that nothing would interfere, when the mayor of our town, whose family I have known, died suddenly. OK, nothing but death will interfere!) Glen Kreiner, Elaine Hollensbe, and Mathew Sheep investigated the ways Episcopal clergy men and women negotiate demands between work and home life.[62] "Boundary work" is a proactive step clergy can take to "stop the madness" and find more sanity for themselves. They found physical, behavioral, cognitive, and temporal tactics that clergy use to maintain boundaries between work and home. Behavioral tactics include *communicating expectations,* both directly in newsletters, meetings, and conversations and indirectly through behavior (e.g., refusing a nonurgent request for help), to lay leaders, other staff, parishioners, and also to spouse/partner and children. For instance, Karen said that she and her pastor-husband Bill carefully guarded Fridays, first as family day and then, once children were in school, as couples time. When something comes up on a Friday, everyone knows what Karen's likely response will be: Someone going into the hospital for tests can be visited Saturday or Sunday, but death or a serious car accident may "trump" part of family day.

Communicating expectations is an ongoing activity. It can sometimes take years to change a set of expectations accepted by a previous rector, or expected by a superior, or even established by someone's own previous habits that are eventually seen as unhealthy. *Confronting violators* is important during or after a problem occurs. An example from the Kreiner et al. study, in response to a parishioner who calls daily to discuss the same old issue, is useful: "Well, you need to make an appointment and come and see me. At the appointment we will talk about that."[63] Many women and some men I spoke with found that this was easier "A.C.," after children. Child-care schedules or just the joy of parenting made it become more important to be more efficient at work, setting limits with parishioners or staff who just needed to talk, dedicating time for certain tasks and honoring those tasks rather than being distracted by urgent but not important interruptions. A huge part of confronting violators for me is giving myself permission to honor my needs rather than assuming that I need to accommodate everyone else's schedule. I suspect that there would be differences between men and women, and maybe between older and younger clergy, in their comfort with directly confronting violators.

Leveraging technology is another important skill in days of almost twenty-four-hour accessibility. Some suggested techniques include separate work and home e-mail accounts and screening phone calls, especially during nonwork hours. I find myself getting too distracted with e-mail — the third time the bathtub overflowed and my child wandered off to play because Mom was on the computer was a good clue — and have slowly gotten better about setting specific times to read and respond to it. Kreiner and Hollensbe's respondents also *used other people,* such as parish administrators or other staff, to maintain boundaries. Several men said that they used their wives to answer the phone, screen calls, or take messages. They did not cite any example of a clergy woman saying her husband helped her maintain boundaries, though there were very few examples from women at all. Without hard evidence to compare actual data, I wonder if there's some lingering expectations of clergy wives dynamics going on there. They didn't analyze sex differences in how boundaries are communicated, maintained, and honored.

Temporal tactics included using a calendar to schedule fairly regular "family" and "work" times, or "banking time" to be used later (so that if in one week four evening meetings were unavoidable, for example, the clergy person took other time for the family during that week), and carving out two consecutive days off every so often. Kreiner and Hollensbe noted that older priests seemed more able and felt less guilty about doing that.

Cognitive tactics are the internal rules clergy develop for themselves about how to deal with home-work conflict. Madison, a woman whom I interviewed who has four young children, said that nothing helped her learn triage for the parish better than the habits she developed sorting out "which child needed what kind of attention when." She also gave an excellent example of negotiating work-home boundaries with a parishioner. Madison lived next door to the church, where there was a day-care center. She was having a picnic with her children on their lawn one day when a fire started at the church school next door. She knew the rector was not in the office, and she was needed at church, but she couldn't leave four children under age seven alone either. Before she had time to think, a parishioner noticed the problem and offered to watch her children so Madison could deal with the fire department.

Kreiner and Hollensbe noted that triage is most effective when basic priorities are set before any particular crisis. One quote from a male Episcopal priest illustrates the tensions between home and church well:

> Family has always been important ... when I would interview with parishioners, I would always inform them up front that my priorities were God, family, and church, in that order. ... It is interesting that every parish I have gone into, it's always been the expectation that clergy will drop everything for a parish need or demand. That's been a tough stream to fight against ... I would have to fight for family time and family priorities.[64]

Kreiner et al. also observed that with the more creative parts of ministry, sometimes home and parish enhance each other. One woman said that one way ministry comes home for her "is that when I'm home and I'm in the garden or I'm cooking or even doing laundry, that is where I get my best ideas about a number of things [in church]. I think I am more creative in my time off than I probably am when I'm in my office."[65] It is important to set boundaries, to set and honor priorities, and to balance home and work obligations. Underlying this work, however, is a basic sense of "being present" as a whole person at home and church. So sometimes the parish interrupts home, when someone calls with a real emergency or Holy Week services are scheduled for every evening. Sometimes home interrupts the parish, when children are sick, or holiday concerts are scheduled at exactly the same time as the midweek Eucharist. That's when a basic sense of trust that eventually what is important will get done allows what's forgotten, overlooked, or left undone to be forgiven.

Participation in a clergy support group

Practically every study strongly suggested participation in a clergy women's support group. A regular place to talk with trusted peers about parish and home life counteracts women's tendencies to blame themselves rather than system for some failings, reminds women of the history of struggle, reinforces creative responses to slow systems, and helps distinguish sexism from other sources of resistance. It is still all too common to be the only clergy woman in the community, or in denominational clergy groups, or on denominational staff. Solo pastors are by definition alone in their workplace: There are lots of people, but none with whom it is appropriate to reveal one's deepest struggles and worries. Vashti McKenzie cited mentors and support groups of professional colleagues and of "girlfriends" as essential resources for African-American women in ministry.[66] She offers ten commandments for African-American clergy women, and number three is "Thou Shall Network."[67]

Simply saying that support groups are important is not enough; help in creating, maintaining, and valuing support groups is essential in seminaries, in continuing education, and in denominational venues. Charlene Kammerer is insistent on the value of women staying connected with other women in order to serve effectively in ministry. "Clergy women do not thrive as 'lone rangers' in the ministry. They need to see each other, to hear each other's stories, to support each sister's struggles, to be advocates, to speak up on justice issues, ... to hear women preaching, singing, and reflecting together."[68] Denominations, or ecumenical groups of churches, could offer annual retreats for clergy women, with relevant topics and lots of time in small groups for sharing and reflection. If such retreats were consistent annual events, with appropriate provisions for child-care, a significant amount of trust-building, mentoring, empowering, and networking could strengthen all women's ministry. There are models in biblical Judaism of "the red tent," where menstruating women gathered apart from their homes, or Jepthah's daughter's friends, who spent a month away together supporting each other (although at the end of that month the daughter was sacrificed as part of an unfaithful promise her father made, so maybe that's not such a good example!).

Attention to the gifts, not problems, women bring

Women entered mainline Protestant seminaries in significant numbers in the 1970s, a few years after most mainline denominations opened ordination to women. Clergy women have been a noticeable presence in parish ministry in mainline denominations for over thirty years, and yet the resistance is still sometimes fierce. Statistics and stories throughout this book have illustrated resistance, but they've also demonstrated many of the gifts women bring to ministry, including resourcefulness in the face of recalcitrant institutional structures. As more women of child-bearing age lead parishes, Pamela Cooper White hopes that "the relatively sudden juxtaposition of *metaphors* of birth with the *actual enfleshed experiences* of birthing in the persons of the church's ministers may well impact some of the church's deepest rituals and the ways in which Christianity's deepest symbols may now be received by believers."[69]

She recounts one woman's story of chaplaincy in a Roman Catholic hospital. Some of the nuns on staff would ask her for a title. When the woman said she preferred to by called by her name, they asked, "Why wouldn't you just be called Father? ... We don't think of our priests as men!" The woman reflected that you could pretend that men were genderless, "but when you have a pregnant woman standing up there it's very different ... you can't pretend I'm not female!"[70] And if the person standing leading worship is female, then women and men may indeed be made in God's image, which means that God may in fact not be only male. That transition will only happen when other symbols and language in worship provide an accepting context within which women are not anomalies. A woman in Cooper White's study rued that fact that her two-year-old daughter insisted that God was a boy and boys were better. A confirmation class I led for five teenaged girls echoed this sentiment in a discussion of the inclusive language used in our worship service. In general, they didn't like using feminine images for God, and didn't understand why I felt it was important to use images other than "Father." "It doesn't matter that God is male, we know we're God's children." "But," I asked, "do you think you're made in God's image, too?" "Of course not," they chorused. "We don't need to be made in God's image to be his children."

Development of systemic resources for clergy families

Families of Clergy United in Support (FOCUS) is a national group in the Episcopal Church dedicated to clergy family wellness. They have assembled a resource guide with specific tools for clergy families at almost any point in the clergy member's career path, from seminary, to first call, to family, marriage, and parenting, including:

* wellness assessments,
* suggestions for a parish transition team when a clergy family leaves and another arrives,
* how to deal with conflict and crisis in the parish when it affects the home, and in the home while minimizing interference by the parish,
* retreats and workshops for clergy family members,
* job descriptions for chaplains for clergy families, and
* lists of contact people and resources in each Episcopal diocese.

It is the source of much of the information described below.

This resource guide is essential, timely, and it sits on shelves because there is no effective distribution system to get resources to clergy families. It was impossible for me to find information from other denominations about resources for clergy families. The topic is not deemed important enough to be on a denomination's website, for instance. There are no systematic ways to collect data on clergy families in the Episcopal Church, either on a diocesan level or nationally. Surely gathering basic information such as a spouse or partner's name, number and ages of children, or contact information for family members independent of the clergy could be part of some denominational official's job description, so that the information could be kept current. That staff person could also arrange workshops, retreats, and support networks for clergy family members — adults and children — and make one-on-one counseling resources available at reasonable prices, ideally subsidized by the denomination in whose service the stress is building. Clergy family members need clergy who are independent of their clergy's deployment or evaluation structures, who can keep confidences, and who have some insight into the unique demands of clergy family life. The absence of people to turn to when problems, large or small, arise in the clergy family is the biggest complaint I have heard from clergy family members. (Clergy schedules, especially as they conflict with family members' schedules, is the second-biggest complaint.)

The absence of attention to clergy families comes in part from a "not my job" mentality, because there are very few other professions that look out for the family members of their employees. Yet this book and others show that the role of clergy families is unique because, more often than not, the family is part of the job. The health of clergy family members has direct implications for the health of the clergy person and the congregation. Many male clergy have also assumed that care of their own family is "not their job" because of socialization of men primarily as economic providers and because the church is seen as more important than the family. Clergy moms know that care of the family is their job, even as they feel that parish ministry impedes their ability to perform that job as well as they would like. Knowing that there are resources for their family members could relieve some of their anxiety about "being all things to all people."

Fair compensation and adequate family resources

There are several issues about fair compensation as it relates to clergy mothers. First, there is a persistent gap, in all denominations, between salaries for women and men, even when experience and job descriptions are taken into account. Zikmund et al. offer some suggestions about how to reduce that gap. One is by using a centralized, denomination-wide employment information system, because that helps the most number of applicants have access to information about the largest number of jobs. They found that denominations that use that system have a wage gap of 6 percent, compared to 12 percent for denominations who don't.[71] Another is to have a denominational staff position specifically dedicated to supporting women in ministry. Such a staff person helps women clergy develop networks, collects information about the status of women clergy, and advocates for needs of clergy women across the system. Zikmund et al. found, however, minimal actual effect on reducing the wage gap, perhaps because they are too far away from the local and regional decision makers to make such a specific intervention.[72]

Second, more women than men are placed in under-resourced parishes, and they tend to stay there longer before finding a parish with a larger budget. This increases the demands on clergy time and energy, and hence increases the pressures of parish expectations on family life.[73]

Third, clergy usually have to negotiate annual salary increases for themselves, even in connectional parishes. In smaller parishes, objective job performance evaluations are less likely to be in place and ever-growing deficits are more likely to be present. It's hard for many clergy of either gender to ask for more money for themselves; it may be harder for women than for men, who have been socialized to value themselves in part by financial earnings and their ability to provide for their family. A clergy salary increase may mean that the parish loses a parish secretary, which will multiply the work expected of the clergy, the equivalent of making bricks without straw. Or the cleric may negotiate reduced hours, but clergy work isn't "clocked" in ways that lend themselves to just working five or ten hours less a week. Without a sustained redistribution of particular tasks to parishioners (e.g., training lay visitors) or off the clergy plate (e.g., eliminating a worship service or program), it's almost impossible to really reduce hours. I return to Loren Mead's observation that the ideal of at least one well-educated full-time professional at every parish, regardless of size, population, neighboring churches, needs, etc. is no longer viable, in terms of either money or parishioner and clergy time and energy.[74]

Parishioners will deny this, will attack the pastor who names the problem, will attack the denominational staff who back up the pastor, because they hear naming of limits, rightly, for the congregation as they have known it. It is hard to do the really creative out-of-the-box thinking about how God wants institutional churches to minister when the survival of the clergy salary line and the congregation itself are so pressing. Many of the women and men I interviewed felt that if they worked less, or took the time they wanted with their families, their congregations would fold. One pastor had been working for five years to reduce parish dependence on him and stabilize social services programs in times of reduced funding sources, and the conscious and unconscious resistance was emotionally exhausting. Would he be a failure if one program closed? Two? Five? On the other hand, his wife was also on staff and she really wanted another baby, but not if they continued to work at their present pace. What will give? What if merging parishes would reduce building expenses and increase parishioner involvement so two clergy could be more fairly paid? What about linking the financial resources of large suburban parishes with the mission needs of inner-city congregations? What about looking at ways (retreats, grants, sabbaticals, in-congregation training) to relieve some of the pressure on clergy who feel called to struggle in difficult, under-resourced or conflict-ridden congregations, so that pastors can be renewed for life at home and in the parish? Sometimes clergy moms, facing exhaustion and burn-out, are the canaries who signal a larger problem in the system.

Fourth, in most mainline denominations there is an ever more formal career ladder for ministry, one that sometimes pits salary needs and standards of professional success against the initial sense of being called by God to serve God's people in the world. One Baptist executive seemed to be equating vocation with sacrifice, financial and otherwise, when he asked, "What if we fashioned the question of ministerial value as calling rather than career? As vocation rather than job? As service and sacrifice rather than security and shortfalls?"[75] I worry that "God's work" becomes an excuse for inadequate compensation, one of the reasons that clergy salaries have been notoriously low and inadequate for family needs. But this executive has a point when clergy and laity lose a sense of God's mission because we can't imagine ways to fund mission other than the status quo. A career-path model assumes that families will have to move to improve their financial situation, and it also assumes that salary, number of parishioners and staff, or complexity of programs define success in ministry rather than naming and working to meet priorities for mission. Salaries are often judged by market standards and sometimes by denominational minimums, but financial support to parishes is based on a theology of voluntary contribution. "If we are going to hold to a career-path model of ministry, it is, of course, essential that we find ways to move women along the path of success. But is that really the best we can do?"[76] What if someone's gifts really are in helping small churches come alive, but small churches can't pay enough to send children to college?

Adequate family resources (in addition to salary) include very basic issues, including maintenance of church-owned housing when it is provided, maternity and parental leave policies, child-care budgets or arrangements at conferences, and development of resources for family members of clergy. Given the complexity of family lives, it may be easier to set aside a pool of money to be given to clergy to pay for child-care in their home than to expect parents to bring children to a common site. One Lutheran woman who left parish ministry to work for the denomination laments that fact that attention to child-care needs is always *ad hoc,* done by volunteers or conference organizers, with no systemic way to address issues when they arise every year. Another woman, complaining about the same issue in her Methodist conference, said that unless there's a plague, clergy with children to care for at required clergy events one year will still have children — a year older — the next year, so why are her conference administrators so surprised that the children are still around year after year? A standing set of procedures for basic child-care issues seems like a very easy thing to implement; funding actual child-care expenses is much more difficult. That this is continually overlooked feels like either disrespect for families or resentment that fewer and fewer clergy have spouses at home to care for all their work as well as family needs. One denominational official said, only half-jokingly, to a woman announcing her pregnancy, "Don't you women know how to prevent these things?"[77] Read: "We didn't have this problem before you women came along." Or you men with working wives. Or you clergy who expect to be whole people with lives outside of the parish.

Respect from denominational officials for church and family responsibilities

Respect from denominational officials for clergy mothers has several dimensions. First, it means advocacy for salary parity for men and women in similar positions, including an analysis of barriers to parity and then steps to eliminate the barriers. There are no denominations where parity exists currently. Second, Lehman's review of six studies of women's ministry found that for women, the strongest predictor of placement was the denomination's formal placement system — the "old boys" network of informal calls and personal connections seems not useful for women. Formal placement systems can increase the number of possible jobs, interviews, preaching visits, and actual calls.[78] Yet before positions even open, denominations need to systematically expose congregations who have never experienced female clergy to women's leadership through interim appointments, supply work, workshops, and any other way to counter stereotypes of women's skills and character. Studies of Baptist and Presbyterian lay people's preferences for male or female clergy performing many different clerical roles showed that initially men are preferred for almost every function, but after seeing women fulfill these roles, the resistance diminishes.[79] One Methodist bishop offers a caveat, however. She found that when she meets with a staff-parish relations committee whose members resist the idea of a woman pastor, "after offering specific examples of successful ministry taking place, and respectfully answering any and all questions, I am astounded by the fact that some lay members don't register the fact that I am a woman!"[80]

Fourth, denominational officials can offer clergy women mentoring and pastoral care that acknowledges the reality and depth of resistance to women in parish leadership and helps clergy identify coping strategies; takes sexual harassment complaints seriously; and listens for new, "nontraditional" gifts, insights, and ways to lead parishes that may help reshape parish ministry overall. Throughout *The Leading Women,* each of these pioneers referred to one or two people, sometimes bishops or district superintendents, sometimes older pastors (male and female) who consistently encouraged them, heard their fear or hesitation at doing something new, and challenged them to take risks.[81] Their stories are too numerous to quote, but again and again I heard echoes of traditional biblical call stories, where God invites, the prophet hesitates, God answers their objection and promises to be with them when they are faithful. Friends can do this too, and should, but the voice of someone with authority and position in the institution carries different and essential weight.

I have linked respect for church and family responsibilities because they seemed like parallel needs for me. I would like to have denominational officials recognize and appreciate my gifts, and help me develop professionally, and I would like some denominational support when I look to make time to be with children or my spouse or accommodate my family's needs. This could be a win-win situation, where as the church implements more and more clergy family-friendly policies, clergy professional gifts also flourish. Yet when vocation is understood as only church responsibilities, it seems as if they are competing or contradictory needs: More attention to family means less attention to church. That's where so much resistance comes from. I hear lay people and some denominational officials often say "you women can't have it all: fulfilling church and family ministry." In God's economy, vocation isn't a zero-sum game: prayer, renewal, a sense of basic competence in home and church fuel both. Fulfillment doesn't have to be measured by number of hours, or programs, or Saturdays worked (although I recognize, as do many of the people I interviewed, that there are real limits of time and energy that cannot be overlooked for long). Yet denominational officials can often see a larger picture of dynamics in many churches. Zikmund et al. found clergy women — but increasingly also young married clergy men with children — leave parish ministry because the struggle to balance work and family life is too great. They suggested that clergy women with young children would probably stay if there were more flexibility and acceptance of combining motherhood with parish ministry. If they respect women's desires to be "good enough" parents and "good enough" pastors, they can help identify new ways of combining resources.[82]

Including clergy families in maps of congregational systems

Nancy Myer Hopkins described the often-overlooked role of the clergy family in the congregational system. A systems theory map of a particular church usually considers clergy and congregation, and perhaps a denominational context. It looks at how clergy family-of-origin issues parallel some congregational dynamics, and how greater self-differentiation in both arenas leads to more satisfying and less conflict-ridden situations. Hopkins suggests that the map also make space for clergy families, since many clergy families are routinely present and participating in congregational life.[83] Even when they're not, lay expectations of what the last pastor's family did create a "ghost" that needs to be recognized and exorcised. In a conflicted parish, some of the conflict usually comes home, and its effects can be seen in family behavior. Often children or spouse or partner are triangulated, so that lay people mad at the pastor insult the spouse instead, or criticize clergy children's behavior in church. Clergy families need to know that someone in the institution hears them, cares about how they are impacted, and is trained to help the family develop effective coping strategies. When clergy are alcoholic, or are abusing family members, there are often signs in the way the clergy person functions in the congregation that could become an entrée to an intervention. Chaplains for clergy families, trained counselors who are not connected to the deployment process and who can be trusted to keep confidences, are essential resources for clergy families. All too often clergy family members feel that they are to be "seen but not heard," which hurts even in everyday situations and can be devastating when conflict erupts.

Ongoing support for clergy families

There is a small amount of information available on the Episcopal, United Methodist, Presbyterian, and Lutheran Church websites about clergy spouses, partners, and families, although I couldn't find it easily. (Once I found the appropriate staff person, they could usually give me the web address.) Many Episcopal dioceses offer annual luncheons for clergy partners and spouses, or clergy and family retreats, or activities organized by the bishop's spouse. I expect other denominations do too, but the resources may only be known locally. The United Methodist website included an article about a district house that that was going to be designated as a "getaway" vacation home for clergy families in need of rest and relaxation. Literature about clergy families seems to have expanded and contracted over the years, as the role of clergy wives changed and then as women became ordained. There is a much larger body of literature about clergy wellness, but it focuses on the clergy person as clergy, not as parent or partner or adult child. One woman told a story about preaching on St. James' Day with her three-year-old son, James, in the front pew. When he heard his name in the sermon, he came running up to her, saying "I'm James, too!" She scooped him into her arms and set him down again quickly, a "mom moment" in the midst of the clergy role, to both delight and dismay among the congregation. Some congregations are more accepting of such moments than others, but our culture, our institutions, and we ourselves are used to maintaining tighter barriers between the personal and professional parts of life, when often they should not be bifurcated.

So what would it be like if we asked the clergy in families to take appropriate responsibility for the well-being of their families? If family members, members of the congregation, and clergy themselves no longer acted as if the parish is automatically the best place in which to serve God? There will be times when the congregations' needs should come first — holidays, worship, pastoral calls, many meetings. Clergy schedules of flexible weekdays and busy evenings and weekends usually reflect the priorities of the congregation. But some meetings can happen during the day instead of in the evening — couples planning a wedding often take time from their work to meet with the florist or photographer but request evening time with a priest when days are only slightly less convenient. In many cases, the behavior of mutual support and choosing among responsibilities as faithfully as possible is already in place. Sometimes clergy desires to be needed, or feel important, or please parishioners can lead us to choose the parish over family. Clergy have to take some responsibility for monitoring our choices. Clergy family members, too, could sometimes question choices made by the clergy — are you really honoring the family as you should? Why suddenly are there four evening meetings a week? Sometimes the answer is procrastination, sometimes it's life: two weddings, a funeral, a convention, and a grant deadline can happen in one crazy week. Capital campaigns or every-member canvasses or starting new programs also take sustained amount of attention and more time than usual for a while. The task of clergy, parish, and family together is to plan how to compensate for that time soon enough for the family not to be really neglected. Here are some ideas to help clergy and family members and congregations juggle competing claims as faithfully as possible.

Chaplains for family members. One of the most consistent complaints of clergy family members is a lack of ongoing denominational support for them. Spouses, partners, or children of clergy usually have no priest. Friendships in the parish are not safe places to talk about stresses within the clergy family or that the clergy person brings home. Some clergy spouses and partners call each other, or develop more or less formal meeting times. *Community of Spice*[84] offers a newsletter; FOCUS has an e-mail list of spouses and partners to share reflections anonymously. Some denominations are intentional about helping clergy family members network. There are times, however, when clergy family members need a safe professional with whom they can talk freely about their own issues, family needs, or concerns about their spouse or partner without fear of consequences for the clergy person at least until the family member it willing to act. Part-time or full-time chaplains for family of clergy, perhaps paid by the denomination but not part of denominational staff with responsibility for clergy, are expensive but invaluable resources to help clergy family members with issues they can't take anywhere else. The FOCUS resource guide offers several job descriptions for part-time and full-time chaplains who are available for short-term pastoral care, some program planning, phone conversations, and general support. Confidentiality is carefully built into these job descriptions.

Marriage/commitment review.

> Over 90 [percent] of female spouses of male clergy work outside the home, with the figure being near 100 [percent] for male spouses of female clergy. The cost of easing financial anxiety has come in the form of a time crunch, with approximately 20 [percent] of clergy reporting that their spouses regularly complain about the amount of time they spent working. Moreover, among clergy women with children, 30 [percent] report that they felt that their ministry did not allow them to spend enough time with their children . . . almost one-fifth of rectors with children in the home regularly consider leaving parish ministry for another form of ministry.[85]

These findings from a survey of Episcopal clergy give a valuable context for understanding the pressures on couples where at least one member is ordained in many denominations. Conversations with lesbian clergy with children at home suggest little difference. One deacon who had been working three-quarters-time in a housing program and volunteering diaconal services at a local parish had to find a different church placement when she and her partner needed to put their children in private high schools; she found a lucrative full-time secular job and a Sunday-only deacon's schedule, allowing her partner to continue lay social services ministry at a lower salary. A lesbian couple, both of whom are ordained, and have two children at home, have spent most of their careers as mothers alternating between one full-time and one part-time position to provide adequate care. A gay male couple, also both ordained, with an adult child with special needs, offer room and board and a small stipend for a nanny to cover times they are both at work. Constant juggling is the norm, and greater daytime flexibility of many clergy means that "family time" is often given to children rather than spouses or partners.

The FOCUS Resource Guide includes a Health Index for Clergy and Clergy Partners and a marriage health assessment tool, based on the Book of Common Prayer wedding vows, and a modified tool for gay and lesbian couples. It is an instrument that couples can use on their own, or it could be the focus of a three-hour clergy couple workshop. But assessment is just the beginning. Many large churches offer regular weekend marriage retreats for lay congregants. Denominations could help fund some one- or two-day "commitment renewal" opportunities. Scheduling of lay and clergy two-day affairs is tricky when we assume that clergy can't be gone on Sunday. But what if denominations said to their congregations that once every few years clergy in marriages or committed relationships ought to have a Sunday off, with pay, so they could participate in a workshop designed to strengthen their relationship? Arranging child-care and Sunday coverage are manageable hurdles when a systemic commitment to the health of relationships is clear.

The care and feeding of clergy children. FOCUS also designed an evaluation of time with children based on the Book of Common Prayer liturgy for the Thanksgiving for the Birth of a Child, to help clergy reflect on their parenting. The resource guide offers examples of four retreats specifically for clergy families, from four different dioceses, ranging from a day to a weekend. Topics included naming the specific joys and pressures for clergy and spouses and partners, attitudes and behaviors conducive to family growth, how parishes can create a "clergy family-friendly environment," an appreciative inquiry session around the question "In light of the baptismal covenant, where is God calling us as individuals, couples and as a community?"[86] For a few years, the Diocese of Newark found funding to subsidize clergy family weekends, when congregations were told that clergy needed to be away and the congregation had to arrange substitute clergy or lay-led worship. The families who participated were very pleased with the connections they were able to develop with other families and with the opportunity to have their role in the church system validated. Several models of clergy family retreats are available in the resource guide.

Bruce Hardy, a Baptist pastor, offers several recommendations specifically for the care of clergy children by parents, congregations, and denominations:

- Encourage children to be themselves, freed from expectations of perfect manners, church knowledge, and behavior, and in an environment where their unique identity as an irreplaceable child of God is nurtured.

- Be sensitive to the grief clergy children experience when the family moves. Rituals of departure and arrival, some help in saying good-byes to important people, and just acknowledgement of their losses can help them make the transition to a new place.

- Provide the clergy more time to be with their family. This could happen through fun, through partially subsidized denominational or ecumenical activities for clergy families or children, through more vacation time for the clergy member, and by reminders from lay leaders and denominational officials that God values family time too!

- Provide the ministry of adult advocacy for clergy children. A lay person known and trusted by the child whose parish job it is to nurture the child's growth, help in times of parish crisis, and advocate for the clergy children's well-being would address the imbalance of power that children experience as youth in an adult institution.

- Let clergy children choose among resources to nurture their own faith.[87]

Sometimes having the pastor and parent in one role is just too much. Heidi Neumark described one particularly trying day when her two-year-old child was on the altar with her in the absence of other child-care options, wanting desperately to receive communion when it was not the custom in that parish to let children receive. As the priest, she had to refuse her child communion; as the mom, she couldn't provide the solace her screaming child needed. She concluded, "I went home feeling like a two-headed monster: Mommy-Pastor, a horror to one and all."[88] I've been there, done that, and it's not fair to the child. Fortunately, in a week full of interactions between parent and child, most are more positive than that. Most Sundays or shared worship times aren't like that, either — we tend to forget the many positive or neutral incidents of conflicting roles.

Preordination discernment. Different denominations include spouses or partners of people considering ordained ministry in different ways and at various parts of the process. Research about what kind of support for family members is most helpful is necessary before any generalizations can be made, but FOCUS lists some issues that ought to be addressed early in the process of deciding to pursue ordination: time, money, involvement in the process, self-care for the potential clergy person and for their family members, unique stresses on clergy families, and theology (e.g., how do family members relate to the biblical injunction for disciples to "hate" their family, or leave the family to follow Jesus, or be a wholesome example for the congregation?).[89]

The Rev. Dr. Ellen Sloan is chaplain at the General Theological Seminary in New York City. For the past three years, she has offered biannual retreats for seminarians and their significant others. In those retreats and in conversations through the years, she has noted the level of serious identity issues for many spouses and partners that are often simply not seen by the seminarians, engaged as they are in their own exciting, scary, new career, or by the sponsoring congregation or denominational office. Huge changes in financial resources, often a forced change in a spouse's job that may or may not be as satisfying as previous work, often geographical relocation — including, in many cases, moving to a seminary campus where privacy is at a premium — and pressing needs or stresses of children also experiencing change can place a strain on any relationship. Dr. Sloan found that many couples don't seem to have the communication skills to talk with each other about the effects of these changes on themselves or their relationship. Suddenly one spouse's or partner's needs are cloaked in a language of holiness or faithfulness to God that makes that person's needs seem automatically more important, even as resentment or jealousy flare. She has suggested couples' counseling for many couples, but couples' counseling is not covered by many health plans and is often too expensive for people living on an already reduced budget. The FOCUS resource guide includes several outlines of programs at Episcopal seminaries also designed to meet some of these needs.

Support for families in transition. Many denominations now offer a module of continuing education when pastors begin a new cure. In the Episcopal Church, *Fresh Start* is a popular model; the Alban Institute's *New Beginnings: A Pastorate Start-Up Workbook*[90] by Roy Oswald offers another approach. Unfortunately, these models don't include much attention to clergy families, and they make no provision for members of clergy families to participate in any structured program when they have recently relocated. The FOCUS resource guide offers a model for an hour-long discussion involving clergy and their families, to help bring attention to family needs at the beginning of a new ministry. It asks clergy and members of their family to think about how the congregation perceives the family in the local church system, and how and when family members are either especially visible (e.g., when the spouse or partner hosts — or doesn't host — events in a different pattern than the previous family, or when the children raise holy hell in a church event) or invisible (e.g., same-sex partners, family members who must not be important because they don't attend church frequently, partners who care for the family behind the scenes and free the clergy person for church work). It asks all members of the family to name and claim their own baptismal ministry independent of the needs of the congregation. It emphasizes the need for someone to function as a pastor for family members, providing a safe, confidential, and supportive place to deal with tensions arising from the clergy person's work with the congregation. And it encourages family members of clergy to develop their own support networks outside of the congregation for ongoing support.[91]

FOCUS also offers a guide to help congregations prepare for the arrival of a new family, to reduce the sense of panic at having to reconstruct basic family resources — doctors, schools, children's activities, take-out restaurants, maps of the town, and the like.[92] They recommend specific tasks for denominational officials, lay leadership boards, search committees, and transition committees (a group of people specifically designated to help the new family become acclimated, which could make themselves available for up to a year).[93] They recommend that lay leadership boards and willing members of the clergy family spend some time together talking about the history of previous clergy families in the congregation, and the history of the clergy family in previous congregations. This helps surface possible differences from the beginning, and prevents some disappointment or resentment at unmet (because unknown) expectations.[94] Finally, it offers a list of "exit issues" for clergy family members to consider, to help them say good-bye well to one place and get ready to move on.[95]

Support for clergy families in crisis or change. Birth, illness, death, addiction, divorce, or other crises can affect any family, and have ramifications for parents' work schedules and career. Yet the public role of the clergy member's family in the life of the church brings added stress and support to clergy families in crisis. A parish I know was aghast one Easter when the rector's two teenaged daughters came to church very late on Easter Sunday, dressed in leather and chains. This fired a "secret" parish-wide discussion about loud arguments in the rectory, daughters' problems in school, clergy parenting styles — no one seemed to remember that gossip is one of the sins Paul most frequently railed against! Ordinary stresses and strains of adolescents can be magnified to no one's advantage.

Then there are the not-so-ordinary stresses: The pastor's spouse shows up drunk again at a church function. Or a pastor is charged with sexual misconduct with a parishioner, or the rector's wife moves with her children into the local battered women's shelter. Even the positive changes — birth, or adoption, meeting and making a lifelong commitment to a partner, marriage or civil union ceremony, children's or spouses accomplishments — bring stress. Denominational officials often can't be trusted to provide necessary help because of systemic conflicts of interest with supervisory roles of clergy. Chaplains or a network of referrals to professionals are essential resources for clergy families.

Conclusion: slouching toward vocation

Listen to this story of a multicultural lesbian couple, both of whom are ordained, and their two adopted children. In it you hear systemic help and hurt, personal choices, crises and resolution, and an ongoing weaving of family, church, social service, and justice ministries with the quest for "a life" for all involved.

The two women met in seminary in the late 1980s. Michelle was ordained in 1989 and on staff of a large church full-time for the next three years. Pat worked in social service agencies during that time, and was eventually ordained as well. In the mid-1990s, they wanted to start a family, and both started doctoral programs because that gave them more control over their schedules than either agency or parish, although it depleted their savings.

But the doctoral programs didn't affect their finances as much as adopting children. Their first child arrived in 1997; Pat was working full-time and Michelle did workshops, supply preaching, and adjunct teaching. In 2000, a full-time and part-time position opened in the same town at the same time, which worked well for everyone in their family. Then the adoption of a second child was held up at the last minute because of concerns in the adoption agency about their sexual orientation. Michelle said that they'd never lied about their orientation during the first twelve months of paperwork, but once a child was available, and despite having the birth mother's blessing, the agency balked and the two moms and the three-year-old daughter were stranded in another state for a month as they fought for their second child. The unanticipated extra month in hotels emptied their savings account and used up their maternity leaves, so when they returned home with their newborn son, he came to work with them daily until he was six months old. The parish was supportive, but multitasking full-time work with a newborn (and a toddler in day-care) was exhausting. At six months of age, the baby could start at the same day-care center as his sister, which was wonderful for a year, until the day-care closed suddenly and they were back to juggling two young children and had no extended family to help.

This led to a decision to move to be near extended family, and became a huge blessing: When Michelle told a potential employer, the senior pastor of a multistaff parish, of her need to put her family first, his response was "you're hired." So she was, but it took Pat another six months before she was working steadily in a social service agency. Six months later, the senior pastor left, the parish decided not to hire an interim in order to save money, and Michelle was working up to sixty or seventy hours a week. Two years later, Pat's social service agency folded suddenly, the new senior pastor gave Michelle a year to find a new position, and the financial merry-go-round started again, this time complicated by their older child's special educational needs. Fortunately, one of their denominations has an "emergency family needs fund" that helped them generously with covering the cost of special educational needs — a good example of concrete help for clergy families that enabled them to do what they needed to do.

The search for stable employment for both parents, in a congregation and town that welcomes multiracial families, continues. Michelle says that while they have no financial safety net, and discrimination in the hiring process is often obvious, they have consistently been able to "make a way out of no way" and offer their gifts to their children, their churches, and their world. Faith in their vocation balances clarity about their gifts, limits, and needs with flexibility in how those gifts and needs will be met. God takes the pieces of their lives and knits them into a whole both more fragile and more secure than they could ever imagine.

This story and many throughout this book remind me of the stories of Mary and Joseph in the infancy narratives. The angels' invitation to both of them paralleled in structure the prophetic calls of Hebrew Scriptures. God, or a messenger of God, brings an invitation. "Mary, will you bear the Son of God?" "Joseph, do not be afraid to take Mary as your wife." Mary and Joseph both hesitated and voiced at least one objection. God addressed the objection, and they agreed. Garland compares Mary and Joseph's calling to be Jesus' family to Jesus' later calling of the disciples to leave everything behind and follow him.[96] The command to Joseph to take the baby and his tired mother and flee to Egypt was also a call to leave everything and follow, but here the family follows together, trusting each other and God.[97]

In a different way in Luke, Anna and Simeon sent the holy family back to Nazareth having fulfilled all the temple obligations decently and in order. In Nazareth "the child grew and became strong, filled with wisdom, and the favor of God rested on him."[98] My life, and the lives of the people in this book, has included periods of journeys into the unknown and periods of settled stability in family life, in professional work, in self-discovery, and in local or global community. It may be clear in retrospect how God was present, but on the way either to Egypt or to Nazareth, I expect that Mary and Joseph wondered, worried, prayed, and hoped that they would be able to do the right thing for themselves, God, and their new son. I expect that the worry never stopped; even when Jesus was an adult, Mary tried at times to give him advice and keep him safe. There was no more divine protection for this family than for any other, though also no less. The Scriptures are clear about how Mary, Joseph, and Jesus fulfilled their role in God's plan of salvation, but they may have understood how only in retrospect. Parenting, parish ministry, social service work, social justice advocacy, nurturing a relationship, rejoicing at some times, crying desperately at others, and finding glimpses of God along the way — this is vocation. The desire to be faithful starts us on a path of intentional choice. The risk of the unknown and the reassurance of unexpected blessings along the way keeps us juggling the joys and trials of commitment to God, self, others, and creation. Scriptures are clear that the world is never ready for all that God wants to offer. Vocation includes clearing away some of the barriers to abundant life created by fear, injustice, and indifference. And some days we look back and see so clearly how we were led to ever-expanding experiences of the love and grace that truly sustained us and blessed the world. The other day I complained to a friend about feeling stuck in a very messy period of life. Her answer was "it all works out in the end." I rolled my eyes — at that moment I was convinced that both girls would end up on the streets, the parish would go bankrupt, and I would be alone for the rest of my life. "And if it hasn't worked out yet," she continued, "it isn't the end."

God's promise is not that we will be free from suffering or struggle, but that a love deeper than any suffering we will know will sustain us. A new mystery will unfold. Hearts and households and commitments will expand. The gifts of God's commonwealth will be shared more broadly, one victory at a time. And ultimately each particular person, family, and congregation will know how their story advanced God's story of salvation. We will be "strengthened in our inner beings with power through [God's] Spirit . . . rooted and grounded in love . . . so that [we are] filled with all the fullness of God."[99] It will indeed work out in the end, more marvelously than we could ever ask or imagine.

Notes

Preface

1. Nelle Morton, *The Journey Is Home* (Boston: Beacon Press, 1985).

Chapter 1: The First Invitation

1. "A Complex Life" is the title of chapter 1 of Barbara Brown Zikmund, Adair T. Lummis, and Patricia Mei Yin Chang, *Clergy Women: An Uphill Calling* (Louisville, KY: Westminster John Knox Press, 1998).

2. In Barbara Glanz, *Balancing Acts: More than 250 Guiltfree, Creative Ideas to Blend Your Work and Your Life* (Dearborn, MI: Dearborn Trade Publishing, 2003), 1–6, Patricia Roehling prefers "blend" of work and family life to "balance." "Blend" seems truer to my experience of more permeable boundaries and more fluid movement between commitments.

3. Zikmund et al., *Clergy Women*, 29.

4. Jeremiah 1:5, Psalm 139.

5. Dag Hammarskjold, *Markings* (London: Faber and Faber, 1964), 169.

6. Carol Ochs, *Women and Spirituality* (Boston: Rowman and Allanheld, 1983), 136.

7. Luke 7:7, Psalm 8:4.

8. *The Book of Common Prayer* (New York: Church Publishing Incorporated, 1979), 299.

9. N. T. Wright, *Surprised by Hope* (New York: HarperOne, 2008), 288–89.

10. Lisa Belkin, *Life's Work* (New York: Simon and Schuster, 2002), 14, 16.

Chapter 2: Collisions of Joys

1. This has been attributed to Bishop James Pike, in *US News & World Report* (May 16, 1960), at Bartleby's Quotations website; "In his sermons, Martin Luther King Jr. was fond of quipping that 'eleven o'clock Sunday morning is the most segregated hour and Sunday school is still the most segregated school of the week.'" At *http://jmm.aaa.net.au/articles/17314.htm.*

2. Louie Crew, "Black Priests in the Episcopal Church," ©1998, 2002, at *http://rci .rutgers.edu/~lcrew/blkpr.html#fem.*

3. Based on data found in "A Report on Episcopal Church in the United States" prepared by C. Kirk Hadaway for the Office of Congregational Development of the Domestic and Foreign Missionary Society of the Episcopal Church, April 2002. Cited by Louie Crew, "Black Priests in the Episcopal Church."

4. M. Wyvetta Bullock, cited in an April 2005 *Leadership Initiative,* at *www.elca.org/leadership/initiative.*

5. 2007–2009 Directory of Black Presbyterian Congregations, online at *www.pcusa.org/blackcongregations/aapc.htm,* 71–75.

6. Barbara Brown Zikmund, Adair T. Lummis, and Patricia Mei Yin Chang, *Clergy Women: An Uphill Calling* (Louisville, KY: Westminster John Knox Press, 1998), 6, 155.

7. Edward Lehman, "Women's Path into Ministry: Six Studies," *Pulpit and Pew Research Report* (Fall 2002): 14.

8. Ibid.

9. "Clergywomen of Color Build Unity to Build Influence," at *www.gbhem.org/site/c.lsKSL3POLvF/b.3833613,* January 2008.

10. UMC Global Ministry in Higher Education Report, "The Status of Racial-Ethnic Minority Clergywomen in the United Methodist Church," 2004, at *www.gbhem.org/ResourceLibrary/RacialEthnicCWStudy.pdf.*

11. Lehman, "Women's Path into Ministry," 14.

12. Zikmund et al., *Clergy Women,* 6.

13. Matthew Price, "State of the Clergy 2006" (New York: Church Pension Group, 2006), 12–14. At *www.cpg.org/formspublications/research.cfm.*

14. Cf. Sally Purvis, *The Stained Glass Ceiling* (Louisville, KY: Westminster John Knox Press, 1995) or Zikmund et al., *Clergy Women,* 6.

15. *www.religioustolerance.org/hom_chur2.htm* lists "Policies of 47 Christian Denominations about Homosexuality"; I confirmed the facts that I cite on the denominational websites.

16. *www.mccchurch.org.*

17. Mary Jane Hitt, "Shape the Debate by the 'Upside-Down Gospel'," in Lehman, "Women's Path into Ministry," 43.

18. Max Weber, *Protestant Ethic and the Spirit of Capitalism,* trans. Talcott Parsons (Mineola, NY: Dover Publications, 2003).

19. Mary Blair-Loy, *Competing Devotions* (Cambridge, MA: Harvard University Press, 2003), 19.

20. Ibid., 19–20, summarizing William Whyte, *The Organization Man* (New York: Simon and Schuster, 1956).

21. Blair-Loy, *Competing Devotions,* 21.

22. Ibid., 21 and chapter 3, "Reinventing Schemas: Creating Part-time Careers."

23. Blair Loy, *Competing Devotions,* 19.

24. Ibid.

25. Ibid., 52, citing several sociological studies in the 1990s.

26. Evelyn Kirkley, "'Mrs. God': The Role of the Minister's Wife, 1930–1980," master's thesis, Union Theological Seminary, 1985, 22.

27. Leonard Steinhorn, *The Greater Generation: In Defense of the Baby Boom Legacy* (New York: Thomas Dunne Books/St. Martin's Press, 2006), 94.

28. Kirkley, "'Mrs. God,'" 25.

29. Ibid.

30. Ibid., 36.

31. Diana Garland, *Family Ministry: A Comprehensive Guide* (Downers Grove, IL: Intervarsity Press, 1999), 251.

32. Ibid., 251, quoting Frances and Joseph Gies, *Marriage and Family in the Middle Ages* (New York: Harper and Row, 1987).

33. Garland, *Family Ministry,* 263.

34. Ann Douglas, *The Feminization of American Culture* (New York: Farrar, Straus, and Giroux, 1977; 2nd ed., 1998), 24.

35. Ibid., 33–34.

36. Ibid., 48.

37. Douglas' carefully nuanced argument is found in *The Feminization of American Culture,* chapter 2.

38. Ibid., 86–87.

39. Linda Gordon, *Pitied but Not Entitled: Single Mothers and the History of Welfare* (Cambridge, MA: Harvard University Press, 1994), 18.

40. Lenore Weitzman, *Marriage Contract: Spouses, Lovers and the Law* (New York: Free Press, 1981) or *The Divorce Revolution: The Unexpected Social and Economic Consequences for Women and Children in America* (New York: Free Press; London: Collier Macmillan, 1985).

41. Stephanie Coontz, *The Way We Never Were: American Families and the Nostalgia Trap* (New York: Basic Books, 1992).

42. Gloria Albrecht, *Hitting Home* (New York: Continuum, 2002), 21.

43. Garland, *Family Ministry,* 261.

44. Coontz, *The Way We Never Were,* 240.

45. Garland, *Family Ministry,* 253.

46. Ibid., 265.

47. Ibid., 268.

48. Ibid., 266.

49. Ibid., 265, quoting Paula England, Carmen Garcia-Beaulieu, and Mary Ross, "Women's Employment among Blacks, Whites, and Three Groups of Latinas," *Gender and Society* 18 (2004): 494–509.

50. Garland, *Family Ministry,* 264.

51. Lisa Belkin, "Family Needs in the Legal Balance," *New York Times,* July 30, 2006, Section 10, 1.

52. Garland, *Family Ministry,* 268.

53. Coontz, *The Way We Never Were,* 276.

54. Stephanie Coontz, *Marriage: A History* (New York: Free Press, 2003), 262.

55. Ibid., 271.

56. Ibid., 274–79.

57. Garland, *Family Ministry,* 38.

58. Coontz, *Marriage*, 264.

59. Garland, *Family Ministry*, 50.

60. Pew Research Center Social Trends Report, "From the Age of Aquarius to the Age of Responsibility: Baby Boomers Approach Sixty," released December 8, 2005, at *http://pewresearch.org/assets/social/pdf/socialtrends-boomers120805.pdf*.

61. Family Caregiver Alliance, "Women and Caregiving: Facts and Figures," May 2003, at *www.caregiver.org/caregiver/jsp/content_node.jsp?nodeid=892*.

62. Ibid.

63. Sara Curran, "Choice or Struggle: Overcoming the Cult of Motherhood and the Cult of the Successful Worker," Gender and Policy Network, Princeton University, November 2006 (*curran@princeton.edu*).

64. Joan Williams, *Unbending Gender: Why Work and Family Conflict and What to Do About It* (New York: Oxford University Press, 2000).

65. Blair-Loy, *Competing Devotions*, 117.

66. Vashti McKenzie, *Not Without a Struggle: Leadership Development for African American Women in Ministry* (Cleveland: Pilgrim Press, 1996), 31–33.

67. Lehman, "Women's Path into Ministry," 4.

68. Advocacy Committee for Women's Concerns, The Presbyterian Church USA, "Clergywomen's Experiences in Ministry: Realities and Challenges," 2003, 10.

69. McKenzie, *Not Without a Struggle*, xvi.

70. Jackson Carroll, Barbara Hargrove, and Adair Lummis, *Women of the Cloth* (San Francisco: Harper and Row, 1983), 77–78.

71. McKenzie, *Not Without a Struggle*, xvi.

72. Pamela Cooper White, "Becoming a Clergy Mother: A Study of How Motherhood Changes Ministry," *Congregations* 2004-07-01, no. 3 (Summer 2004): 7–8.

73. McKenzie, *Not Without a Struggle*, xvii.

74. Robert Putnam, *Bowling Alone* (New York: Simon and Schuster, 2000), 19.

75. Ibid., 289.

76. Ibid., 283.

77. Ibid., 72.

78. Ibid.

79. An interesting observation: The teenaged children of clergy who responded said that their best support group was friends, in or out of the church; adult family members never mentioned friends as a source of support.

80. Jay Sidebotham, 2006 Church Pension Fund Calendar, December.

81. Jackson Carroll, *As One with Authority: Reflective Leadership in Ministry* (Louisville, KY: Westminster John Knox, 1991), 42.

82. Ibid., 57.

83. Barbara Brown Taylor, *Leaving Church: A Memoir of Faith* (San Francisco: Harper-SanFrancisco, 2006), 159 for particular image; chapter 13, 155–66 for general points.

84. Ephesians 4:11–16.

85. Matthew Price, "State of the Clergy 2003" (New York: Church Pension Group, 2003), 6–7. At *www.cpg.org/formspublications/research.cfm*.

86. Becky R. McMillan and Matthew J. Price, "How Much Should We Pay the Pastor? A Fresh Look at Clergy Salaries in the 21st Century," *Pulpit and Pew Research Report* (May 2003): 2.

87. McKenzie, *Not Without a Struggle*, 87.

Chapter 3: Differentiating Service to God and Service to the Church

1. "Blessing of a Marriage," *The Book of Common Prayer,* 423.

2. Violet Fisher, in Judith Craig, *The Leading Women: Stories of the First Women Bishops of the United Methodist Church* (Nashville, TN: Abingdon Press, 2004), 64.

3. Susan Wolfe Hassinger in Craig, *The Leading Women*, 81.

4. Barbara Brown Zikmund, Adair T. Lummis, and Patricia Mei Yin Chang, *Clergy Women: An Uphill Calling* (Louisville, KY: Westminster John Knox Press, 1998), 7–14.

5. Jackson Carroll, *As One with Authority: Reflective Leadership in Ministry* (Louisville, KY: Westminster John Knox, 1991), 57–58.

6. See, for example, Lloyd Edwards, *Discerning Your Spiritual Gifts* (Cambridge, MA: Cowley Publications, 1988).

7. Ruth S. Osborne, "Releases, Fertility, Women," U.S. Census Bureau News, October 23, 2003. See *www.census.gov/Press-Release/www/releases/archives/fertility/001491.html.*

8. Ibid.

9. Table 5, "Employment status of the population by sex, marital status, and presence and age of own children under 18, 2005–06 annual averages." United States Bureau of Labor Statistics. At *http://pewresearch.org/assets/social/pdf/WomenWorking.pdf.*

10. Carol Ochs, *Women and Spirituality* (Totowa, NJ: Rowman and Allanheld, 1983; rev. ed. 1996), 134–44.

11. Margaret Hebblethwaite, *Motherhood and God* (London: Geoffrey Chapman, 1984).

12. Suzanne Guthrie, *Praying the Hours* (Cambridge, MA: Cowley Publications, 2000) or *Grace's Window* (Cambridge, MA: Cowley Publications, 1996).

13. Zikmund et al., *Clergy Women*, chapter 6, "An Expanding Ministry."

14. Barbara Brown Taylor, *Leaving Church: A Memoir of Faith* (San Francisco: Harper-SanFrancisco, 2006), 4.

15. Matthew Price, "State of the Clergy 2003" (New York: Church Pension Group, 2003), 4. Online at *www.cpg.org/formspublications/research.cfm.*

16. Taylor, *Leaving Church*, 37.

17. Melissa Martin, *For Better or for Worse: A Blessing or a Curse, Domestic Violence in the Christian Home* (Phoenix, AZ: It's Women's Work, 1999).

18. I know this from experience working at a battered women's shelter; it's confirmed in Marie Fortune and James Poling, "Calling to Accountability: The Church's Response to Abusers" in Carol J. Adams and Marie M. Fortune, *Violence Against Women and Children: A Theological Sourcebook* (New York: Continuum, 1995), 452.

19. Stanley Grenz and Roy D. Bell, *Betrayal of Trust: Confronting and Preventing Clergy Sexual Misconduct* (Downers Grove, IL: InterVarsity Press, 1995), 118–24.

20. James Nelson, *Embodiment: An Approach to Sexuality and Christian Theology* (Minneapolis, MN: Augsburg Fortress, 1978); Marie M. Fortune, *Love Does No Harm: Sexual Ethics for the Rest of Us* (New York: Continuum International, 1998); and Karen Lebacqz, *Professional Ethics: Power and Paradox* (Nashville, TN: United Methodist Publishing House, 1985).

21. Diana Garland, *Family Ministry: A Comprehensive Guide* (Downers Grove, IL: Intervarsity Press, 1999), 276.

22. Leonard Sweet, *The Minister's Wife: Her Role in 19th Century American Evangelicalism* (Philadelphia, PA: Temple University Press, 1983), 3.

23. Evelyn Kirkley, " 'Mrs. God': The Role of the Minister's Wife, 1930–1980," master's thesis, Union Theological Seminary, 1985, 53–54.

24. Richard Schori, personal conversation, quoted with permission in March 2008 e-mail correspondence.

25. Zikmund et al., *Clergy Women*, 156–57.

26. Eugene Peterson, *The Message* (Colorado Springs, CO: NavPress, 2002), 135.

27. Exodus 18:15–40:38.

28. Exodus 18:23.

Chapter 4: Life on the Tightrope

1. Dean R. Hoge and Jacqueline E. Wenger, *Pastors in Transition: Why Clergy Leave Local Church Ministry* (Grand Rapids, MI: William B. Eerdmans, 2005), 180.

2. Ibid., 178–79.

3. Advocacy Committee for Women's Concerns, "Clergywomen's Experiences in Ministry: Realities and Challenges 2003," *Presbyterian Church USA* (2005): 25. At *www.pcusa .org/acwc.*

4. Ibid., 17.

5. Kenneth Inskeep and Victoria Flood, "35th Anniversary of Ordination of Women Rostered Leader Survey 2005 — Report 1," Research and Evaluation, ELCA, September 2006, 3.

6. Ibid., 10–11.

7. Pamela Cooper White, "Becoming a Clergy Mother: A Study of How Motherhood Changes Ministry," *Congregations* 2004-07-01, no. 3 (Summer 2004): 4.

8. Advocacy Committee for Women's Concerns, "Clergywomen's Experiences in Ministry," 22.

9. Judith Craig, *The Leading Women: Stories of the First Women Bishops of the United Methodist Church* (Nashville, TN: Abingdon Press, 2004), 85.

10. Janice Riggle Huie, quoted in Craig, *The Leading Women*, 111.

11. Vashti McKenzie, *Not Without a Struggle: Leadership Development for African American Women in Ministry* (Cleveland: Pilgrim Press, 1996), 36.

12. Kate Moorehead, "Raising a Family as a Priest," *www.episcopalchurch.org/34303_ 34100_ENG_HTM.htm?menu=menu4540.*

13. Inskeep et al., "Rostered Leaders," 10. Seventy-five percent of white male clergy found their first call within one to four months, compared to 56 percent of male clergy of color; only 3 percent of white men waited more than a year for a call, compared to

15 percent for male clergy of color. Statistics for women were not different because of ethnicity, and were similar to numbers for male clergy of color.

14. Quotation from a survey distributed to clergy in the Episcopal Diocese of Newark in January 2007.

15. Craig, *The Leading Women*, 85.

16. Cooper White, "Becoming a Clergy Mother," 3.

17. Bruce Hardy, "Pastoral Care with Clergy Children," *Review and Expositor* 98 (Fall 2001): 551.

18. Barbara Brown Zikmund, Adair T. Lummis, and Patricia Mei Yin Chang, *Clergy Women: An Uphill Calling* (Louisville, KY: Westminster John Knox Press, 1998), 122.

19. Ibid., 123.

20. Matthew Price, "State of the Clergy 2006" (New York: Church Pension Group, 2006), 10. At *www.cpg.org/formspublications/research.cfm.*

21. Ibid., 12–13.

22. Zikmund et al., *Clergy Women*, 89, citing Paula D. Nesbitt, "Marriage, Parenthood, and the Ministry: Differential Effects of Marriage on Male and Female Clergy Careers," *Sociology of Religion* 56 (Winter 1995): 397–419.

23. Zikmund et al., *Clergy Women*, 87–91.

24. Karen Powers edits a newsletter for family members of clergy called *Community of Spice*, which had an issue devoted to adult PK's reflections on their experiences. It can be found at *www.communityofspice.org.*

25. Bruce Hardy, "Pastoral Care with Clergy Children," 550.

26. Kate Moorehead, "Raising a Family as a Priest," *www.episcopalchurch.org/34303_ 34100_ENG_HTM.htm?menu=menu4540.*

27. Quotation from a response to a survey distributed to clergy in the Episcopal Diocese of Newark in January 2007.

28. Zikmund et al., *Clergy Women*, 41.

29. Ibid.

30. Hoge and Wenger, *Pastors in Transition*, 151.

31. Ibid., 144.

32. Zikmund et al., *Clergy Women*, 23.

33. Jackson Carroll, *As One with Authority: Reflective Leadership in Ministry* (Louisville, KY: Westminster John Knox, 1991), 21–23.

34. Cooper White, "Becoming a Clergy Mother," 3.

35. Barbara Brown Taylor, *Leaving Church: A Memoir of Faith* (San Francisco: Harper-SanFrancisco, 2006), 98.

36. Ibid., 46.

37. Cooper White, "Becoming a Clergy Mother," 3.

38. Edward Lehman, "Women's Path into Ministry: Six Studies," *Pulpit and Pew Research Report* (Fall 2002): 24.

39. Advocacy Committee for Women's Concerns, "Clergywomen's Experience in Ministry," 21.

40. Ibid., 26.

41. Ibid., 20.

42. Ibid., 21–23.

43. J. Elise Brown, "The Story Is Still Unfolding," response to Lehman, "Women's Path into Ministry," 39.

44. Lehman, "Women's Paths into Ministry," 25.

45. McKenzie, Not Without a Struggle, 36–37.

46. Ibid., 67.

47. Charlene P. Kammerer, "View from the First Wave," response to Lehman, "Women's Path into Ministry," 44.

48. Taylor, Leaving Church, 73.

Chapter 5: Unchosen Dimensions of Vocation

1. Matthew 16:24–25.

2. Barbara Brown Taylor, Leaving Church: A Memoir of Faith (San Francisco: Harper-SanFrancisco, 2006), 47.

3. Valerie Saiving, in "The Human Situation: A Feminine View," in Womanspirit Rising: A Feminist Reader in Religion, ed. Carol P. Christ and Judith Plaskow (San Francisco: Harper & Row, 1979), 25–42, was one of the first women to name this dynamic; bell hooks, Feminist Theory: from Margin to Center (Boston: South End Press, 2000) analyzes this idea in more depth, as do other feminist and womanist theorists.

4. Jean Baker Miller, Towards a New Psychology of Women (Boston: Beacon Press, 1987) named this dynamic clearly, and the work of the Stone Center at Wellesley College elaborates on it in the development of relational-cultural theory.

5. Vashti McKenzie, Not Without a Struggle: Leadership Development for African American Women in Ministry (Cleveland: Pilgrim Press, 1996), 89.

6. Ibid., 86–87.

7. Dean R. Hoge and Jacqueline E. Wenger, Pastors in Transition: Why Clergy Leave Local Church Ministry (Grand Rapids, MI: William B. Eerdmans, 2005), 178–85.

8. Karl Jaspers, Philosophy, trans. E. B. Ashton (Chicago: University Of Chicago Press, 1969–71), 2:178, quoted in Carol Ochs, Women and Spirituality (Totowa, NJ: Rowman and Allanheld, 1983; 2nd ed., Rowman and Littlefield, 1996), 59–60.

9. Ochs, Women and Spirituality, 117.

10. Joanna Trollope, The Rector's Wife (New York: Random House, 1991).

11. Arch Hart, Fuller Seminary, at Glen Eyrie Conference Center, Colorado Springs, CO, November 7–10, 1991, quoted in Fred Lehr, Clergy Burnout (Minneapolis, MN: Augsburg Fortress, 2006), 4.

12. Matthew Price, "State of the Clergy 2003" (New York: Church Pension Group, 2003), 2. At www.cpg.org/formspublications/research.cfm.

13. Hoge and Wenger, Pastors in Transition, 74.

14. Ibid., 178–79, 184.

15. Loren Mead, Financial Meltdown in the Mainline? (Bethesda, MD: Alban Institute, 1998), 144.

16. Becky R. McMillan and Matthew J. Price, "How Much Should We Pay the Pastor? A Fresh Look at Clergy Salaries in the 21st Century," *Pulpit and Pew Research Report* (May 2003): 12–13.

17. Ibid., 2.

18. Matthew 10:34.

19. Matthew 10:37–38.

20. John 15:12–15.

21. Ochs, *Women and Spirituality*, 135.

Chapter 6: A Wider Vision of Vocation

1. Pamela Cooper White, "Becoming a Clergy Mother: A Study of How Motherhood Changes Ministry," *Congregations* 2004-07-01, no. 3 (Summer 2004): 4.

2. See Leviticus 18:21, a prohibition against child sacrifice that immediately precedes the prohibition against male homosexuality in a context of sexual offenses.

3. Marie Fortune, *Sexual Violence: The Unmentionable Sin* (New York: Pilgrim Press, 1983), 71.

4. Ibid.

5. Margaret Farley, "The Church and the Family: An Ethical Task," *Horizons* 10, no. 1 (1983): 51.

6. Diana Garland, *Family Ministry: A Comprehensive Guide* (Downers Grove, IL: Intervarsity Press, 1999), 35.

7. Ibid., 38.

8. Ibid., 39.

9. Mark 4:31–35.

10. Reinhold Niebuhr, *Moral Man and Immoral Society: A Study of Ethics and Politics* (first published in 1932 by Charles Scribner's Sons; reprinted with a new introduction by Westminster John Knox Press, 2001).

11. Farley, "The Church and the Family," 63.

12. Michael Strassfeld, *A Book of Life: Embracing Judaism as a Spiritual Practice* (New York: Schocken Books, 2002), 301–3.

13. Beverly Wildung Harrison, *Our Right to Choose: Toward a New Ethic of Abortion* (Boston: Beacon Press, 1983), 265. Harrison explains here that she prefers the Puritan political term commonwealth "as a theological symbol for our shared humanity under God."

14. Deirdre Good, *Jesus' Family Values* (New York: Church Publishing Incorporated, 2006), 90.

15. Ibid., 114.

16. Garland, *Family Ministry*, 321.

17. Ibid., 307.

18. 1 Corinthians 1:3–9; 2 Corinthians 1:3–7.

19. Excerpts from Colossians 1:3, 5, 6, 10, 20.

20. 2 Corinthians 1:20.

21. Colossians 1:3–6.

22. Ephesians 1:18.

23. Ephesians 3:14–20.

24. Gail O'Day, "John," in Carol A. Newsom and Sharon H. Ringe, eds., *Women's Biblical Commentary* (Louisville, KY: Westminster John Knox Press, 1992), 300.

25. Ibid., 302.

26. Kathleen O. Chesto, *Why Are the Dandelions Weeds?* (St. Louis, MO: Ligouri Publications, 1993), unpaged, paraphrased.

27. Tikva Frymer-Kensky, "Deuteronomy," in *Women's Biblical Commentary,* 52.

28. John 13:35.

29. O'Day, "John," 304.

30. John 17:21.

31. Amy-Jill Levine, "Matthew," in *Women's Biblical Commentary,* 254.

32. Ibid., 252.

33. Ibid., 253.

34. Genesis 1:27–29.

35. Genesis 2:18.

36. Mark 10:6–8.

37. Dante Alighieri, *The Divine Comedy: Paradiso,* trans. John Sinclair (New York: Oxford University Press, 1939), 484–85.

38. 1 Corinthians 10:23–24; Ephesians 4:29.

39. 1 Corinthians 1:10–14.

40. 2 Corinthians 8:12–15.

41. Cf. 1 Corinthians 5.

42. Galatians 5:13–23; cf. also Ephesians 4:25–5:1; Col 3:5–17; 1 Thessalonians 5:14–24; Hebrews 13:1–7.

43. Luke 12:48; the parable is Luke 12:35–48, with parallels in Mark (13:33–37) and Matthew (24:42–51).

44. Anne Underwood, Esq., presentation at the "Celebrating the Religious Search" group of the Society for Values in Higher Education, North Central College, Napierville, Illinois, August 2006.

45. Wendy Mogel, *The Blessings of a Skinned Knee: Using Jewish Teachings to Raise Self-Reliant Children* (New York: Penguin Books, 2001), 32.

46. Callie Marie Rennes, U.S. Department of Justice, Bureau of Justice Statistics, "Intimate Partner Violence 1993–2001." (February 2003). From the NCADV website: *www.ncadv.org/files/DV_Facts.pdf.*

47. "National Child Abuse Statistics," online at *www.childhelp.org/resources/learning-center/statistics,* 2006.

48. Ched Myers, *Binding the Strong Man* (Maryknoll, NY: Orbis, 1988), 266–68.

49. John 15:11.

50. O'Day, "John," 303.

51. John 15:11.

52. Barbara Brown Zikmund, Adair T. Lummis, and Patricia Mei Yin Chang, *Clergy Women: An Uphill Calling* (Louisville, KY: Westminster John Knox Press, 1998), 122.

53. Fred Lehr, *Clergy Burnout* (Minneapolis, MN: Augsburg Fortress, 2006), 4.

54. Edward Lehman, "Women's Path into Ministry: Six Studies," *Pulpit and Pew Research Report* (Fall 2002): 23.

55. Vashti McKenzie, *Not Without a Struggle: Leadership Development for African American Women in Ministry* (Cleveland: Pilgrim Press, 1996), 92.

56. Barbara Brown Taylor, *Leaving Church: A Memoir of Faith* (San Francisco: HarperSanFrancisco, 2006), 135.

57. Ibid., 98.

58. McKenzie, *Not Without a Struggle*, 87.

59. Michael Jinkins, "Great Expectation, Sobering Realities," *Congregations* 2002-05-01, no. 3 (May–June 2002), at *www.alban.org.*

60. Patricia Hayes, "Clergy Self-Care Strategies for Good Times and Bad," *Alban Weekly* no. 40, 2005-04-25, 1.

61. Ibid., 2.

62. Glen E. Kreiner, Elaine C. Hollensbe, and Mathew L. Sheep, "Boundary Work Tactics: Negotiating the Home-Work Interface," unpublished paper available through first authors at College of Business Department of Management University of Cincinnati, PO Box 210165, Cincinnati, OH 45221-0165.

63. Ibid., 25.

64. Ibid., 35.

65. Ibid., 37.

66. McKenzie, *Not Without a Struggle*, 86.

67. Ibid., 105.

68. Kammerer, "View from the First Wave," in Lehman, "Women's Path into Ministry," 45.

69. Cooper White, "Becoming a Clergy Mother," 1.

70. Ibid., 2.

71. Zikmund et al., *Clergy Women*, 79.

72. Ibid., 80.

73. Matthew Price, "State of the Clergy 2006" (New York: Church Pension Group, 2006), at *www.cpg.org/formspublications/research.cfm*; also Lehman, "Women's Path into Ministry," 15.

74. Loren Mead, *Financial Meltdown in the Mainline?* (Bethesda, MD: Alban Institute, 1998), 144. See also chapters 5, 10.

75. Robert Dale, "The Intersection of Church and Market," response to McMillan and Price, "How Much Should We Pay the Pastor?" *Pulpit and Pew Research Report* (May 2003): 26.

76. Mary Jane Hitt, "Shape the Debate by the Upside-Down Gospel," response to Lehman, "Women's Path into Ministry," 43.

77. Cooper White, "Becoming a Clergy Mother," 6.

78. Lehman, "Women's Path into Ministry," 20.

79. Ibid., 24–25.

80. Kammerer, "View from the First Wave," response to Lehman's "Women's Path into Ministry," in *Pulpit and Pew Research Report* (Fall 2002): 44.

81. Judith Craig, *The Leading Women: Stories of the First Women Bishops of the United Methodist Church* (Nashville, TN: Abingdon Press, 2004).

82. Barbara Brown Zikmund, Adair T. Lummis, and Patricia Mei Yin Chang *Clergy Women: An Uphill Calling* (Louisville, KY: Westminster John Knox Press, 1998), 30–31.

83. Nancy Myer Hopkins, "We Are All One in the Body of Christ: Looking at the Church from a Family Systems Point of View," in the *FOCUS Resource Guide,* available from Families of Clergy United in Support, at *www.episcopalchurch.org/focus.htm,* 22–25.

84. *www.communityofspice.org,* or write to Karen D. Powers, publisher and senior editor, 1505 Deerfield Drive, Oshkosh, WI 54904.

85. Price, "State of the Clergy 2003" (New York: Church Pension Group, 2003), at *www.cpg.org/formspublications/research.cfm*; 8.

86. FOCUS Resource Guide, Section 3.H and I.

87. Bruce Hardy, "Pastoral Care with Clergy Children," *Review and Expositor* 98, no. 4 (Fall 2001): 552–55.

88. Heidi Neumark, *Breathing Space: A Spiritual Journey in the South Bronx* (Boston: Beacon Press, 2003), 82.

89. FOCUS Resource Guide, Section 4.

90. Roy M. Oswald, *New Beginnings: A Pastorate Start-Up Workbook* (Bethesda, MD: Alban Institute, 1989).

91. FOCUS Resource Guide, Section 3.B.

92. Ibid., Section 5.B.

93. Ibid., Section 5.C.

94. Ibid., Section 5.D.

95. Ibid., Section 5.E.

96. Diana Garland, *Family Ministry: A Comprehensive Guide* (Downers Grove, IL: Intervarsity Press, 1999), 308.

97. Ibid., 312.

98. Luke 2:40.

99. Ephesians 3:16–20.